MW01714772

DREAMS & PROMISES

THE STORY OF THE ARMAND HAMMER
UNITED WORLD COLLEGE

DREAMS & PROMISES

THE STORY OF THE ARMAND HAMMER UNITED WORLD COLLEGE

A CRITICAL ANALYSIS
BY THEODORE D. LOCKWOOD

SUNSTONE PRESS
SANTA FE

© 1997 byTheodore D. Lockwood. All rights reserved.
Printed and bound in the United States of America. No part of this book may be reproduced in any form or by any electronic or mechanical means including information storage and retrieval systems, without permission in writing from the publisher, except by a reviewer who may quote brief passages in a review.

Sunstone books may be purchased for educational, business, or sales promotional use. For information please write: Special Markets Department, Sunstone Press, P.O. Box 2321, Santa Fe, New Mexico 87504-2321.

FIRST EDITION

10 9 8 7 6 5 4 3 2 1

Library of Congress Cataloging in Publication Data:
Lockwood, Theodore D., 1924—
Dreams & promises: the story of the Armand Hammer United World College / Theodore D. Lockwood. — 1st ed.
p. cm.
ISBN: 0-86534-260-1
1. Armand Hammer United World College of the American West.
I. Title.
LD247.L63 1997
378.789' .55—dc21 97-2020
CIP

Published by SUNSTONE PRESS
Post Office Box 2321
Santa Fe, NM 87504-2321 / USA
(505) 988-4418 / *orders only* (800) 243-5644
FAX (505) 988-1025

front cover: Montezuma campus
inset: top,clockwise; Armand Hammer and Charles, Prince of Wales;
Cri Chandrariani (Indonesia);
Yvonne Akpalu and Joseph Poku (Ghana).

DEDICATION

This book is dedicated first and foremost to my wife, Lu, who not only shared in establishing the college but who also brought to the account her own recollections, and corrections.

To all the other people who worked so hard to make certain that the college succeeded we wish to extend our thanks for a job well done. And to their successors we add our best wishes.

Finally to Sunstone Press and in particular to Jim Smith, editor and publisher, we owe both thanks and gratitude.

CONTENTS

ACKNOWLEDGMENTS

The Richard Lounsbery Foundation graciously offered to help with the publication of this book and for their continuing support and encouragement I am most grateful.

Three individuals, long interested in the United World College movement, deserve special recognition for their ideas and assistance: Dr. William McGill, Sir Ian Gourlay, and the late Honorable Kingman Brewster.

To the editor and publisher, James Smith, I am indebted for his enthusiasm and careful scrutiny of the book. His staff, and particularly Vicki Ahl, have been most helpful throughout the project.

And to my wife, Lu, I am happy to acknowledge her help in reading and rereading the text to catch those unavoidable omissions, mistypings, and infelicities. Moreover, in many instances it was her memory of some incident that lent the text some relief and humor.

To the staff at the Armand Hammer United World College I am indebted for their willingness to share archival material, and to Diane Nieto in particular for so expertly transcribing all the oral records I made of trips, meetings, and calls.

—Theodore D. Lockwood

FOREWORD

This is the story of the founding of an International Baccalaureate College in a remote part of the United States, northern New Mexico. Around the world there are 500 pre-university schools offering this two-year diploma program, the equivalent of the 12th and 13th grades in this country. Rigorous, traditional in its curriculum, the typical IB college attracts a talented and diverse student body. Part of a movement known as the United World Colleges, this particular institution came upon the scene quickly, with a flourish that only unusual circumstances could provide. And those circumstances centered around a man known worldwide, Dr. Armand Hammer, a physician by training and a businessman by choice.

Thus, in another sense it is the story of an extraordinary man's generous decision to make possible in the United States what others, despite their good intentions, had not been able to create—a new and different educational venture linked with what has been undoubtedly the finest collection of international schools the world has yet known. Hammer brought to the task the entrepreneurial skills that had built a petroleum empire and had brought him both praise and criticism. His acquaintance with world leaders helped in recruiting students and staff. But his name has always evoked controversy, now fueled by latter-day detractors. There was no question that he liked power and publicity, but he was also a philanthropist who genuinely believed in the need for peace. And it was to that end that he made possible the founding of a college, to be named for him and to become his memorial.

Necessarily, therefore, this story revolves around those, particularly Hammer, who were most directly involved in creating The Armand Hammer United World College of the American West. It does not recreate life on the campus. It does not chronicle all those events which occurred in Montezuma, a small village five miles from Las Vegas,

New Mexico—events which absorbed all the energies of faculty and staff. But it does seek to explain why and how it happened and then how the first 12 years were influenced by the founder in ways that rendered its future continually uncertain.

Nor did Hammer limit his action to the local scene. He had undertaken the project at the instigation of British royalty, and this association with His Royal Highness The Prince of Wales led to both spectacular events and unrealized expectations. Moreover, the history of any United World College must include reference to the International Office in London and to the movement's governing board since, in many instances, the gap between the ideal and what was actually happening provides the only explanation for the missed opportunities to achieve even more than will be noted here.

So, this is the story of both dreams fulfilled and promises not kept. In bringing the drive and notoriety required to launch this kind of institution, Hammer led everyone to believe that he would guarantee its future. Not so. Shrewd as ever, he kept people guessing and no one had the temerity to try to outguess him. Yet, in fairness, he did not interfere with daily operations at the college. As with other Hammer ventures, this was linked closely to Occidental Petroleum, again a most unusual and fortuitous situation for a non-profit, independently chartered institution. Hammer took great pride in the success of Montezuma, but then he chose not to underwrite it in the fashion he had repeatedly promised to do.

Therefore, this story relates how the programs were sustained amidst massive uncertainty and how, despite all the ups and downs and dreary financial discussions, the college did provide young people from around the world the best education they could possibly obtain. Misled at times by its founder, yet generously supported by him, his friends, and associates, the college survived his death in late 1990 and planned for a future that inevitably reflected the conditions of its founding and, most importantly, the strength of the mission which it had undertaken.

In telling the story I have not sought to eliminate my own bias just as I have not forsaken including those anecdotes which may entertain but may not enlighten. In sum, it is an account of an impulsive, brilliant man who had few friends and many enemies, an assembly of dedicated academicians, and a collection of individuals whose entrances and exits are quite unpredictable.

—Theodore D. Lockwood
Santa Fe, NM/1996

1: TO THE HALLS OF MONTEZUMA

It was raining in Hartford, Connecticut, that April afternoon in 1981 when Kingman Brewster came to the president's office at Trinity College. The former ambassador from the United States to the Court of St. James's and President Emeritus of Yale University opened the conversation by asking what I knew about the United World Colleges. The answer was easy and brief: nothing. He then provided a scanty version of the three existing "colleges" in Wales, Canada and Singapore. He was even less precise about something called the International Baccalaureate. And his final comments included a vague reference to His Royal Highness The Prince of Wales, a Dr. Armand Hammer, and Lord Louis Mountbatten.

But there was a point to the conversation: "Dr. Hammer, head of Occidental Petroleum in Los Angeles, has proposed to establish a United World College in the States. He wants to make it part of the United States International University in San Diego. We in London are worried that this may not be the appropriate location. We want you to help assess the situation." When I asked where the "Dr." came from, he replied that Hammer had studied medicine at Columbia University and had received his M.D. in 1921, but before he could take up his internship he went to Russia.

I begin with this meeting simply because it was my first association with the project; and, as this accounting of the early history of The Armand Hammer United World College of the American West will carry my personal bias throughout this book, it seemed the logical place to begin.

But clearly the proposal to found a new college in this country had received extensive consideration much earlier. In fact, for at least a dozen years there had been the hope that such an institution might be established in this country. The committee in

New York City which had been responsible for selecting students to send to the United World College of the Atlantic in Llantwit Major, Wales, and to the Lester B. Pearson United World College of the Pacific in Victoria, British Columbia, had tried to find an existing institution in the northeast that might serve as a United World College. Lord Louis Mountbatten had toured the States in the hopes of recruiting financial backing for a college shortly after he had become president in 1968 of the new movement which he hoped to create as one means of preventing a third world war. Nothing happened. A site in Vermont proved too expensive and corporate America was not yet ready to invest in this kind of international education. Meanwhile the development of the International Baccalaureate academic program had gone forward and the first trial examinations were ready in 1969. Sir Alec Peterson worked valiantly to implement this standard credential for the many international schools around the world and had proposed that Atlantic College adopt it for use in the UWCs. Thus the academic program was well in place years before a college in the United States.

The next step came on November 8, 1978. Prince Charles invited Dr. and Mrs. Hammer to a reception at Buckingham Palace. Lord Mountbatten was present to honor the Friends of the United World Colleges. As Hammer would often tell it, the two English gentlemen steered him into a corner and would not let him leave until he had promised to help with the project in the United States. Lord Mountbatten told him: "I witnessed the horrors of two world wars and I came to the conclusion that, if we are ever to have peace in the world, we would have to start with the young people of an impressionable age who would learn to live together, regardless of their nationality or religion or their ideology." (From Hammer's official autobiography, written with Neil Lyndon and containing surprisingly little reference to the college.)

The rest of the conversation is equally familiar to those who worked at Montezuma. Prince Charles suggested to his great-uncle that he approach Hammer, but Lord Louis countered: "I'd be delighted to, but I don't see why he should succeed where others have failed." The retort was predictable: "Well, in my opinion," Prince Charles replied, "if anybody can do it, Doctor Hammer can." Hammer agreed to help.

But not until 1980 did Hammer's staff begin a serious search for a site and formulate some plans, based primarily on the model in Canada. By then Prince Charles had become President of the International Council for the UWCs, actually just prior to Lord Mountbatten's assassination. This preliminary exploration had led to the idea of renting space from the United States International University in San Diego. It was clear the new college would be located somewhere in the western United States. (For those unfamiliar with the UWCs, the term college derives from the British use of the word to designate institutions preparing students in their last two pre-university years.) Whether San Diego appealed because of the proximity of the ocean for the kind of sea search and

Louis, Earl
Mountbatten of
Burma.

rescue required of students in Wales and Canada or whether it seemed like an inexpensive way to begin remains unclear, but in other ways it represented a considerable departure by yoking a small cadre of younger students to a university based on recruiting overseas students on a paying basis. That approach worried the London office, which also wondered if anyone on Hammer's staff knew much about education as opposed to petrochemicals.

The London office, a term which will appear frequently in this story, consisted of a small staff, headed by Sir Ian Gourlay, whom Mountbatten appointed as Director General in 1975. Sir Ian had been Commandant General of the Royal Marines. His was the unenviable task of serving a board that met seldom, of helping three colleges at long distance, and of trying to clarify roles in an organization lacking sufficient funds and experience to operate effectively. Housed in small and unimpressive quarters in London

House at Mecklenberg Square, the office had recently become more active as the Chairman of the International Board, Professor Thomas Symons from Trent University in Canada, devoted more and more hours to the founding of additional colleges. Under the guidelines for the organization, the International Board alone could authorize a new college. On paper the board set the basic principles according to which each college must operate, leaving the financial arrangements entirely to the institutions themselves. The International Council, of which Prince Charles was the President, met once every five years and served mainly to involve the chairmen of the various national committees in a review of policies and procedures, especially as they applied to admissions. Thus the London office's main tool was persuasion and its chief need was communication. It was the "center" but not the central player.

The speed with which Hammer was prepared to move must have disconcerted London and everyone else. But Prince Charles was pleased and agreed to a meeting at the British Embassy in Washington, D.C., on May 1, 1981, to confirm the plan for San Diego under which Hammer would pay one million dollars a year to rent space at the United States International University there, plus all normal operating costs. Therefore, when I agreed to assist Kingman Brewster and others, I did not have much time. I began inquiring among fellow presidents on the west coast as to the situation at USIU. Jack Sawyer, whom I had known for many years when he was president at Williams College and then head of the Andrew King Mellon Foundation, was familiar with the UWCs and sympathetic to the cause but reluctant to comment. Quickly I learned that there were some severe financial strains at USIU and that at that time the institution was on probation from the Western States Association. Those facts raised questions as to the appropriateness of the proposed affiliation.

But more serious reasons for not proceeding rested on what I was learning about the programs of the United World Colleges. They sounded like an admirable effort to involve young people in an idealistic goal; for they combined cold showers with lots of math and languages. The common examinations were no doubt formidable, but the service concept represented an interesting and proper move away from typical high school activities. I wondered how many kids made it, what kind of staff it required, and why there was so little interest in the States. It seemed to me also that these two-year institutions needed to stand on their own feet in locations appropriate to the mission they had set themselves. As my report began to take form, my wife Lu and I went to Vermont for the weekend. Hammer called to suggest we fly out to the San Diego site. He had learned of my involvement in ways to which we would become accustomed as time passed! He said he was also sending me a copy of the proposal which his office had prepared. It sounded as if he had concluded that it was a good proposal and that the site would be appropriate. Only months later did I learn he personally never went to San

Diego. Not only did my schedule preclude such a trip, but I also felt that it might prejudice my own judgment on educational grounds.

The meeting in Washington was set for four in the afternoon. Edward Adeane, the Prince's private secretary, met the guests and indicated which chairs we should occupy once we had had tea. As we stood with our teacups, I was introduced to Tom Symons, Chairman of the International Board, Jack Matthews, director in charge of Pearson College, George Franklin from the Trilateral Commission, Russell Palmer from Touche Ross, Hammer, and his assistant Jim Pugash. When the Prince arrived, he went down the line and spoke graciously to each person. He was ruddy of complexion, and much less stuffy than I had feared. We all sat down in our appointed chairs. Prince Charles then asked Ambassador Brewster to outline the status of the project. With his usual diplomatic charm and imprecision, Kingman told of the rising interest in the movement that would, he hoped, lead to the successful choice of a site for a UWC in this country. Knowing nothing about the position of the U.S. Committee in New York, I missed the full import of these comments. Certainly the Prince was puzzled by the tone of this introduction.

"Well, what is the problem?" he asked. There was a long pause. Kingman then suggested that it might help if I made a few remarks. (I had been carefully told not to speak without first being asked.) I replied more crisply than usual.

"Educationally it will not work to associate the new college with USIU. The university is in a precarious position with both financial and academic problems. It is too large and would overshadow a UWC. Given the general ignorance of the UWCs in the States, it should have its own identity and not appear to be an apse chapel attached to a university. Practically, it might not be wise to enter into a financial agreement which would be primarily to the advantage of USIU. Moreover, the service programs might be difficult to carry out in San Diego." I sensed all too quickly that these words of caution, if not of disapproval, were unwelcome.

The Prince was not pleased, quite understandably, for he had assumed all was ready for a final blessing. Now Hammer might withdraw his support. He asked others if they shared my views. In succession others expressed comparable reservations less harshly but still effectively. As Jack Matthews explained years later, he had even seen the proposed site, was not impressed, and had, therefore, warned the London office after informing Hammer that he needed time to think about the idea. Then there arrived that moment when the outcome would be determined. Hammer was a master at sensing when to speak at the critical time: "If there are reservations, then we should go look for another site as quickly as possible."

That eased the tension. The Chairman, Tom Symons, used the occasion to suggest that we proceed. Then the Prince, Dr. Hammer, and he withdrew. But no one knew quite what that meant and would have welcomed another cup of tea. We chatted informally, stared at the carefully prepared folios Jim Pugash, Hammer's special assistant, had distributed, and wondered whether we had seen another attempt to start a UWC in the United States go down the drain. Professor Symons returned and assembled a few of us to form a site-selection committee. Russ Palmer of Touche Ross offered to release two of his staff to work full-time with realtors in identifying possible locations. The Prince returned in his bathrobe to go for a swim, and added: "I do hope we can get on with the task as rapidly as possible so that we may take advantage of this splendid and very generous offer of Dr. Hammer's."

We got the message. Although I was on the committee, I was uncertain as to what that might involve. I assumed that my consultancy might end that night at dinner until, as I was leaving the Embassy, Hammer asked me to outline where they might look for a site. Therefore, as I flew back to Hartford that night, I jotted down some ideas favoring the southwest over California where I sensed real estate prices were too high. It was fortunate that I had organized my response because the next day Hammer phoned to ask my ideas—a practice to which we all would become accustomed.

There was more than curiosity on my part because I was leaving Trinity College in June and had already agreed to help part-time the Association of American Colleges in its proposed study of American undergraduate education. When it appeared in 1985 under the title *Integrity in the College Curriculum: A Report to the Academic Community,* it was Professor Frederick Rudolph from Williams College who wrote the final version, a person who in 1993 joined the board of directors at the Armand Hammer United World College. It remained conveniently unclear during the next two months while I was busy preparing for the Commencement at Trinity, and Lu and I were sorting out prior to moving up to Quechee, Vermont. By then, also, we had concluded that we had made the right decision to leave after 13 years, to strike out on our own in the Green Mountain state. The parties at the Trinity graduation were better than ever. We began packing for Vermont.

Meanwhile, out in LA, Jim Pugash, a Rhodes Scholar with an odd mixture of organization and abandon, carried out Hammer's instructions to find a site for the United World College. California, Arizona, and New Mexico became the primary targets in the search. My function was to list the criteria which the location should meet. We had concluded the size should be the same as Pearson College: 200 students all in residence. We needed a place where community service would be possible and some kind of search and rescue. The spirit behind the UWC program, Kurt Hahn, strongly believed in using the outdoors to test one's stamina, physically and emotionally. Hahn had come from Germany to England after having established a very successful school at Salem. A Jew, he had been arrested by Hitler but the intervention of the British saved him and brought him to London. He became involved with Gordonstoun School where Prince Charles had received his education—an important happenstance in the history of the UWCs. Hahn passionately believed in changing education so that it would transform the lives of young people, make them active leaders in fighting prejudices and in learning to share with others in serving humanity. It was clearly he who set the moral tone for the programs established first at Atlantic College and then at other UWCs. Antonin Besse, a French businessman deeply interested in international education, recalled how Hahn had persuaded him to join two British leaders from the Second World War, Sir Lawrence Darvall and Rear Admiral Desmond Hoare, in establishing a new institution to be called Atlantic College because of the example of the Atlantic Alliance. They succeeded in 1962 when Besse purchased St. Donat's, a castle in South Glamorgan, Wales, which William Randolph Hearst had renovated.

There were rumors that a convent in San Francisco might work. Then the Governor of Arizona proposed to give land east of Scottsdale. As we moved up to Quechee in July, there were more calls from Occidental, the import of which was to think ahead to what would be needed if the college was to open in September of 1982. Pugash had called in June to ask if I could join Jack Matthews in Albuquerque to look at a piece of property in Montezuma, New Mexico. We could not find it on the map, an experience others would have. Ironically, Lu and I had flown to Albuquerque in May for a Trinity reunion and, having an extra day, had driven to the famous city of Santa Fe. Then we had flown on to San Francisco where our Trinity colleagues warned that we would "leave our hearts in San Francisco" as Tony Bennett's song proclaimed. That did not happen; in fact, Lu told her friends that it had been Santa Fe (despite rain and clouds) that we had found enchanting, not San Francisco.

When I arrived at the Albuquerque airport, I was told to meet Jack at the AMFAC hotel. An agent would meet us early the next morning for the drive to Montezuma. Accordingly Jack and I sat around the pool and I learned about Pearson College and the IB. Since there was so little in print, it was an invaluable orientation. Jack was the kind of buoyant Canadian whose enthusiasms were contagious. As we drove up to Las Vegas, a city of 15,000 some five miles south of Montezuma, we were struck by the combination of the dryness and the long views in every direction. It was not the desert we had anticipated, for there were numerous low evergreens, but it was obviously an area with a small population. The Sangre de Cristo mountains made a majestic backdrop. We first talked with local priests in Las Vegas about the city and then about the property since it belonged to the Catholic Church and had been a seminary for Mexican priests from 1937 to 1972.

We drove out to the site. There stood the famous Montezuma Castle. On the plain below were a number of old and newer buildings—seventeen in all. As we would learn,

Aerial view of the Armand Hammer United World College in Montezuma, New Mexico.

the Santa Fe railroad had built the hotel in 1882 as a tourist attraction at a time when New Mexico was still a territory and very much the Old Southwest. The railroad spur ran farther up the Gallinas River Valley to ponds whose winter ice was used by the trains. There had been two older hotels on the property, one of which was a stone hotel erected in 1879, a building that was still standing but like all the others abandoned, vandalized, and unpromising. We walked around the Castle. We did not say much. We then toured what had been the dormitories for the seminarians. Fortunately the sun was out because it was forlorn. The utility poles wandered around in haphazard fashion; the main field where we entered was a dust bowl; and the terrain was sufficiently rugged that it would make integrating the campus difficult. We returned to Albuquerque.

As we talked that evening, Jack and I concluded that it would work. Although Jim Pugash had intimated on the phone that we might be able to put everything into the Castle, neither of us felt that such a concentration was desirable: we would recommend using some of the other buildings as well. We worried about a place for dining facilities. But overall we concluded Montezuma might work. Not having seen the site in

Scottsdale, we could not compare. What we also recognized was that search and rescue would have to be in the mountains since the Gallinas was but a trickle of water. There were enough good rock faces around, in my judgment, for that kind of strenuous training. We had no illusions about the basic utilities: everything would have to be replaced.

As we parted, we agreed to submit separate reports to Hammer recommending Montezuma. We also had had sufficient fun working together that we agreed it would be nice if we could both continue as consultants once the project got launched. Back in Hartford, I called Dr. Hammer. I explained what I thought to be the virtues of the location: a fascinating area to study, a mixture of three cultures, ample places for Hahn's outward bound component, a nearby city for community service, adequate medical facilities in Las Vegas, and a university with whom we could collaborate as appropriate. It would be as much an entirely new experience for Americans as for foreign students. But I also said that it would cost a lot of money to fix the utilities, renovate the buildings, and put everything in readiness.

"Fine, and don't worry. I am quite prepared to spend two million to buy the property and renovate it." As Hammer would later say in his autobiography: "When I had first visited the site in 1981, I had been immediately enchanted with the place but daunted by its dereliction. The buildings were almost in ruins. The grounds were completely overgrown [*sic*], and we walked around them through mud up to our ankles. Nonetheless, my mind was made up immediately. This was the place."

In the middle of July Hammer offered the Catholic Church $900,000 for the 110 acres on which the buildings stood. There were another 600 acres available, but he was not interested because they were not contiguous to the campus. Summertime in Quechee was proving quite interesting as the mail brought various materials from Los Angeles and the telephone rang at odd hours. One of those calls asked me to come out again to go over the property with Tom Symons, Sir Ian Gourlay and his wife, Lady Natasha Gourlay, from London, Bill McGill and Arthur Groman from the Occidental Board, Linda Bastedo, the head of the U.S. Committee's office in New York, and staff. Again we walked around. Hammer was obviously intrigued by the Castle. He had decided we should move ahead even though Bill McGill expressed caution at the possible expense.

I had not seen Bill for a number of years. He had left the presidency of Columbia University and gone back to San Diego. Later we all had dinner at the Doolittle Ranch in Watrous, some twenty miles north of Las Vegas. Jim and Barbara Doolittle raised cattle and were involved in many New Mexico business operations. They were most genial hosts. Jim and I discovered we had a common background and interest in skiing. Hammer was already lining the Doolittles up for a prominent role in the future college. Everyone departed enthusiastic.

Armand Hammer and Ted Lockwood leave the municipal airport in Las Vegas, New Mexico, to inspect the campus.

2: MOVING WEST

Vermont in August was green. We went bicycling and swam almost every day. We settled into the house and began to reorganize the furniture, build more bookshelves, and watch our border collie, Tippy, and the two cats cavort in the tall grass. We were enjoying the scenery and the new pace. New Mexico seemed very far away indeed. Word came from Hammer's office that he had stopped in Washington in mid-August, on his way to Brazil, to buy the property. When he entered the office of the bishop handling the sale, he encountered a lawyer who indicated that there might be some problems, even though Hammer had upped his offer to $1,000,000. Another bidder was waiting outside with a larger offer. Hammer countered quickly by saying that he had negotiated in good faith and would not be a party to this kind of blackmail. He had a check for the full amount in hand. At this point the bishop intervened and said that he would honor Hammer's agreement. Hammer always delighted in telling the story.

What he learned later was that the other bidder was the son of a friend in Texas. Wid Slick had moved to Las Vegas and wanted to restore the Castle as a resort hotel. Subsequently Slick bought the Plaza Hotel in Old Town in Las Vegas and renovated it completely. He and his wife, Katherine ("Kak"), became close friends and supporters of the College.

What would happen next? I had no formal agreement to continue consulting. Having been paid only my expenses, I was uncertain as to any future arrangements. Jack Matthews called and said that Hammer had asked him to indicate what the next steps might be. He deferred to me since he was unfamiliar with the American educational scene. Thus in a most casual manner, we both became involved in planning ahead. It was easy to compile a list: recruit faculty and staff, find 100 students, renovate the facilities we would need for the first year, locate the requisite books and supplies, develop appropriate literature, find out what New Mexico required before opening, etcetera. In fact, it was rather entertaining to enumerate all the tasks for someone else to tackle. Lu disagreed. She sensed that all this involvement with the UWC was going to lead to something. But we went on working on the house at Quechee, and I flew down to Hartford regularly on the puddle-jumper out of Lebanon, New Hampshire, for Connecticut General meetings. And Hammer or Pugash were calling regularly.

One such call asked: "What can you and Jack do about getting the place going so that it can open in 1982?"

"You will have to find someone to put all the pieces together in a hurry. Frankly, I doubt that it is possible. You just can't slap together a school in 10 to 12 months, with good faculty and good students," I replied. I promised to send him a list of candidates.

On August 22 we were in the living room watching the mist settle. We scolded the cats for scratching on the new furniture. There was a scent of fall in the air, and we speculated on how soon the leaves would turn and we could enjoy the colors. The phone rang. "This is a conference call. Please wait for others to join." Matthews, Hammer, Pugash, and Symons were on the line. Hammer asked how we were. No clue as to the purpose of the call as he meandered for a few more minutes. Then:

"I read your letter about helping to find a director. We have found one if he will agree." The trap was sprung: Lu and I should take on the assignment. "Everyone we have consulted has said that your experience alone would make it possible." I wondered if they had actually talked to anyone else. "Would I accept?" The question was a bit awkward since I was considering a request to seek the job as head of the New York Public Library—which I did not because it would have involved primarily fund-raising. There was also an interesting idea that I serve as assistant to the President of Botswana. While turning that one over in our minds, we suggested that it would help us decide if we could visit the site, especially as Lu had never been there.

"Fine. We will arrange transportation for you to come out on the 24th to Albuquerque. Jim Doolittle will meet you there and fly you to Las Vegas." The conversation ended. We talked and agreed that it might be interesting to go for a few years, not more than five, and then return to Vermont. Out came the suitcases. We stayed overnight at the AMFAC hotel near the airport in Albuquerque after our flight from Hartford.

The next morning Doolittle met us along with Jim Pugash and an architect from Albuquerque, George Pearl. He had been appointed to oversee the renovation. Pearl was a watercolorist and a fascinating gentleman who had always lived in New Mexico and felt very strongly about the restoration of the Castle and other buildings in Montezuma. As we took off, Lu's white knuckles showed. We flew over the Pecos, across the campus, and into the small airstrip at Las Vegas. The weather was superb and the 6500 feet of elevation did not bother either of us—a good omen.

First arrival in New Mexico: left to right, Armand Hammer, William McGill, Ted Lockwood and his wife Lu.

We all piled into Doolittle's red Lincoln Town Car and drove out to the campus. Hammer was in the front seat. As we passed the Montezuma post office, Hammer turned to Lu and said: "Lu, did you see that post office? That's where you'll be mailing your letters back home." Lu laughed, but thought to herself: don't count on that. Warren Wildenstein, the security guard, opened the Castle for us. As we toured the second floor, Hammer remarked to Lu: "You and Ted will have the entire second floor as your residence." Certainly that would have been adequate for two people, a dog and two cats! Everything would be wonderful, he assured us.

After lunch at the Doolittles we got into the two planes and headed for Santa Fe: Hammer, the Gourlays, Doolittles, and Tom Symons. We called on the Governor, Bruce King. With the Governor was Leonard Delayo, head of the New Mexico Department of Education. It was an intriguing half hour. First, Hammer gave Governor King a copy of the biography Bob Considine had written. "That's a mighty nice picture of you, Armand." "That's not me; that's the author." So the banter went back and forth. Sir Ian Gourlay asked King how many hats he had to wear as governor of a state, at which point King pulled out a fireman's hat to show Ian—or "Eye-an" as he pronounced it.

In Governor King's office, Armand Hammer and Leonard Delayo share a humorous tale.

Hammer introduced us as the people who would run the college, and the governor assured us of his full cooperation and hoped I and "the little lady" would come by often. He also put in his bid to attend whatever opening ceremonies we had, adding that it had better be before the end of 1982 because his term would end then. Hammer concluded on the spot that the dedication should take place in October before the cold weather set in, at a time when Prince Charles could attend. Delayo promised to cut through the red tape—something he did to our great benefit. The meeting ended with the feeling that it would not be complicated to operate in New Mexico unlike, say, New York or California.

We flew back to Las Vegas with the Doolittles again. For dinner they took us to the El Alto Supper Club, "the best place to eat in Las Vegas." It was disconcerting in comparison with what we knew in the east; but the food was good and the chunks of lemon in our martinis were certainly adequate. We returned to the ranch and we planned to spend the next day looking around Las Vegas and seeing some of the countryside before returning to Quechee.

The next morning as we were having breakfast, the telephone rang. It was Hammer again. "Wouldn't you like to go to Canada to see Pearson College? George Pearl could go along and study their layouts. Then you could come down to Los Angeles so that we can discuss when you begin." I muttered something about our air tickets to Hartford for Thursday. "Don't worry; we'll fix your tickets. Jim (Pugash) will meet you at noon today in Albuquerque." We were learning that once Hammer had made up his mind, there was no relaxation or deflecting his intentions.

Doolittle used his small plane at the ranch to get us to Albuquerque, where we boarded the Oxy G-2 for Victoria, Canada—hoping that we did not need our passports. Unlike other citizens of the United States, we had assumed they were not needed to enter New Mexico and accordingly had not brought them. It was a magnificent flight, not only because of the comfort in the plane but because clear skies permitted us to see the recent eruption of Mount Saint Helens.

We touched down in Victoria late that afternoon, bypassed immigration, and drove to Pearson College, an hour away and apparently as remote as Montezuma. Jack Matthews greeted us. The setting was beautiful. The campus had been built all at one time in 1973 and thus had an architectural integrity seldom found at colleges. The giant pines rose above the buildings; Peddar's Bay sat just off the edge. It looked so attractive that Lu proposed that Jack go to Montezuma and that we remain in Victoria. Jack had founded Pearson and we soon began talking about what would be needed for us to open. He had taken three years; we had only one. We studied the facilities, had dinner in their dining hall overlooking the water, and then talked some more. As it was prior to the opening of the next school year, we did not get a feel for what it would be with 200 students present.

At some point the name of the new college entered the conversation. Originally it was to be the United World College of the Southwest. How many knew where that was and whose southwest was it? We settled on the United World College of the American West. Some thought it sounded too much like John Wayne or that it implied that some day there would be a UWC of the American East. Why not seemed a reasonable response.

We had breakfast with Jack and his wife, Jane. Then, as if on cue, Hammer called to ask us to take off as soon as possible so that we could meet with him that afternoon in

LA. Again our leisurely tour of the area did not take place. We met with Hammer that August 27th and he wanted to know if we had made up our minds. We hedged. "How long will it take?" To our surprise we said next week since I had to be in LA on Monday for a Connecticut General real estate committee meeting. That was acceptable, and we walked back to the Westwood Marquis, an excellent hotel we would come to know well over the years. Jim Pugash asked us for dinner at his apartment and we accepted. Then Hammer called to ask us to dinner. Pugash was not surprised and said he would just keep his dining room table set for another two weeks against the day he hoped he would be able to entertain. Hammer took us to a private dining room at his favorite Italian restaurant, Perino's, chosen because he was entertaining the head of EMI, an Italian petrochemical company with whom he hoped to swing a deal. He told them about the college, which he assured them Lu and I would be creating. During dinner we were serenaded by an Hungarian violinist. Hammer wanted to give him a tip; therefore, he leaned over to the person on his left and asked: "Do you have any money?" The person, an Oxy executive, let Hammer choose from among his bills a crisp $100. Later, Hammer asked for more money. Lu was worried that he would turn to her next. When he did speak to Lu, he asked how old I was. Lu indicated 56. "Good," Hammer replied. "That means Ted can do the job for at least 30 years." Hammer was 83 at the time and considered that his most important work had taken place after age 55.

Not an easy conversationalist unless on his own turf, Hammer was far more soft spoken than his controversial reputation as an old style capitalist suggested. We had been reading about him and his remarkable career. His well-known association with Lenin after the First World War was what most people remembered. That he had had about three other careers was less well-known. Once, sitting at a table with Lu on our back lawn in Montezuma, Hammer burst out laughing when Lu said: "You have had three very interesting lives." Hammer thought she had said "wives."

People assumed he was wealthy, one of the Fortune 500. We did not know then, nor did the others who welcomed his support of the college, that much of his wealth consisted of the art which he had collected over the years. He had only a modest home in Westwood, actually the property of his third wife, Frances. He had kept the apartment in Greenwich Village in New York where he had stayed during his days as a medical student at Columbia, and he had an apartment in Moscow. The balance of his wealth consisted of Occidental Petroleum stock and the Hammer Galleries in New York City.

We flew back to Hartford. Subsequently we learned that Symons had urged Hammer to set up a board of directors as quickly as possible so that it would conform to the pattern of the three other UWCs and permit the International Board to accept the new institution into the movement. We had also assumed that the property which Hammer had bought would be shortly conveyed to the college once we officially became a 501C-3 charitable corporation in the State of New Mexico. It did not take us long to conclude that we should accept the assignment. Hammer had told us in LA that we need not plan to move out, if we preferred, until January of 1982, and that we could spend our holidays and summers in Vermont. When I returned to LA the next week, I signed a contract for five years with the understanding that, if everything went smoothly, we would leave earlier. We would set up the college; then someone else could take over.

The first address for the United World College of the American West was Box 383, Quechee, Vermont. We prepared some light brown stationery suggestive of the southwest; we rented a typewriter; and we set up some files. We wrote the first brochure for a nonexistent school, using photographs of the campus that would not show the broken windows, the large expanses of dirt or the tangle of overhead wires. We talked with Linda Bastedo in the U.S. Committee office. We assumed that, since the committee had been recruiting students and was familiar with the UWCs, it could help us as we moved along. What became quickly apparent was that the committee had not been much involved with the Hammer initiative. Ironically in 1973 Vermont had been the focus of their effort to found a new college. When that did not materialize, the committee concentrated on finding students, not sites. We had trouble understanding just how it operated. The committee had raised money and had plans for more events through which they could find the scholarship assistance needed. We did work out an arrangement subsequently that, in return for $5000 a month from us, they would undertake to find us 25 Americans for the entering class.

All of this lay ahead, however. In the immediate future we had two major tasks: planning for the renovation of the campus and bringing some structure to our own procedures. In keeping with Symons's recommendation, Hammer formed a small board of directors of which he would be the Honorary Chairman and Bill McGill the Chairman. McGill had joined the Oxy Board in 1981 and Hammer had promptly asked him to help out. Hammer's lawyer and close friend, Arthur Groman, would also join the board along with Paul Hebner, an officer of Oxy who would serve as Secretary-Treasurer. I carried the curious title of Executive Director of the Board, presumably since I was director of the college. It was not clear just how much time any of these people would have for the college's business, but Jim Pugash was told to help as much as possible—a fortunate decision since he had both the talent and energy necessary to follow up on matters that needed resolution in LA.

George Pearl began to develop some rough notions of how we might use the existing buildings. The older buildings from the 19th century were in bad shape. In fact there were so many questions about the Castle that I suggested to Hammer that we bring in an engineer from LA to go through the structure with me. The result was an estimate of eight million to restore the Castle properly, in keeping with its being a designated historical landmark. Hammer did not want to spent that much; in fact, it took some effort to convince him that we needed two million for the first phase of the project. I discovered that he did not like my estimate of four million. We began to look at the other structures, especially those which had been built in the 1960s when the seminary had some 600 students. Pearl began to lay out how we might use the Stone Hotel and four of the recent rectangular, cement-block buildings down on the lower tier. But we had a long ways to go before schematics would become available from Pearl's firm. We also needed a project manager; for I could only very generally oversee any construction. Hammer had a young man in mind, a person who had repainted his house. Accordingly Joe Cohen was appointed.

As Matthews and I talked over the phone, we concluded that it would not work for us to remain in Vermont. Lu and I heartily concurred. We could not bring the pieces together from that distance. We decided to move on October15 with a minimum of furnishings since we would be back often. We took our little VW bug in the van and left the Eagle wagon for someone to drive out later. We took the two cats and Tippy, Occidental having kindly agreed to provide cages for these remarkable animals. We were heading west.

But before we went, Pugash, Hammer and I met with the U.S. Committee in New York on October first. We were taken aback by the carping that occurred. Clearly many of the members did not like Hammer; they did not see how they could raise money for students coming to our college; and they were sufficiently busy with planning for a gala next June at Broadlands, Lord Mountbatten's home and now home to Lord and Lady Romsey, that they could not assist us much. To me it was clear that relations with the committee would be difficult. No doubt one explanation was that they were disappointed that, after having tried over the years to find money for a UWC of their choosing, they had been outflanked by Hollywood. Our original thought had been that members of the committee would serve on a board of visitors; but that idea did not surface again until much later when the whole question of possible ties between the two bodies would become poignant. For the moment we could only speculate on how much assistance New York could provide. No doubt they were equally skeptical of our ability to move ahead.

The middle of the month arrived and we flew to Albuquerque again with our three companions. We rented a car to drive to Watrous where we would stay in the ranch manager's house at the Doolittle Ranch for a week until we could move into a rented house in Las Vegas. The adventure had begun. That evening I took a photograph of the sunset to send to the family —and to use in the first color brochure, as it turned out.

Jack Matthews joined us since we could not do much until our furniture arrived; but we could talk and plot. We went over the staffing requirements, again using Pearson

College as a model. I had decided that the arts should have a prominent place in our programs since art was so much a part of the southwest. That would be one variant. Depending on who came as dean of studies, we put teaching the Theory of Knowledge course to one side. Our basic situation would be awkward the first year since we would have only one-half of our total student body but would need a full program of courses. But what was very obvious was our good fortune in having Matthews available to help. He had been through starting up a college and knew what was needed and what could wait. He knew the IB as I clearly did not. And we had fun working together. We had established a mailbox (#248) at Montezuma so as to avoid the possible confusion the name Las Vegas might cause.

We visited the site. Nothing was happening, and Jack wondered out loud whether we could ever make it in less than a year's time. We talked about student recruitment, and Jack promised to make available the Canadian embassies where we could not make other connections. It was all quite unreal as we drove to Taos that weekend to view the yellow aspens, the snowcapped peaks, and the rolling fields south of Mora.

We moved to a furnished rental house at 801 Erb Place in Las Vegas on October 23 and chose two of the rooms for our offices. Lu got the one with the mammoth flying fish mounted on the wall. We then looked for equipment in Las Vegas. We took the one desk available. There were no electric typewriters in town. Lu went to Santa Fe and the IBM offices. The representative, Mike Donlan, tucked one under his raincoat and put it in our car. We ordered an IBM display writer, the size of an upright piano, indispensable then but obsolete within a few years. We searched for supplies, and I began to assemble the first brochure. We began to hear from the local community also. Even before we had accepted the position, a woman had called us in Vermont from Las Vegas to congratulate us on the project and to offer her help. Rheua Pearce, who was older than Hammer, became a great promoter of the UWC. But more immediate was our concern that we get to know local people and clarify what we were going to try to do. Already rumors abounded: some thought it was a front for the CIA to train young people; others wondered if it would be another jet set school for rich kids; and a few even claimed that it was a communist training school since Hammer was putting up the money.

Las Vegans had two questions on their minds: how many people would we employ from the area, and what were we going to do about the hot springs that were on the property? To the first we replied, "As many as possible if they are qualified." To the other we could say little, but we gathered it would be a sensitive matter. We did tell them it would be a while before we renovated the famous Castle. We met with virtually every local group over the next few months, trying to convey some sense of our program. Basically the city was happy to have us there and to see the property in use again. Our main problem was that we really did not know all that much about what would happen. We hoped for the best.

Then came the question which would never disappear: "Why did you choose Montezuma?" Since in this instance the truth was inadequate to people's expectations, we elaborated in a manner that would become the standard answer after the fact. First, we wanted a multicultural setting. Second, we wanted the mountains for our outdoor programs. Third, we wanted a city nearby where our community services would be not only welcome but also needed. Finally, we were convinced that the Montezuma property had the facilities necessary for our operation. Of course, we also admitted that the price was right. Lu and I began to appreciate still another reason: the weather was superb, the sun shining all the time in the dry air.

The first priority was to decide which buildings would meet the needs of the first year. George Pearl had come up with some interesting ideas on the four rectangular buildings on the east side which would become the student residences. He proposed painting them a soft buff adobe and adding porches on front with arches similar to those on the Castle. He had also tinkered with the Old Theatre, as it was called, on the west side of the campus, as our residence. But his firm admitted that they could not produce the specifications required for a contractor to begin work by the first of the year. We were obliged to change architects, to Flatow, Moore, and Bryan. John Moore took over and George Pearl remained as a consultant. Everyone agreed that we should leave the Castle for a later day, but that we should weatherproof it and then close it. All of us were disappointed, especially as the dust bowl at the bottom of the hill seemed so uninspiring.

Least complicated of the renovations would be the four dormitories, originally built in1966. Although we had hoped that we could reconfigure the small, dark cell-like interiors to provide for four students to each room as at Pearson and Atlantic, that would have meant removing too many partitions. We settled for two to a room. The built-ins already there would continue to work although they would require mattresses specially designed to be narrower but longer than regular twin size. On the ground level we would put apartments for faculty and the resident tutor (a phrase we coined as preferable to housemaster and less sexist) would live in what had been deanery apartments at the end of the middle floor—an idea that did not work out after a year's trial. Some thought we could squeeze in three living quarters on the ground level, but the absence of cross ventilation and windows on the north suggested we start with one larger apartment in each of the two south-facing dorms.

We were also concerned about adequate lounge space. Fortunately in the middle of each of the upper two floors there was an area which the seminarians had used for study, adjacent to the wash rooms. We figured the cost of renovation would run about $5000 per bed as opposed to $20,000 per bed for new construction. Pearl recommended that, in addition to the porches, we add wing walls at each end. Everyone felt comfortable with the residence halls: we would do two the first year and then two more the following summer. Experience led us to redesign the faculty apartments in the next phase. As each dorm could hold 50 students, we were mesmerized by the coincidence that we would thus have just room for 200, our goal. We agreed to carpet the entire building since sound traveled so easily in cement block structures.

More complicated was the decision where to locate the dining room. In this case we had to plan for the maximum number of 250 persons eating in the building. Originally we had thought that the Casino to the east of the Castle would make a good dining room/theater/kitchen area; but that made no sense when we concluded that the Castle would await the future. We turned to the rectangle known as C-2, the southern one of two residences on the west side of the lower tier—across the road from the Stone Hotel which we had identified as the most likely place for administration, library, and some classrooms. But the dining room and kitchen would not fit on one floor. We decided that only solution was to extend the dining room out to the south of the middle floor, with the kitchen on the north side—its service door close to the road. We did not know what to do with the rest of C-2 until we had decided on our classroom/laboratory requirements. As it turned out, the dining room was too small when it was nearly finished in May; and we had still another projection added—two steps down, on the south side, an adjustment which worked very well indeed.

Of course, this was a heady time when we could dream and still assume that we could finance all that we needed in the highest quality available. Joe Cohen, the indefatigable project manager, and I agreed that we must watch that we got value for every dollar, but we also wanted the place to look like the best UWC in the world. McGill and I talked about the construction budget and warned Pugash and Hammer that it would be double what they had allotted. "No problem." We quickly concluded that we could never complete science laboratories, and equip them, within our time schedule. Therefore, I talked with John Aragon, the puzzling but pleasant president of Highlands University, about using their labs in biology, chemistry, and physics during the late afternoons for the first year. He kindly agreed.

By this time we had concluded that we would use the other dorm on the west side (C-1) as the location of labs and classrooms to be finished during 1982-83. Since this building could be used in the meanwhile with minimum renovation, we put the project management office there and assured ourselves that, if our enrollment came in heavy, we could put students in this hall.

We still had to find classroom space. Matthews and I decided we could get along with only six regular rooms and two seminar rooms. Our *modus operandi* had become apparent by then: we were following the easy route by using the buildings that required the least amount of work and then fitting into them what we required. Even so, all these decisions took a distressingly long time to make. First, the architects had to do some plans; then Cohen and I would review those proposals before sending them to Pugash to review. He in turn wanted to make sure he asked all the questions that Hammer would think appropriate for the simple reason that, should anything cost too much or work out badly, Jim Pugash would be blamed. Second-guessing was common under such circumstances. On the other hand, Jim was committed to the project, he was an extraordinarily hard worker, and he served as a buffer.

As we tried to sort out where to put the remaining facilities, one issue grew in importance: housing for faculty. The prospect of 200 teenagers careening around the campus led Lu and me to feel that we should have as many faculty present on campus as possible. Matthews heartily concurred, for that was the pattern at Pearson and Atlantic. We thought of using the annex next to the Stone Hotel for three apartments, but it then became clear that it was the only structure that could be remodeled to serve as the director's residence and guest house for the college. Los Angeles did not have much sympathy for faculty housing anyway; let them live in town. In the end we provided for only seven faculty, including ourselves, to live on campus.

The Stone Hotel was another historic landmark. We studied it carefully before concluding that we could provide for staff, the library, and faculty offices quite easily and, during the second phase, open up the second and third floors for classrooms. We would house the infirmary in C-1 for the first year. Interestingly, in the area to be occupied by the library were murals done by *La Raza* in the 1970s; these were preserved by building out over them.

Time was passing all too quickly. It was November already; winter was approaching. We had to find a contractor; we needed better cost estimates; and, even though Cohen and his assistant, Catherine Shuster, had moved out to New Mexico, we still lacked a precise idea of what we could do about the utilities—beyond burying the electric and telephone lines and thus ridding the campus of the laundry lines going every which way. We were worried, especially when we realized that the largest local contractor, Jim Franken, could not handle so big an assignment. He could and would weatherproof the Castle, but we had to turn to Albuquerque for help from Bradbury and Stamm, a fine firm. It would cost us probably 15% more, but Hammer wanted to get moving. In another sense that decision to hold to our opening in September 1982 was remarkable since not only would it cost more, but it might also lead to hasty mistakes, and might not work out anyway. But fools and optimists share some things in common.

Meanwhile, back in Erb Place, the word processor had appeared, a second phone line had been installed, and the correspondence began. When the post office issued a

Renovation of the Stone Hotel during the spring of 1982.

stamp featuring desert cacti, we bought all we could for our mailings. The Montezuma post office was happy also since they had been threatened with closure under the Reagan consolidation plans. Our business saved them, but it did not qualify them for either a postage meter or even a sponge to wet the stamps!

Recognizing that I should learn more about the International Baccalaureate, I went to New York City to confer with the senior officer for North America, Gil Nichol, an old friend who had worked for Homer Babbidge at the University of Connecticut. He assured me that, as soon as I knew what we would offer from the IB curriculum and who the basic staff might be, he would be prepared to request the approval of the Geneva Office to proceed. In the hallway where he had his unprepossessing quarters, Nichol filled me in on the requirements and some of the political struggles then occurring in the IB. As IB approval was all we would need technically to operate, that was a relief; but I still felt that we should seek approval from the North Central Association of Schools and Colleges and the State of New Mexico. That meant having in place an outline of our programs—in short, a catalog.

That thought led to searching first for a dean of studies who had had experience with the IB and, if possible, with the UWC routines. I wrote to the other UWCs to ask if they knew of someone or, even better, if they would allow me to raid one of their senior faculty. They all offered to help, which gave the new folks on the block a good feeling.

It was now October 30. There was snow on the ground, and we were getting ready to leave for a visit to Atlantic College in Wales and to attend our first International Board meeting. David Bennett would take care of our animals. Bennett had been caretaking the Montezuma property for a number of years and in particular knew the history of the property better than anyone else. He would remain on our staff for many years. The snow prevented our jogging that day—exercise that we found much more strenuous at 6500 feet than in Vermont. As others would discover, elevation also reduced the blood pressure and pulse rate. It might even be healthier for everyone to come to New Mexico.

3: OFF TO LONDON

Our pulses beat a bit faster when we went to London. We had yet to realize how much travel we would be doing. For the moment it was exciting to land at Heathrow, go to Paddington Station and catch the train to Bridgend. A taxi took us through the hedgerows to Llantwit Major and St. Donat's. David Sutcliffe, the headmaster and by far the best informed person on the history of the movement, met us. It was dark and rainy as we looked toward the Bristol Channel. We had a bite to eat and then Sutcliffe showed us to the Lady Anne room in the tower of the brooding castle which M. Antonin Besse had bought from William Randolph Hearst for around $300,000 in 1961.

We knew the story of Hearst and his companion, Marion Davies. Hearst had redone St. Donat's and then presented it to her. A few days of the Welsh prospect and she had decided she would be better off in some other house. As we entered the room, the rain was whipping through the mullions and dead flies covered the floor—a portent of problems we would have later. But it was all most romantic and Sutcliffe most gracious. Lu read the fire procedures on the back of the door, concluded they were too complicated, and we went to bed. In the middle of the night a siren went off. We remembered the instructions but concluded that we would wait and see what happened—or perish. It was the sea rescue horn, our introduction to the significance of the search and rescue program.

The next two days were spent meeting with faculty and staff. We toured their facilities and wondered if we would ever have anything comparable—especially as we looked down across the terraces to the water beyond and visited their two pools. We even met with the entire student body to assure them of our future. The atmosphere was most encouraging until an American student asked what our policy on drugs would be. I said that we would not permit them and anyone using, buying or distributing drugs would go home immediately. That disappointed that questioner. But what most impressed us was that, despite their young age, these students were extraordinarily articulate, friendly, and confident. Obviously the program worked very well at Atlantic and we began to doubt if we could ever put anything comparable together in New Mexico.

Returning to London, we found that our hotel room was not available and we were sent to another place on Queen's Way where Sir Ian Gourlay and Anne Marie Nylander, chairman of the national committee in Sweden, picked us up to have dinner in Greenwich at the Gourlays's home. What no one expected was the sudden appearance of the Hammers for dinner. They were passing through and would leave dinner early to lift off in the Oxy 727 before the runways were closed for the night.

The next day I went to the UWC offices in Mecklenburg Square. It was really too early to ask questions and I certainly did not know how best to respond to the repeated inquiries about Hammer's intentions, always a matter of curiosity. But the fact that an American college might appear the next year caused some excitement.

Other prospects were stirring elsewhere. In a manner reminiscent of the confusion that had arisen over which was the second UWC, Pearson or The United World College of Southeast Asia in Singapore (and that had been a dead heat in the spring of 1975), plans were progressing for the opening of a college in Duino, Italy. In 1974 a distinguished Italian diplomat, Gianfranco Bonetti, and others had received enthusiastic backing from the regional government of Friuli-Venezia-Giulia for a UWC in northeastern Italy. The earthquake which struck the area in 1976 stalled the project for understandable reasons. Activity resumed in 1977, and Tony Besse, deputy-chairman of the International Board, and David Sutcliffe with his experience as head of Atlantic College began refining the details for the site near the castle owned by the Prince of Torre and Tasso in Duino, some 20 kilometers west of Trieste. And in Venezuela the Prince of Wales had responded favorably to a proposal for the establishment of the United World College of Agriculture. Luis Marcano was asked to head up a founding committee in 1978. A change in government the next year slowed the process down. But in 1981 FUNDACEA was set up as a non-profit foundation to develop the college. For some this move to a more practical education was an appropriate departure from the emphasis originally placed on leadership in the international community. For others, as later discussions would reveal, it was a very worrisome departure from the very strong academic reputation achieved by the IB schools. My first impressions of the central office were mixed: dreary quarters, good people, and an unclear mandate.

That evening we went to a dinner of the International Board members held at the Stafford Hotel. Security was impressive since Prince Charles would be present. We had drinks in the wine cellar and there met His Royal Highness. He quickly asked: "What are you going to do for search and rescue since you have no water?" "Take to the mountains, sir." He wished us good luck. Others who asked about our plans could not conceal their skepticism that we could open in 1982. Dinner was pleasant, especially as Michael Colborne, secretary to the Prince of Wales's office, was seated next to Lu. He was just about to leave the Prince's service and entertained the table with Palace stories. When the Prince spoke, he expressed great concern about the scholarship policy; he felt parents should contribute because the costs were running so high. During the discussion we learned that the majority felt strongly in favor of full scholarships for everyone to assure admission on merit. Only Singapore demurred. When asked, we came down on the side of a financial means test. We would return to this topic innumerable times.

The next day the International Board met. Kingman Brewster was the only other American present. Except for Anne Marie Nylander from Sweden, all were men showing a lot of gray hair. These were largely people who had been involved, like Corrado Belci from Italy and Sir John Partridge from Atlantic, with the founding of the colleges. Symons presided with infinite patience. The only major item of business was the formal acceptance of a school in Swaziland as the fourth UWC. Waterford kamHlaba, located in Mbabane, had been started in 1963 as a multi-racial school funded largely by liberal South Africans opposed to apartheid. Unlike Singapore which had been a typical international school for foreigners living and doing business in that country, Waterford had sought some association in the seventies with the UWC movement since it felt isolated. At that time, following the pattern used with Singapore as an associated school, the board was sympathetic to admitting Waterford to full status although it could not pay the normal annual subsidy to the central office. It was the first UWC in a developing country and thus addressed one of the criticisms leveled at the movement for being too western, first world.

I was asked to give a brief report on our plans and progress to date. I was then bombarded with questions about Hammer's role and the extent of his commitment. It was the first public encounter with the skepticism many held about his involvement. One reason was that this would be the first UWC dependent on one man's pledge. Members were also puzzled by the choice of Montezuma, New Mexico. Dagfinn Paust, clearly unimpressed with American education and wondering aloud whether any Norwegians would ever want to attend, asked: "Not having been able to find the city on any map and discovering that New Mexico is at least a day from anywhere else of any importance in the United States, how is anyone going to get there?" Later he rescinded his criticism and often came to our defense on the matter of parental payments. And we uncovered the fact that, when he was a Norwegian pilot training in Canada in 1942, he had skied against me in Lake Placid, New York, when I was at school there.

In retrospect it was a curious meeting. Little business of any importance took place; everyone accepted the plans for the Adriatic College as splendid; and most had limited enthusiasm for a U.S. UWC. Some openly questioned whether we would insist on high enough standards. That was surprising in view of the fact that the United States was the fastest growing area for new IB schools presumably meeting that standard. In Texas alone there were more IB schools than in any country outside of the U.S. and Canada. In the midst of this tepid reception Jack Matthews spoke up with great enthusiasm and assured them that we would be operating next year, "because that is way they do things in North America."

No doubt, part of the unease derived from views expressed earlier by the U.S. Committee in New York. Part also can be attributed to our announcement that we would follow a different policy on financial assistance to students. I explained that, in keeping with the policy of private schools and universities in the States, we would expect parental contribution according to the financial needs analysis. Some jumped to the conclusion that we would favor those who could pay and not accept merit as the sole criterion.

There was irony in all this talk, not only because of what Prince Charles had said the evening before, but also in light of what we had been told about support from national committees. As Hammer would never forget, or forgive, the international office and the chairman had assured us that we could count on about half of our students coming with support from their committees—a most important projection in terms of our tuition income. That it never happened was unfortunate; but even this first meeting suggested that not all was well with the finances of the movement—something to which we would return frequently.

But it had been a good introduction to what lay ahead.

4: HURRY UP THE CONSTRUCTION

We returned to sunny New Mexico. The snow had melted. And we had to get on with the recruiting of a dean of studies. We would look for two people in English, one of whom would specialize in English as a second language; a person in Spanish who could help students offering another language; possibly some help in French and German on a part-time basis; two mathematicians; a chemist, biologist, and physicist to fill out the sciences; an historian and an economist for The Study of Man section; and part-time help in art and music. We looked for 11 full-time faculty and three to six part-time people. We put out advertisements, and received over 400 replies. That challenged the word-processor in this day of affirmative action. Many responses came from overseas, a quick confirmation of the international network that exists, especially among IB schools. Sorting, checking references, thinking about scheduling interviews: all this made us wonder if we could finish by April. We did wish to bring all serious candidates to New Mexico to see where we were and what they might encounter.

We were fortunate to have two excellent suggestions for dean immediately. However, when we brought in the candidate from Singapore, it was clear that the family was not yet ready for the wide open spaces and the absence of urban amenities. Andrew and Heather Maclehose from Atlantic College came over in the early winter and hiked up Hermit's Peak in street shoes, a good sign. Andrew had held the equivalent position in Wales and had taught Theory of Knowledge, a required segment of the IB. They accepted our offer, a most fortunate decision for us. Once that appointment was in place, we could jointly proceed with a catalog for the first class.

We had begun recruiting that class as early as possible since communications with many countries, the London Office had forewarned, was slow indeed. Matthews offered to help with the international student quota of 75 since he knew many of the chairmen. We would concentrate on the 25 Americans, of whom two, we decided, should be Native Americans. We set a deadline of March 15 for all applications to be in, optimism that has never been warranted in practice. We inquired of the Department of State what procedures would be necessary for the students to enter this country. They promised to notify the embassies and work with them. No one mentioned any other requirements, an oversight that later proved very upsetting. But at least we were moving forward on the major decisions.

In truth our operation was quite modest. We estimated that it would cost us $250,000 for our expenses until July of 1982, to cover recruitment, admissions, printing, general operations, and personnel salaries. We had talked with people about the security of the property, for instance, and were told firmly that we must have people as we began construction. Therefore, we had two people on eight-hour shifts around the clock beginning with the new year. We maintained our own books. That was not easy since we did not have either a set advance on funds or even an indication as to when we would get paid. Los Angeles was generous and responsive, but we needed to establish procedures if we were to handle the purchase of equipment and supplies properly. The proposed construction would only complicate matters of cash flow.

Having sorted out how to handle the legal and architectural fees, we ran further projections on the total renovations for the first year: $4,000,000. Hammer's office wanted much of it put out to bid; but if we followed that process, we would not get the job done on time. We settled on one contract with Bradbury and Stamm, with an upset figure and a penalty clause if there were delays. For the next two years this decision brought periodic complaints as having cost far, far more. But, in my judgment, it did not cost us much more than going out for bid; and it did make it possible for us to open on time. It is well also to recall that none of this would have been possible without the generosity of the Armand Hammer Foundation and the hard work of people like Joe Cohen, Jim Pugash, John Moore, Bob Stamm, and Catherine Schuster who helped Cohen by searching for mattresses, lamps, and library card indexes, as well as special deals on furniture. Through their efforts we located our dining room chairs and tables at Pomona College in California for $10 each, as one example of the frugal approach we insisted upon.

Among other early decisions was the selection of a food service company. We talked with ARA, Saga, and Sun West, a New Mexican group. We asked for bids and chose Saga, largely because they appeared to have the requisite managerial backup and could also assist in planning the layout of the kitchen equipment. Again the ominous timetable prodded us. It was not cheap, however: we would be spending almost $1800 a student for food each year.

Another decision we had to make was the kind of fringe benefits we would provide faculty and staff. In keeping with current trends, we wanted the basic program to apply equally to all salaried personnel and a comparable package to be available for the hourly wage earners. Many of the fine details would have to await the construction of a budget and the establishment of a business office, which we anticipated opening in July of 1982. We chose the CIGNA corporation because I was familiar with their programs and they could offer comprehensive coverage and thus limit our dealings to one vendor providing health, disability, and life insurance, a strong annuity program, and the appropriate liability protection. We could then provide an outline as we sought to recruit personnel. Not so easy was procuring fire and casualty insurance. No one wanted to include the castle except Aetna, and after two years they canceled that policy. A similar problem arose in getting student health insurance. Finally we worked out an agreement with a firm in Albuquerque. It was disappointing that we could not use local brokers; but they were neither competitive nor able to draw up a package that would meet our needs. Perhaps, like many local merchants and suppliers, they had not confronted a schedule such as we insisted on following: tradition had accepted a certain relaxation in meeting deadlines. That did change, but we learned repeatedly that in New Mexico we were not operating in a large city—a condition Los Angeles did not always fully grasp.

The weather was a further reminder. Heavier snow came in December, and the mornings were beautifully crisp, with the smell of *piñon* from the fireplaces hanging in the air. We went back east for the Christmas break and we had two days in Quechee before the family arrived. There was plenty of snow, high enough for some *luminarias* and outdoor lighting. It was our last holiday of this kind, and we admitted that it was unlikely we would spend much of the future there. And in fact, we eventually sold that home in favor of a place in New Mexico—yet another indication of the wisdom of having chosen the southwest for the setting of this United World College.

When we got back, the local contractors, Jim Franken and Company, were at work weather-proofing the Castle. They had also begun work on the Stone Hotel. But we had not started on digging for the new utility lines. We concluded that we could retrofit the existing boilers for heat, and Jim Pugash had located a stand-by septic-lagoon system at the Sandia ski area outside of Albuquerque. We would dig a lagoon on the south side, put in a liner and then hook up the filtration system. This lagoon water could then be fed into the irrigation system we had planned for the front playing fields.

But we had one major obstacle to overcome: how to get heavy vehicles to and from the campus across the Gallinas. The bridge from the post office was old. The state highway department estimated that it would carry five tons safely. How had they arrived at the estimate? "Oh, a windshield estimate: we look out the windshield as we drive over." That was not reassuring. We also heard that the State was going to replace route 65 with a new road up the canyon through the middle of the playing fields. After frequent conversations with various officials over the next six months, we were back to where we started; namely, using the ford, thinking about repairing the bridge, and using the road up the canyon as an alternate. We also learned repeatedly that everyone wanted to cooperate if Hammer would pay for the bridge, the road—or the world. Locally the assumption was that Hammer had a pot of gold from which all local charities and enterprises could expect a contribution. We had to inform people gently but firmly that such was not the case.

As winter settled in and we realized that we had only six months left to complete the project, the tempo increased. We began to bring faculty prospects to campus. Interviews in our house at 801 Erb Place were appropriately stilted; then lunch at El Rialto on Bridge Street would relax the candidates, especially if they were unaccustomed to chile; and after dinner at the El Alto Supper Club, we had usually reached a decision on whether to hire or to wait for the next interview. The setting did challenge the wardrobe: should one dress up or down? Visits to the campus led to questions about readiness, and the answers had a delightfully fictional sincerity about them. Matthews and I speculated about foreign faculty and went ahead with the search "hopefully," an adverb that became well-worn that first year. We did not know, of course, how people would get along with each other. In the end we did very well indeed.

Tragedy struck in February, 1982. Jim Doolittle, who had been so helpful, crashed in his helicopter during a night take-off and died. An experienced pilot, he nonetheless caught his blades in the telephone wires near his ranch. Thus we lost one who was well-known in New Mexico, genuinely interested in our programs, and a close personal friend.

A recital of this year of preparation needs to be placed in some perspective. It may be fascinating to know that the first 4000 books for the library were going to cost $45,000 instead of the original estimate of $30,000; but even when estimates were really only guesstimates (something that haunted our construction), this activity occurred within a climate that was to prevail for years and affect the style in which our business took place. Decision-making followed an unusual course. On most everyday matters Lu and I decided what should be done and paid the bills. On construction and the purchase of furnishings et al, Joe Cohen would recommend to us what we should do, we would review it, and then we would talk with Pugash in Los Angeles. He was quick in either providing an answer or getting one from Hammer; but he did not have experience in the myriad of matters that necessarily came up. Bill McGill always reminded me that Hammer's assistants had short tenure and that, therefore, we might lose something "in translation" as it worked its way around the top floor on Wilshire Boulevard. With no member of the board in the area and infrequent visits by anyone from

California, we were operating in an atmosphere quite different from anything we had known before. I had also been unable to keep in touch with my former associates in the east, with whom I might have compared notes. As time went on, it was increasingly remarkable that this transformation of an historic site into a college commanded so little outside oversight. But that only made the tension greater since a bolt from the blue might strike at any moment. The main constant was haggling over costs.

As the winter wore on, we went through the normal debates about alternatives. Original plans for the Stone Hotel and the Annex were too grandiose. Therefore, the hotel's front porches (later installed as a gift from the contractor) were eliminated; fireplaces in the president's home and the library were cut; we chose to use cheaper stacks for the library (which arrived in late August unassembled); and we were severely disappointed in the landscaping design. We discontinued the landscaping company's work and improvised, mainly after school had opened. Early consideration of our telephone service was essential if we were to be able to operate in July and August. It proved to be a frustrating arrangement since US West did not have much equipment in Las Vegas; but to their credit, it was up and running on time.

Meanwhile we were jumping over the ditches that snaked their way across virtually the entire lower tier. With nearly 100 men working on various parts of the renovations, we began to think of it as some kind of theater; but no one knew which act it was or when the climax would come. We had a master plan for four phases, but no one was interested in anything except phase one. Thus those to whom it seemed logical to know the ultimate layout of the campus and alternative uses of the open spaces were disappointed. No doubt Hammer was critically concerned that the lower part be presentable when Prince Charles and others arrived in October.

Putting the pieces together involved matters other than plumbing and electricity. We had to expand the board. We held a meeting in Los Angeles on February 17, 1982, to review our progress. Present were Hammer, McGill, Arthur Groman, Pugash, and Lu and I. As would be typical at many such meetings, such major matters as the architect's plans and the budget for phase one of the construction were calmly approved without discussion. We changed the opening date from September 9th to the 14th; faculty guidelines, salary scales, and fringe benefits were all accepted without objection. Even the budget for the first year of operations ($2,005,000, of which half was for further capital improvements) was approved; but Hammer wanted it reviewed at every meeting.

Then Hammer mentioned he would be suggesting a number of prominent people as possible board members. No one demurred or suggested that the board first review such names. When Hammer told Groman, his lifetime legal adviser and close friend, "I'm going to ask Dear Abby (Abigail Van Buren) to come on the Board," Groman demurred. "Dear Abby won't agree." Hammer argued that she would be a natural.

Groman countered, "But every school and university in the USA wants her." "Do you want to bet she'll say yes?" Hammer challenged. Groman yielded because, as he told us, "In 1956, when Hammer was acquiring Occidental, I bet him that the stock, then selling at 20 cents a share, would not reach $2 within a year. I lost."

Setting the comprehensive fee at $8500 a year did evoke some questions. I explained that we were in a strange situation; namely, that the UWCs tried to keep their fees comparable so that there would not be a "cheap" UWC or an inappropriately expensive one. We pegged ours above Atlantic but below Pearson. Obviously Waterford was an exception. No one knew what the Adriatic college would charge—just millions of lire! Against our estimated costs that would mean a subsidy of nearly $1500 per student at the outset. Hammer accepted that feature on the assumption that half of the students would be paid for by committees. This issue never died as budget succeeded budget.

On other issues we were proceeding smoothly. The International Baccalaureate Office gave final approval for our using the program. We inquired again about student visas, only to discover that we had to obtain other approvals from the Department of Justice as well as State. We sought that permission only to learn that we must have had sufficient operating experience that we could demonstrate what happened to our graduates. We would need state and regional accreditation before we could invite foreign students. We called Delayo's State education office in Santa Fe; they were surprised. We talked with Washington. They found our financial information insufficient. The Office of Education was perplexed as well. Hot water lines might be important, but this dilemma was alarming in its implications. It was a Catch-22. Obviously the government did not want to endorse a program about which they knew little, which was not up and running, and whose finances appeared shaky at best. We tried every avenue of both reason and influence. Nothing happened: Immigration and Naturalization was unresponsive. We felt that we had made some ghastly mistake.

In the end it required political pressure from various quarters to get the I-20 forms delivered. By then foreign students were becoming uneasy since they had to go to the local U.S. embassies which, as it turned out, had not read their mail and thus knew nothing about an institution not listed in any handbook in their libraries. We quickly found out that there were jurisdictional boundaries that prevented Justice from talking to Education or to State. Having finally resolved this sticky issue, we learned from Poland and China that they required IAP-66 cultural exchange forms since they wanted their students to return home after the two years. We applied and went through the same frustrating delays again. Oddly enough, Russia, whom we expected to insist on the IAP-66 as well, did not; but they were alarmed to find out that their embassy officials could not check out the college since it was located in New Mexico, an area off-limits for Russians.

We were in a juggling act by May. We had not heard from some countries. Matthews had run into complications with the Canadian embassies since Ottawa insisted on involving the U. S. cultural affairs officers in the U.S. embassies in Egypt, Turkey, Israel, Yugoslavia, etc.. Communications were shockingly poor, and many embassies ignored us. All of this totally surprised London which could not understand the strange and wonderful ways of American bureaucracy. Jack and I would review the admissions list every time he came down. Panama would come on to replace Papua New Guinea. No one knew what was happening in Senegal or Zambia or Bolivia. As we were branching into countries new to the UWC like Nepal, Pakistan, Chile, and Palestine, the guessing game became even less certain. In particular, Nepal illustrated a new hazard. The application papers we received had a name and description that did not correspond with the student whose name had been submitted. We later learned that this student, Pradesh Shrestha, had heard about the college through U.S. friends and had sent us his documents in the hope we would give him a scholarship too. Our contact in Kathmandu had encouraged him as well since he felt the first candidate, Shiva Gurung, would do better if he had a countrymate. India did not reply until August with one candidate; but Hammer had seen Indira Gandhi and we ended up with three, chosen by means unknown to anyone. France would be similar: Hammer talked with Madame Mitterand who found two students. Lu was finding that most of her time was spent on student recruitment and accompanying correspondence.

Everyone liked our first brochure and fact book, a deliberately thin substitute for the traditional catalog. But mailing it was a challenge. Our first effort at Montezuma took hours because the post office did not have any stamps larger than 50 cents. So all of us valiantly licked the postage for overseas ($2.80 each envelope). As replies came in, we began a whole new stamp collection. More serious was another consideration: boys versus girls. Our plumbing and sleeping provisions required an even distribution. At first, it appeared we would have too many girls; then in July the trend went to boys and remained that way. We had to plan on using three bedrooms in another dorm (C-1). U.S. recruitment had been disappointing. We had run a large ad in the New York *Times*; very few responses. The New York office was not finding many well qualified candidates although they had a goodly number of applications. I began recruiting directly. Which led to an amusing episode in April when Hammer paid a visit to the campus. We were sitting around in the house Joe Cohen had rented. He asked about admissions. I explained how complicated it had become with national committees and their payments, and with finding U.S. students. "In that case, you will have to interview every candidate personally. And make sure they don't have long hair." By this time I had learned to listen to such statements, try not to respond, and then go about the normal routines.

We also encountered some resistance from parents who could pay. They pointed out that, if their son or daughter went to Pearson, they would get a full scholarship whereas at Montezuma they would have to pay. This issue was too important to go away, and we petitioned London to help. It was put on the next agenda for October. The problem did not end there. We had counted on London assisting with national committees, especially in providing financial support for their candidates. It was not happening. Our tuition projections would be woefully below budget. I had forewarned of some of the implications in a letter to Groman. I wrote: "I think the board needs to recognize that we could conceivably have as many as 60% of our 100 students on some form of scholarship aid from the U.S. UWC. We shall never have enough tuition revenue to balance the budget: we shall have deficits that must be covered annually by contributions or endowment income. That worries me over the long haul, because our fee structure is hedged in by those set in Wales and Canada—and by fees at the best preparatory schools [where Exeter and Andover have large endowments]. It will be creative financing for a while." And so it turned out.

As I suggested earlier, the enterprise came to resemble a very strange and wonderful theatrical production. Everyone was scurrying around looking for make-up, only to discover that the actors had not been hired. Rehearsals were impossible since the stage had not been fixed up, but the props were piling up in C-2. The mattresses were the wrong size, but there was no one to sleep on them anyway. We were printing the tickets for opening night without knowing what we would do on that date since none of the faculty and staff had yet arrived to arrange the reception. We were inviting students from all over the world but with little appreciation of what it means to work with people who basically know nothing about us, are properly skeptical of going to the superpower land, and cannot find Montezuma on any map in any atlas they consult. And we had no notion of what the admissions results would be when the doors opened and the stage was all lit up.

We had incredible optimism. The unlikely combination of ignorance and experience may have been ideal: ignorance of what other problems lay ahead but with enough experience to improvise whatever the challenge. Haggling over money was the only truly upsetting matter.

The next meeting of the board was in Montezuma on April 19, 1982. By that time we had some new board members: Mrs. Morton Phillips (Dear Abby), a Los Angeles developer, Guilford Glazer (whose wife, Diane, would subsequently join the board), and Rosemary Tomich, a California rancher and member of Oxy's Board. The first action was to expand the board to thirteen with the addition of friends and associates of

Board members: Arthur Groman, long-time lawyer for Hammer, and Guilford Glazer, generous supporter.

Hammer: the ceramicist Helen Boehm, Metromedia financier John Kluge, Paramount Pictures director Sherry Lansing, and a Washington lawyer, Francis Saul. With astonishing optimism the board agreed to meet four times a year, presumably half of such meetings being held on the campus. Then the chairman, Dr. McGill, explained the evolution of the name of the college; for in March it had become evident that, in return for his philanthropy, Hammer would like his name inscribed. Therefore, we became Armand Hammer College: The United World College of the American West. Other reports were optimistic since the U.S. Committee had told me that 350 people had applied. Later we learned it was the number of inquiries. In any event, the board wanted the director to make all final decisions on who was admitted. I then alluded briefly to our problem, prospectively, with faculty housing since all candidates wanted to live in Montezuma, not Las Vegas. Since we could accommodate only six families free on campus, we were subsidizing the rentals in Las Vegas with a stipend of $5000 so as to avoid differentiation in salaries. The other curiosity of this meeting was a comment by the Honorary Chairman that "the Board of Directors should consider the possibility of developing the Castle as a resort hotel or spa, so that the income generated from the development could be used as an endowment for the College." It is all part of the history.

In that same meeting we indicated how much we had spent thus far. We had set up our accounts in the pattern approved by the American Council on Education despite urging from Oxy to use corporate accounting. Even so, the American form of fiduciary bookkeeping would make comparisons with the other UWCs difficult. In total we had dispersed $169,000 by the end of February 1982, most of it for general institutional purposes. Our projected expenditures for the construction, through August, were $5.5 million, a figure that proved high as well as unacceptable. On the other hand, we were working against the unknown, and a generous figure seemed safer than one we would readily exceed. Equipment and furnishings would probably cost around $300,000 for the first year, without the science laboratories for the second year.

Spring had come early and seductively to Montezuma after the five snow storms that had blown through that winter of 1982. With May came hailstorms, however, and we began to appreciate what it took to grow a garden in this region. In May McGill, Hammer, and I concluded that it might help the college if we had an Honorary Board of Trustees. To our European friends, already disaffected by the name change, this decision appeared to add further confusion and a suspiciously fund-raising twist to the governance. But then, some never did recognize American ingenuity with respect to raising money. The proposed list sounded sufficiently impressive: Phyllis George Brown, Mary Lee and Douglas Fairbanks, Jr., Phyllis Rothschild Farley, Arthur Gilbert, Merv Griffin, Fred L. Hartley, Bob Hope, Phoebe and Pompeo Maresi, Suleiman Olayan, James Roosevelt, Carola Warburgh Rothschild, and Frank Sinatra. Obviously we were trying to associate the prominent members of the U.S. Committee in New York with our undertaking as well as what would be known as "Hollywood types."

The timing was in anticipation of a second Broadlands Ball in England at the end of May. But there were some reservations about that affair, another fund-raising effort by the U.S. Committee. It had become all too clear that the committee expected Los Angeles to play a major role in getting financial backing and in recruiting prominent couples to come, at the cost of $1000 per couple in addition to travel expenses. We hesitated about spending the money to go, but in the end did attend the Gala—and it proved to be a memorable occasion indeed, well organized and done in a style one could only compliment. It raised everyone's spirits.

Events began on May 28 at the Guild Hall in London. Dr. Aldo Gucci had arranged a fashion show, to be followed by dinner. Not many of the people there knew anything about the United World Colleges. Above the inevitable din, we did our best to explain what we were doing; and it was most encouraging to see so many present and presumably ready to support the movement. On Saturday afternoon, May 29, we took the bus to Broadlands, the estate where Lord Mountbatten had lived and now occupied by his daughter, Lady Patricia Mountbatten and her husband Lord Brabourne, and the grandson, Lord Norton Romsey and Lady Penelope Romsey who, we discovered, were close friends of Prince Charles.

It was a magnificent setting on the River Test, originally made famous by Lord Palmerston. This was the occasion on which those who had paid to attend would finally meet the Prince and Princess of Wales. Hammer had arranged for a private reception in advance of the main dinner-dance for donors to the American college. As Lu and I went down the reception line, Charles looked up and said: "What are you doing here? I thought you would be in New Mexico getting things ready." When I alluded to the fund-raising possibilities, he laughed and said, "You Americans are always ready to catch the money when it drops."

The parade to dinner was a different world from Montezuma and a reminder that people do cross the Atlantic to shake the hand of the future King of England and sit, preferably, where they can view royalty. Seating had proved a problem, as it turned out. As a result, to avoid offense, Dr. Hammer sat on the right hand of Lady Diana and I sat on her left—and Lu joined the Prince's table. The Princess, very much with child, may not have found the white-haired flanking all that intriguing and conversation was not always brilliant—at either table. In the course of this dinner, Prince Charles asked Tom Symons and myself to confer on one side of the large tent which protected us from the showers.

"I want to announce the name of your college tonight, but I find the present title too cumbersome." Symons and I explained its origin. The Prince was not convinced and thus peering out of one of the false windows of the tent, we agreed to a new name: The Armand Hammer United World College of the American West. In his remarks thanking Dr. Hammer, the Prince proclaimed the new nomenclature. And then came the auction at which the Los Angeles visitors did most of the purchasing. Later we learned that some $300,000 had been raised over the weekend.

Meanwhile McGill, Pugash, and I concluded that we needed to use the occasion for a special dinner of Hammer's guests on Sunday night at Claridge's: it was too good a chance to miss. This inspirational event would follow a polo match to take place at Windsor Great Park. The event had been arranged by Mr. and Mrs. William Ylvisaker and the Palm Beach Polo and Country Club with help from Helen Boehm (pronounced to rhyme with team) and featured the American players, called the Boehm Team, against Prince Charles's team. Back in London for dinner at Claridge's, Guilford Glazer, speaking as a board member and contagiously enthusiastic about the college, agreed to play the lead role in encouraging people to think ahead about their pledges. When we were all sipping cocktails, we announced the pledge drive. Some rose to the occasion; some coughed; and others sought the restrooms. But we did secure promises totaling nearly three million dollars, most of which over time were honored. The dinner closed a remarkable weekend in England.

Heartening as it was to realize that before even opening the new college had some $500,000 in restricted and unrestricted money as a result (and more pledged for the future), the success of the first Broadlands proved misleading. Some of our foreign friends quickly assumed that, therefore, the United States could provide the necessary financial support for the entire movement. No one was paying much attention to the projections we had prepared. We estimated that we would need an endowment of at least $20 million to offset annual deficits. Otherwise, we would need to raise at least a million each year to underwrite the scholarship costs. Even Dr. Hammer was enthusiastic about the results since he felt others would take some of the burden off his shoulders. We were caught: to diminish the achievement would seem ungrateful; but to exaggerate the support of these early donors would mislead everyone.

The summer schedule was further deflected by my returning to England in June for the meeting of the International Board. Again the question of scholarships arose. Besse proposed the creation of an international endowment for this purpose. No one dissented, but no one knew where the money would come from. We reiterated our policy of a financial means test, and that led others to insist that all students be on tuition scholarships. We could not disarm the notion that we would insist on admission by merit even where parents could pay. At this meeting it was also clear that each of the United World Colleges faced a tremendous annual challenge to find the money to support their programs. And we had our first discussion of a possible college in India, a discussion which illustrated another characteristic of the movement; namely, its penchant to consider new undertakings when it was unclear whether the present institutions could sustain themselves. For years the movement would be torn by its desire to expand and its need to consolidate its resources to make certain it represented the very best quality in international education.

5: THE FINAL PUSH TO OPEN

We moved to our new quarters on the campus in the third week of June. There had been amazing progress, but the plumbing and electrical work was not yet completed; and the offices were not ready. As we had begun to hire staff for an opening date of July 1, we could only hope for the best. That was not enough; for, when we assembled our six people on July 1, plugged in the computers and typewriters, and adjusted the desk lights, we found there was no electricity. So we improvised for a day or so. Deliveries of furnishings arrived daily, and we stashed them away in places not yet renovated. As we should have expected, we ran into some major problems that summer. First, we could not arrange for the pumping station at our new lagoon until September. That meant we would just let the water build up temporarily until we could then test out the irrigation system later. Most of the utility lines had been buried, but we decided not to extend the lines up the hill to the Castle. In a sense that was illogical since we had the main water line to the top of the hill where our holding reservoir received city water and then distributed it, holding enough to provide for the fire hydrants. But we could not justify the expense at that time. More serious was the collapse of the floor under the new boiler when it was delivered: that delayed testing of the heating system for weeks. And then the coal which was delivered from Colorado for the tests was the wrong size anyway. The kitchen was ready to go by September 7th despite the late addition to the dining room. Seldom do we remember these unglamorous details, but they were vivid at the time. But nothing compared to the mud.

When the first monsoon rains struck—an afternoon phenomenon in these mountains during six to eight weeks in the summer, the acres of dirt turned to gooey adobe mud. Cars and trucks got stuck; our L.L. Bean rubbermocs became encrusted with the

Ted and Lu Lockwood at the time the College opened, 1982.

stuff; and, as luck would have it, that summer's rains exceeded anything the region had known for ten years. Then again, we found that everything in San Miguel County was measured ten years at a time. It was this mud which would lead one of our first Indian students, S.P. Kumar, to exclaim as he descended from the bus in a downpour, "To think I left India for this!"

Time was passing and there remained many tasks to complete before we could begin operations. In this respect Highlands University was most helpful. We worked out the schedule for science laboratories, and we conferred about salaries for all the personnel in the administration so as not to disturb expectations in the region. We also took their associate librarian, Lucy Cruz, to establish our library, especially since the books which we had ordered were already arriving. But we had not had time to organize community service. Lu and I had spoken with various groups in Las Vegas; but it was not until Peggy Baker arrived from Connecticut that we were able to divide up our incoming students so that everyone had exposure to both wilderness training and in-town service. Tom Callanan was going to handle our Search and Rescue Program, and we planned to introduce all students to the outdoors during our orientation.

We learned more from the students who came down as volunteers from Pearson College. Nine students arrived ready to work on the campus center although the girl from Malta was shocked at how much had yet to be done. "I came prepared to mow the lawns." After a day or two of digging out drainage ditches, they enjoyed working on the Queen Anne house even when it demanded a lot of scraping and sanding before the paint went on. Lu's sons, Michael and Nicholas Abbot, undertook to reshingle the roof. The two groups who came from Pearson were both a pleasure and such good help that we speculated as to whether we should not exchange groups of UWC students each summer in the future. It did not happen although it may have been the prelude to later conversations about Third-Year Options. The students also were in the film which Hammer Productions began to put together that summer.

Even before the college opened, the name Montezuma was the adopted shorthand, comparable to Pearson and Atlantic. As the summer wore on, not only was the progress of our construction a daily worry, but also plans for opening and for the dedication in October. One concern in particular loomed large: facilities for exercise. We had always assumed we would have soccer and softball on the fields along the road, but they were mud now. Therefore, we surveyed the area northwest of the Castle where there seemed to be room for three tennis courts and a shrunken basketball court. Los Angeles kindly agreed to let us proceed with their construction. They even agreed that we should think seriously about a swimming pool. We began planning—and are still planning for a pool. To add to our distractions, Hammer's office wanted to know how much the second phase would cost; in short, what was the minimum we would need for September 1983? We came up with a figure. Actually we felt fairly confident in August as our staff and new faculty started working. Maybe we simply took refuge in saying, "They will understand if everything is not ready."

Our lean administrative staff was performing extraordinarily well, with Al Romero supervising the development of our business systems. We had discovered that our word processor could not handle the accounting needs, and it would take some time to develop the appropriate machinery for our financial affairs. Moreover, it was complicated because Los Angeles wanted information we could not easily generate. We were trying valiantly to put our medical program, insurance policies, and annuities in place; and we were perpetually harassing Los Angeles for cash with which to function. In turn, their bookkeeping had been confused by the various transfers to the Foundation, in and out of Oxy accounts, and advances for the dedication. Only years later did it become clear that too many people were involved to assure both clear accountability and a smoothly functioning transfer of funds, properly designated.

By now there was some national interest in what we were doing. Inquiries arrived daily. The media would soon enough arrive. *People* magazine would do a flattering interview with Lu and me, and the *Wall Street Journal* did a front-page article on the college. It was no surprise that every analysis expressed some kind of reservation either about the kind of institution or its founder. But, as we needed whatever public relations we could get, we welcomed the press and knew that the dedication in October might well be the last major occasion on which to advertise our programs widely. Local papers had given us coverage but it was not the same—especially when the headline under my picture carried the caption: "Escaped Convict." They had juxtaposed two articles and had kindly assumed that I resembled the convict for whom they lacked, presumably, an appropriate snapshot!

There was no moment at which we could say to ourselves that we were ready. We were not, and the grand opening in September would have to accept the presence of groundskeepers in particular as they worked into the night to finish the basic landscaping. But we had come a long ways since January; in less than a year we had prepared for our first students. It was hard then and still is difficult to maintain a perspective on those months before we opened. We had hurried; we had made fewer mistakes than we might have expected under such pressure; but we had so worthy an enterprise in prospect that we could remain optimistic even when that seemed foolhardy. Certainly the help from the other United World Colleges and from the International Office was both enormous and indispensable. We did not have time to think whether it could have been done differently—or even to check the calendar that closely. We would make it—and that was the atmosphere in Montezuma that summer of 1982.

6: A ROYAL TURNOUT

On September 8, 1982, there were three Italians at the airport awaiting transportation. We had invited only two. Was this situation normal for UWCs? We hoped not since we had too many students. Eugenio Ruggiero, his father, and Enrico Caporale appeared. Thus unexpectedly we had not only two students arriving ahead of time but also a parent.

What we did not know then was that it would be a week before we knew where all the students we had admitted actually were. Lu tried to maintain a log of arrival times and flights. We had bought two used school buses for $8000, a real bargain; but they did not like the hills between Montezuma and the airport. More important at this juncture was the fact that the custom-made mattresses were the wrong size—too short and too wide. There was no choice but to rush out and find 106 futons, which served the students well but displeased, in later years, summer visitors like those from Elderhostel. The company that had made the error in the original mattresses threatened to sue us when we refused to pay "because we are struggling and Armand Hammer is rich." We were to hear such a claim more than once.

The bulk of the students began to arrive on September 11th, and to our surprise all were in by the 13th except for the Chinese who could not gain clearance in Beijing until October and the Soviets who just could not get out of Moscow for a while. The campus was transformed. Then we learned that we did not have not enough bed lamps, and that the showers made too much noise since we had not had time to adjust the hot water system. Otherwise, it was truly a sense of pioneering that took over for both students and faculty.

Of course, we heard horror stories about their travel, none quite so amusing as the two Palestinians. Their agent in Jordan learned that Montezuma was near Las Vegas. Accordingly she booked the students into the Nevada airport. The students were surprised that no one was around to greet them, but they went out to the taxi stand and asked for a ride to Montezuma. "Sure. I can take you," the driver replied. Wisely they asked the fare: $600 was the response. They went back into the airport and sought Traveler's Aid and got a flight to Albuquerque.

Orientation began on the 14th. We had planned to split the students into two groups. One half went to Cimarron for two days of hiking and a visit to Taos; the other half went to Camp Stoney as a base from which to visit Santa Fe. The only trouble at Camp Stoney was the limited amount of food; the chief challenge at Cimarron was the rain. Then each group changed scenery. The program went surprisingly well. Since I had had to enter the hospital for surgery, the official opening was handled by Lu when Dr. Hammer came to greet all the new students. Surely it was with a sense of pride that he shook the hands of all 102 students from 46 countries. As the number of boys exceeded our expectations, we put six of them in C2, the dorm to the north of the dining room building and quickly named "Siberia"—which would work only until we had to begin renovation of this building for a science complex. It was there we would later find illicit beer cans stashed between the wallboard and the outside wall.

Classes began with amazing verve and confidence. Almost all the students knew enough English to follow directions if not yet to grasp the intricacies of economics. But in the dorms we could only wait and see what settled out. We had placed the girls on the top floors of each residence hall; the boys roomed on the middle floor; and the resident tutor lived in the large apartment on the ground floor. We had carefully named each hall with the most prominent peak of each continent; e.g. Sagarmatha and Aconcagua. But the head's brilliant way of avoiding the change in name of each house, as resident tutors changed, did not prevail: the first two houses became Hunter and Roy, named for our new biology and math teachers (both Canadians) who had agreed to serve as RTs. We also had appointed assistant resident tutors to provide relief on weekends and to alternate nightly safety check. We felt that a conservative policy was best: a check on whether everyone was in his or her room at ten seemed a reasonable precaution. For the most part students accepted this restriction, but over the years it would remain an issue open for tiresome debate.

Some students had more acute problems than the time of check-in. The student from Rwanda, Andre Kandy, had lost everything at the Brussels airport, including the paper he had been given as a substitute passport since he was a refugee living in a camp in Burundi. Somehow he made it to New Mexico—as did other students who had inadequate visa papers. In fact, there was considerable variation in the length of stay granted students, and Lu spent all year straightening out these mishaps. Some students tried to impress their colleagues with their brilliance; others clearly were bewildered; only a few were homesick. They did not have much time to worry once the schedule was in full swing. We did discover that our Arab students did not trust the two Israeli girls and wanted to know if they carried arms. The students from this country suddenly discovered that they were outnumbered and perhaps "outsmarted" by all these foreigners. International education was at work.

The persistent rains prevented holding the Open House for Las Vegas until October 10th. It was to be a dry-run for the grand event later in October. And clearly that was going to require more and more of our attention. Hammer wanted trees and grass, and that meant employing people under lights. Janet Jackson, a blind girl from Jamaica, was astonished when she came out of a class and bumped into a tree. "That wasn't there an hour ago!" she exclaimed.

The amount of time spent on arrangements grew ominously. Materials went back and forth between the offices in Montezuma and Oxy headquarters. We were to have ample help, but the planning was already disrupting the normal routines of starting a college. Ron Klink in the dining room was told that he would have all kinds of assistance from Saga operations on the West Coast. A big tent had been ordered, etcetera. Peggy Baker was learning that she would have to do more on this front than on handling changes in registration. For all of us it was a bit hard to concentrate. I was just relieved to feel well and be back at work after ten days of recuperation. And not least among the concerns was just how to get 800 guests to Montezuma and accommodate them for three days. It was our first experience with this kind of Hammer extravaganza.

On October 7 we received a shock. Word came from St. Vincent Hospital that Peggy Baker had been killed in an automobile accident east of Santa Fe. Our project manager, Joe Cohen, had been driving them to Albuquerque and lost control on a curve. Fortunately he was not badly injured, but it was a staggering tragedy for the college and for us personally. Lu lost her closest friend. Others would need to review the progress of the construction for the time being. Two days later we held our open house, preceded by the first annual Montezuma Marathon which Andrew Maclehose had organized. Five thousand people came to see the displays, to meet the students, and to satisfy their curiosity about this strange school now occupying an historic piece of property dear to their hearts. It was a resounding success although the *Albuquerque Journal* chose to run a picture of our undocumented brethren laying sod for the playing fields rather than of our students performing.

The next two weeks were punctuated with calls from Richard Tallboys, the British counsel in Houston, and from Los Angeles—always concerning arrangements for the Prince and other dignitaries. Robert Creighton from the London office came as well to help with the plans for the International Board. Security would be immense, partly because of fear of some Irish fanatic and partly because of having so many people in the Las Vegas area. The FBI wanted to know where each person would be staying. Los Angeles was preparing a timetable at least 20 pages long. Faculty were muttering about the overkill factor, but the students were getting so excited that scholarly efforts declined. CBS wanted to come in early for some advance filming. On the one hand, it was all very exhilarating; on the other hand, it was one big mess as we watched the crews putting the finishing touches on the campus.

The sunny days continued, but the evenings became cooler. It was entirely possible that we might get a snowstorm near the end of October, as we had the previous year. But the 27th arrived and the weather remained promising. By then the camera crews had arrived; the tent had been erected after having blown down the first night; and the Los Angeles staff arrived with a new set of questions.

Our response: "We're as ready as we will ever be."

"But who is driving the Buick?" And so the script ran.

The day before Tom Symons, Chairman of the International Board, had arrived along with Sir Ian Gourlay, Director General. They worked in the study at the house while we hung the Daumier prints Hammer had sent in the room which the Prince would occupy on the third floor. Lu was coping with the two Betamax machines Hammer had rented for use during the celebration. As a number of other board members arrived on the 26th, we had a reception at the house that evening. We had enough plates and the supplementary cooking crew did well on this dry-run. And additional security poured in, all carrying very heavy looking briefcases.

The International Board began its deliberations the next morning in what was then A-1, a large classroom off the library. Kingman Brewster and Bill McGill would carry the honors for the college (and convince the board to permit parental payments, a decision later reversed) while Lu and I went to the airport to meet the Hammers. As it turned out, I answered that earlier question by driving the Buick myself. We had lunch at the house and then the Hammers rested. We always sensed that the altitude bothered them both. By mid-afternoon it was time to meet the Prince's plane, coming directly from Houston. Five Lincoln Continentals lined up to transport people; the Las Vegas High School band prepared to play at the airport, but a fierce wind took away most of the sound. A thousand spectators practically blocked out the view of the small airport hangar. A red carpet was whipping around in the wind. The plane arrived and Prince Charles stepped on to the soil of New Mexico for the first and only time. He was very tolerant of all the greetings, and he chatted with the crowd while exclaiming about the scenery. He continued to express his surprise as we drove up Hot Springs Boulevard where Las Vegans had painted their fences and planted flowers in his honor. They even lined the roads with placards welcoming the Prince to their city. For years afterwards, local folk would claim that he shook their hands, shared some chilies, and ate in every restaurant in town.

Back in Montezuma, Sir Edward Adeane, the Prince's personal secretary, the Royal Valet, and the Royal Superintendent, John MacLean, all extraordinarily pleasant men, arranged the Prince's suite. Lord Romsey went over to the Maclehoses's house, where he would stay. After freshening up, everyone came down for drinks. We had planned a small dinner party that evening on the assumption that people would be tired after traveling so far. When asked for a drink, the Prince chose, rather tentatively, apple juice. Then he turned to me: "Do you make a good martini, Ted?" Happily, it was the one drink I could make. Accordingly everyone else changed their orders; the mood became relaxed; and an early dinner at the house was both enjoyable and entertaining. Then the Prince and the Hammers retired upstairs. [We gave over the third floor to the Prince and his staff, and the Hammers occupied the guest room on the second floor where we had installed a transom and doors to assure privacy, a bit of construction that would become incredibly controversial later.] Once our guests were settled, the Prince's staff left for town and we decided to have another dinner at Barbara's Doolittle's ranch in Watrous, north of Las Vegas. She had invited, with the help of Maxie Anderson, the famous balloonist, all members of the International Board. When we arrived, it was clear the party was a great success. And by then even those most apprehensive about America's ability to create an appropriately rigorous UWC had mellowed as the margaritas flowed.

Prince Charles and Ted Lockwood confer after HRH's arrival. Joining them is Lord Romsey.

The next morning was clear, crisp, windy, and quite cool. It looked good for our formal ceremony. Breakfast was ready. The Symonses, Gourlays, Hammers and we had all come down when suddenly the Prince appeared. He had indicated earlier that he wished his breakfast brought to his room; but not so.

"I haven't had such a cold shower since Gordonstoun," he observed. The hot water had given out as everyone tried to be ready early! Breakfast was formidable, with steak, eggs, fruit and everything else as our visiting staff displayed their talents. Later, when Lu went to make a telephone call, she found that the lines were dead. She went to the administration building only to find she could not get in to the house lines. The mystery was solved when the Prince explained that the evening before, when the phone rang, he tried putting it in the drawer of the night stand. "When that didn't work, I took the receiver off the hook." The Prince's explanation accounted for more than he realized; for we had been surprised that Hammer had not received any calls during the night. Although it was amusing, his staff began to panic at the thought of all the calls that had never come through. It may well have been the only time in his life that Hammer did not get calls during the night.

Breakfast was interrupted by a commotion at the front door. Unbeknownst to us, the laundry room on the second floor had flooded as the housekeeper was in the process of laundering the bed linens for our guests. A college maintenance person appeared to address both the absence of hot water and the washing machine. But the FBI at the front door were reluctant to allow him in the house because he had not had clearance; that is, he did not have the special small gold pin with the diagonal red and white stripes required to enter the residence. The matter was resolved by having both the FBI and maintenance inspect the plumbing problems. We added a supplementary tank to make sure that the Prince did not suffer yet another cold shower.

Next the Prince and Lord Romsey went on a tour of the campus with Andrew Maclehose and students. While other dignitaries visited the exhibition of New Mexican artists in the Castle dining room, Joan Lunden of ABC-TV's *Good Morning America* interviewed Prince Charles in the lobby. I went to the Inn of Las Vegas, where the press were staying, to explain why they should refrain from photographing our guests doing the ordinary things like eating and drinking, and all such important details. We had a press conference in the dining hall. It went well until the final question asked by a student: "As the future King of England, what are you going to do about Ireland?"

The wind was really up as we began the formal dedicatory ceremonies at 11:30. As the letter of invitation had forewarned, "guests should be prepared for cool weather." The platform was set just west of the dormitories, running east to west, so that the audience would look north and thus avoid staring into the sun. It would be outlined by

Prince Charles speaking at the dedication, October 28, 1982. Left to right: Governor Bruce King, Armand Hammer, William McGill, Thomas Symons, Richard Tallboys, and Andrew Maclehose.

the flags of the countries represented in the student body. We were establishing precedence: not only would we always use these flags but we also used academic regalia for our speakers. As the dean intoned the country, a student placed its flag on the platform. People were moved by this spectacle. The speeches were decorous and surprisingly brief. As Chairman of the Board, Bill McGill welcomed everyone to the ceremony. Governor Bruce King presented his official welcome from the State of New Mexico. Tom Symons extended greetings from the International Board. Then Dr. Hammer reminisced about how he had become involved and read a telegram from President Reagan. The Prince was complimentary of the effort and personal in his references to our having left Vermont so precipitously.

The ceremony seemed to combine the requisite formality with obvious warmth and cordiality and lasted only 45 minutes. Lunch was an impressive feast of New Mexican specialities beneath the mammoth spread of canvas. Of course, the Prince's staff insisted on limiting those who came to the head table. The rest of the afternoon was less daunting since Hammer wanted the Prince to meet at the house the prime donor prospects and do an interview with TV host, Merv Griffin. The students had more fun with Cary Grant in his shetland crew neck sweater. But one amusing episode occurred when the Prince asked how we might sneak over to the famous hot springs. He and I tried and scaled the fence only to hear the sirens of the State Police clearing the road of intruders. The Prince was surprised by the condition of this landmark and in a letter written to me after his visit expressed the hope that his next visit would find them magnificently transformed. A meeting in September with community people had shown that any attempt to curtail public access would lead to a very unfriendly response. Therefore, the springs remained unrepaired.

Meanwhile the other 800 invited guests toured the campus facilities while enjoying the music of several mariachi bands. Some students performed dances in their native costume while others greeted the guests with song and conversation. Japanese businessman and philanthropist Ryoichi Sasakawa was strolling the grounds resplendent in his traditional robes, along with a large entourage from Japan (even though the National Committee would not send students until the following year when they were assured of the College's success). It was a fiesta in true New Mexico tradition and an occasion no one would soon forget.

High tea was served in the dining hall at four o'clock and Prince Charles met with the International Board and members of the college board for an informal exchange. Later that evening the second floor of the library was transformed into an elegant dining room where distinguished donors dined with HRH and the Hammers. Some students came by to serenade, which was a surprise for everyone since it was not on the closely guarded schedule.

Meanwhile, in downtown Las Vegas at the El Alto Supper Club, the college staff and spouses were enjoying pitchers of blue margaritas and 16-ounce steaks with members of the International Board. As a matter of record, parties were held in every watering hole and restaurant in town, and anyone with the slightest connection to the college, HRH, or the Hammers was regarded as a celebrity.

When we returned to the house for a nightcap, our two cats, Leaper and Loper, former residents of the animal shelter, had established their hegemony by stretching out full length on our sofas. Edward Adeane, a cat fancier, was delighted. Charles was polite but not dazzled. "Are these special cats, Lu?"

"To me, they are, sir" was her response about two beasts that survived for years in the wilds of Montezuma.

Our guests retired for the evening and Lu and I joined the Royal staff in the kitchen where clearly there was a crisis of some sort. The Prince had lost his "flannel," something which he said always happened in America. We did not know that the green rag lying on the counter, picked up in his room by the housekeeper, was the famous flannel. After that relief, we talked about skiing and other serious matters—glad that everything had gone so well.

During the night we were awakened by some strange sounds coming from downstairs. When Lu went to investigate, she was surprised to find a stray cat in the living room. Then the front and back doors were flung open and two armed secret service men entered to see who was walking around in the semi-darkness. Whereupon one of the men confessed to having let the cat into the house thinking it was our Loper. He had even found some food in the kitchen cupboard and had fed the interloper. Thus was the cat mystery solved.

On the next day visiting guests were treated to open houses at the ranch of the Duke and Duchess of Bedford in Tesuque and at Baroness Diergardt's ranch in Santa Fe, a luncheon at Fenn Galleries, and tours of the capitol city. The weather continued to be fine. This time the Prince ate breakfast in his room, and the Hammers decided to fly to Albuquerque and pass up the reception scheduled for that afternoon in Santa Fe. After breakfast the campus was closed to the public and the Prince met with students in the dining hall for an hour.

The inevitable happened: the microphone did not work. Lu asked Bob Wade, our physics teacher, to fix it. Security would not let him near it because he lacked the proper security pin in his lapel. He thought they said "pen" and reached in his pocket for a pen, which further alarmed everyone. Lu finally straightened that out. Class visits followed and the Prince fashioned his own pot in the pottery class with students. Everything was behind schedule, but we still felt that we should have student dances for him in front of the administration building. Accordingly we shortened the student presentations, difficult even under ideal circumstances; and everyone joined in the lion dance. A meeting with Hammer, faculty and their spouses led to a discussion of appropriate technology, a volunteer fire brigade for the college (and that led to our procuring a pumper from Pasadena). The Prince was enjoying it, one reason being that his watch had stopped at 20 minutes after eleven! We had a somewhat hurried lunch and then we left for the airport and a short flight to Santa Fe.

Governor Bruce King and his wife, Alice, had arranged for a reception for the Prince of Wales at the Museum of Fine Arts but could not prevent a few drab-looking Irish protesters dressed in Hallowe'en costumes from heckling HRH. As with many such occasions, ostensibly recognizing the new institution, people seemed more interested in royalty than education. Later all of us flew to Albuquerque. On both flights the Prince and I talked openly about the situation, and I sensed that he was worried about Hammer's sustaining his interest in the college. At the Regency Hotel in the Duke City some 1200 people waited to shake hands at the reception. Dinner was delayed, not simply because of the crush of numbers but also because of Hammer's disapproval of the seating arrangements. In due time the Prince left; dinner was served; and a special auction conducted by Merv Griffin gained some additional $170,000. By then everyone was tired but content from the grand occasion.

For those staying overnight in Albuquerque, Maxie Anderson arranged a very early series of balloon rides from his ranch. Some went; others collapsed—satisfied with the whole affair. An unknown poet had used my typewriter at the house to leave a summary of the occasion:

"Students from fifty-nine different nations,
guests of at least that many stations,
dukes and duchesses and balloons,
a prince, and possibility of monsoons,
buses, taxis, and limousines,
caviar and chili beans,
sports-coat style for solemn fete
black-tie dinner for the lordly set:
such is the style of the grand beginning
where luxe has nothing to do with sinning
and festival spirit is joined with knowledge
to inaugurate the life of a new world college."

7: SHAKING DOWN

Our first snow of the season fell the next day and left almost two feet. We returned to the routines, and it was a pleasure to see the manner in which the faculty were responding to students with linguistic or other deficiencies. The dean was working on the winter schedule, and our newly created Search and Rescue Team went looking for a lost hunter. Although the Wilderness Training Program would undergo many changes, there was genuine interest in acquiring the skills needed for mountain rescue and morale was high despite the very difficult terrain in which we worked, in the Sangre de Cristo mountains between Santa Fe and Taos.

We now turned to matters which the dedication had delayed. We began working on admissions for 1983. We changed our forms to coincide more closely with what seemed to be an emerging common form for all UWCs, but still in buff and burgundy. (Our B&B stationery was distinctive and controversial—quite a contrast to the blue and white others used.) Our first entering class had shaken down to 102 students. We wanted to increase the number of countries represented. We issued more offers than we had beds for, but we assumed some countries would not be able to accept. We had to be careful, however, since it was proving expensive to bring so many young people to Montezuma. Not only were we providing far more scholarships than anticipated, we were also paying air travel and pocket money ($200 a term) for students from regions like Africa.

A second major matter was planning our construction for phase two. Hammer wanted to wait until January to review everything before any future commitments. That meant a very tight schedule in prospect; for we needed to complete work in the Old Stone Hotel on the second and third floors for more classrooms and offices; we had the science building to retrofit; and we had two dormitories to get ready. There was even talk of renovating the carriage house, which the Montezuma Baptist College had used for a theater, and making it an arts center. We drew up ideas for additional recreational facilities to the east of the Castle.

As was to become clear, financial concerns dictated what we did. Los Angeles had continued to handle all the construction accounts, but as a precaution we had begun our own files. It was difficult to agree on figures; and these discussions inevitably led to a delay in the transfer of funds to the college for operating needs. The tuition money we received, as well as all donations, went to the Oxy offices where they were invested, as we learned later, in Occidental bonds. Therefore, it was hard to know what happened to gifts we thought were meant for scholarships if they landed in the construction column.

On the other hand, there may well have been an understandable worry on their part about our ability to handle the finances. It was emblematic of a situation that was becoming more troublesome; namely, the question of our independence as an educational institution. The problem had arisen just before we opened. We had not received the deed to the property; it was still in the name of the Armand Hammer Foundation. I insisted that we must have the deed and be in fact, not simply by intent, an institution operating independently in the state in which we were registered and would have to be accredited. Further, we could ill afford to be perceived as an operating subdivision of his company.

Hammer accepted the inevitable, but there was no assurance that similar instances would not continue to arise since Los Angeles controlled the purse strings. Yet, it seemed the better part of wisdom to learn how to achieve our purposes within this bizarre structure rather than force a philosophical clarification at this juncture. The immediate consequence of the financial crunch was to delay plans for phase two until we could sort out the billing for phase one. All in all, the college affairs were far more complex than the size of the institution suggested.

Meanwhile, at Montezuma, students prepared for the first Thanksgiving. Since no one was going anywhere, we held our first "national" day that weekend. Our Spanish teacher, Maria Elena Maldonado from Uruguay, had organized such events at Pearson College and got the U.S. students to plan a special menu and to organize a show. It went surprisingly well, given the inexperience of everyone with such student-talent shows. It was built around dances typical of the decades of recent American history.

That evening we held a square dance in a very cold Castle dining room. We concluded we would have five such days over a two-year span, and thus cover the globe. After this slight break, it was a run for the Christmas holidays. Lu discovered many students could not go home or did not get invitations to accompany North American colleagues. She had to find places for them. We were also learning all the ways in which students can run out of money. To help with emergency funds we had established the Peggy Baker memorial fund, a kind of loan bank which received periodic infusions from the campus store which two students, Bertrand Kan (The Netherlands) and Patrick deGruyter (West Germany) established and ran.

We prepared reports on each student, outlining their academic progress and various activities. We knew each student well and these reports were disconcertingly informative to parents and national committees. They also provided the first predictions of how well our students would ultimately do on their IB examinations; for, unlike the usual grading system, we used a scale of one to seven (seven being the highest) combined with a letter grade on effort. To those teachers unfamiliar with the IB, these procedures were quite a surprise and a lot more work. But they provided a far more helpful summary for each student than the normal grading systems. It also served as an early warning for those having difficulties.

The day of departure for the airport it was snowing hard. Snowballs flew, but everyone was also crying and embracing each other as if they would never see each other again. We were astonished, but by then we had realized that we were not good at predicting, especially the weather, and Maclehose's knowledge of Atlantic College did not apply to Montezuma. We were departing also to ski with my brother and his wife in Lech, Austria, where we would recruit both an Austrian student and a chairman, Veit Burger, to coordinate the Nepalese committee. It was a pleasant time.

It was clear and crisp when Hammer and Pugash arrived on January 7, 1983, to review the construction costs to date with Bob Stamm, Cohen and myself. During December the Foundation had received bills for $1.1 million instead of only $441,000 as Cohen had forecast. They wanted an audit, which succeeded in tying up the business office over the holidays. As we sat in our living room, it was apparent that there had been a loss of trust on all sides. The auditors had not found any fraud or peculation, just sloppiness. No doubt it was true that the hurried schedule had cost Hammer at least $100,000 extra; it had been difficult for Joe Cohen to stay on top of all the estimates sufficiently; and the billings may have been erratic. "You are just taking advantage of me," Hammer interjected. He then went on to illustrate how the contractor had ripped him off. He singled out the doors with the glass transom on the second floor of our house. The cost: $3000. The reply was illogically correct: they had to redistribute costs as they mounted and put that tab next to the doors since they could find no other place for the charge.

The bickering continued. Stamm, an honest and highly respected builder, agreed to tighter controls for the second phase. Los Angeles concluded that, for cash flow reasons, we would not begin phase two until April 1 and we would limit the project to the very minimum— no swimming pool or art center. It was not a happy ending to the meeting. Clearly, if Hammer became increasingly perturbed by such expenditures and lost enthusiasm for the college, long-range stability would prove elusive. Therefore, we put in the files the elaborately prepared master plan for the campus and concentrated on trimming phase two.

Hammer returned a week later, still perturbed and with a different set of associates from Los Angeles to review the situation. He had his colleagues scan all items for overpricing. Stamm was pressing from his side for payment of long overdue billings. We were trying collectively to see what we could pay now and what had to undergo further review by auditors. It was becoming increasingly acrimonious, and it certainly was exhausting to those of us trying to get on with the business of running a college properly. There should have been a better way of handling this dispute, but the personalities did not permit a calmer resolution.

The students returned. For the second term we had not lost anyone, but our two Russian representatives were a week late for inexplicable reasons. The weather was beautiful and everyone wanted to learn how to skate on the pond west of the campus. I had procured skates from the coach at Trinity College, as well as blue and gold soccer uniforms. Some students wanted to try cross-country skiing. We were building up quite a store of equipment, including sleeping bags, and the rooms below the kitchen were getting a bit ripe from airing this equipment. Although we had drawn up estimates on how much equipment, how many textbooks, and how much paper the college would require, we now had to revise them as practice altered expectations. In particular, the copying machine went all day and night.

This second term we received a visiting team from the North Central Association of Schools and Colleges, the agency responsible for peer evaluation in our region of the country. (Edward Jay Epstein was incorrect in his most recent book on Hammer in claiming we would not be accredited.) We had decided that it was important for our reputation and for American parents to have this form of accreditation in addition to New Mexico's. I had arranged for a team of visitors, including some former associates sympathetic to our experiment. They were astonished. They were also uncertain as to just which category we would fit: to them we were beyond a high school but less than a two-year college; we had a fixed curriculum, no interscholastic sports, an unusual student body, and virtually no income!

During the three days they became enthusiastic about our students in particular. We would receive full accreditation retroactive to the beginning of the year and would not have to wait during a probationary period as was customary. To anyone familiar with accreditation procedures, this was unheard of. They did raise questions about our facilities and our financing, so far as they or anyone else could understand that part of our operations.

January was a busy month since we were training everyone in first-aid, conducting cross-country classes on the playing fields, and arranging for downhill at Sipapu, a ski area 55 miles northwest of Las Vegas, for $5 an afternoon for everything. But not all was that promising. Students were becoming depressed as they sensed how long it was until the end of the term. No exciting events like the dedication were in the offing. The dorms were nosier than anyone liked; the tennis courts were still not ready; trips to Las Vegas were not that exciting. Even the introduction of matchmaking for one week did not lift their spirits. Eventually the tempo picked up, but it was a reminder that the winter months would be much harder than the fall term.

On February 4th the board of directors met in Los Angeles. It was clear that, however spectacular our achievements to date, the future was uncertain. I had written confidentially to the Hammers in late January. I acknowledged that they had grounds for feeling some people might try to take advantage of them and that too few realized that they had put more money into this UWC than any single person had in any UWC. Some now expected them to pour additional money into the movement and thus lessen the financial challenges. "In short, in an astonishing fashion the future of the UWCs has become too closely tied to what does or does not happen here." The point of the letter was to remind him that failure to support the college appropriately would have large consequences. He also needed to determine the extent of his support to the International Office so as to disarm those dreaming of endless resources.

In response to his request, and in recognition of his contribution, the International Board would, we hope, offer him a seat. It was not all that easy to predict how Hammer might act, or react. As I wrote to Kingman Brewster at the same time, Hammer had put in—or arranged to have available thus far—some seven million dollars; he was underwriting our deficit to the tune of $125,000 a month. We all knew he had a mixture of motives when undertaking the project: they remained and confused the situation in the minds of some friends of the movement. Nonetheless, if he perceived he was being rebuffed at the international level, he might back out entirely. Hammer wanted to be more involved with London; and he wanted more recognition for his investment. These sensitivities persisted throughout the remainder of his life, whether it was the rebuff on being godfather to Charles's son or on not being offered a knighthood.

At this same meeting the board confirmed that the directors were: Mrs. Aerol Arnold, Guilford Glazer, Arthur Groman, Dr. Hammer, Frances Hammer, John Kluge, Sherry Lansing, Theodore Lockwood, William McGill, Martin Meyerson, Anthony Portago, Abigail Van Buren, B. Francis Saul II, Rosemary Tomich, and Jerry Weintraub.

The board also agreed to enlarge the honorary trustees to include A. Robert Abboud, Jack Campbell, Alec P. Courtelis, Phyllis Farley, George S. Franklin, Dillon Ripley, and Mrs. Walter Rothschild. In anticipation of more donors, it agreed to establish categories: Founders ($250,000-$1,000,000); Benefactors ($50,000-249,999); Patrons ($10,000-49,999); and Sponsors ($1,000-9,999). To provide for officers, Hammer was elected president, McGill chairman, Lockwood executive vice-president and executive director, and Pugash secretary-treasurer. In a financial report, we estimated spending $1.6 million on operations and $2.3 million for new construction. These figures led to the suggestion that we use a movie premiere for fund-raising, an idea never to die but never to be executed either.

8: THE END OF YEAR ONE

During that first winter we began to realize that having 100 more students the following year would indeed be welcome. Some personalities were proving too harsh, and in the absence of recreational facilities that winter (except for skiing and skating), the students began to press against the guidelines. From the beginning the college had established certain expectations as to the kind of conduct that should prevail. Not all the students accepted these guidelines, especially about visiting among themselves after hours. Close relations were leading to questionable conduct, and the resident tutors found they had their hands full. It has always been an irony of the UWC campuses that thievery, drinking, and sexual improprieties persist when, for the most part, all the dreary disciplinary issues with which so many schools have to deal are not common on a UWC campus. Insensitivity to the different cultural attitudes toward all these matters tended to make the situation more complicated but not less inexcusable. Thus whenever a disciplinary issue did arise, we were all disappointed—almost affronted by the failure of someone to sustain the model institution. No doubt also some students became genuinely depressed and anxious as the academic work piled up. In turning to their colleagues they did not necessarily realize that they were creating additional pressures.

An attempted suicide brought the problem before the whole community. We took a day off to discuss it in small meetings before holding one of our famous all-college sessions. We learned again just how intensely students feel about their friends. The whole incident was a demonstration of how remarkably well a UWC can respond to deep personal distress, not always with total success but far better than most institutions. It also convinced everyone that we should have more faculty on campus to assist

Skating on the Montezuma pond: Serge Pelletier (Canada) and Simona Goi (Italy) help Mark Stephens (Jamaica). During winter terms all students were required to practice at least one skill like skating, cross-country skiing or snowshoeing.

during such crises, which would constitute still another expense at a time when such outlays were unpopular. Simultaneously as a faculty we were trying to determine how much involvement faculty should have and how much should be left to the dean and others. The reports which we prepared were certainly helpful in assessing the progress of each student, and there was always ample discussion at meetings about those students not making the grade, but we did not always identify quickly enough those with emotional difficulties. Curiously enough, the faculty was very loath to have committees; at best we would establish some *ad hoc* groups to plan ahead for next year's orientation program. As we talked with other campuses, we learned that this degree of faculty involvement was unusual. It certainly led to long afternoon meetings, every one of which prompted a request to the kitchen to keep dinner warm for the teachers and staff.

This winter also led to a deterioration in the relations between the U. S. Committee in New York and Hammer. Los Angeles had hoped for more substantial fund-raising efforts in New York. When the issue of fund-raising had arisen at the board meeting in February, there had been a motion to put everything together so as to enhance our potential at getting more money. Hammer had offered to have the members of the U.S. Committee join the board. It seemed clear also that we would do better on admissions and know our scholarship needs more accurately if all admissions were coordinated through Montezuma. The U.S. Committee took umbrage at these ideas. So matters had been tabled. As a consequence, we no doubt missed opportunities to find significant new funds; we appeared to some as irresolute; and for most of us the relationship between LA and New York was at the very least confusing.

In February the IB Heads Conference took place in Madrid. It would be the first appearance of two new UWCs. The hotel was sterile; the dining facilities were uninviting; and the meeting rooms were below ground level. We did not find the setting for the conference inspirational. That opinion was reinforced by the absence of our luggage, lost somewhere over the Atlantic. It was clear that the IB organization was going through a major transition in leadership and had a number of complex issues before it. In the four days of discussion the position of the United World Colleges was always lurking in the background since they represented the largest block of examination-takers and were virtually the only schools offering solely the IB. My UWC colleagues warned that we should not appear to act as a *cabal*, a distinct inconvenience when it came to the happy hour. Since the fate of the IB was so important to the UWCs, the apparent split over expansion into countries where there was little interest, and the high costs of servicing small schools around the globe, became important concerns. As always the expense of this kind of collaboration worried everyone. Certainly for us the cost of supporting both the IB and the UWC central office was a significant figure in our budgets, at least 5%. Yet, there seemed to be no alternative if we were to have a common curriculum and examination program.

Another major topic was how best to represent the interest of the schools. The North Americans were well organized by comparison with Latin America or Africa and Asia. Future curriculum development was another important topic. New proposals had been made, but adoption of any changes generally required at least three years. Clearly the weight was still with the traditional subject matter taught rigorously, despite growing evidence that some subject matter was receiving greater attention than others; that is, physics and math overshadowed art and music. Again it was apparent that the United World Colleges would have to take the initiative if changes in courses or in the community service component seemed desirable. I knew that, if the IB faltered, some of our own board members would argue to forget it, simply on the grounds of cost. Years later the heads of the various UWC campuses would argue again as to whether the IB program was sufficiently distinctive, but there was never a realistic academic alternative.

For the UWCs the atmosphere at the conference was not too encouraging: it was clear that some administrative changes were needed, examination procedures needed review and modification, and cost containment was necessary if schools in poorer countries were to remain members. As the heads talked in the shadows of some remote restaurant about these issues, we also realized that all the colleges were facing, in one form or another, severe financial constraints. Everyone agreed that the UWCs had to raise more money more efficiently, especially in light of the impact that both Montezuma and Adriatic had on the scholarships offered by both countries and colleges. For example, Norway could fund only 24 students a year: the addition of two colleges meant Atlantic had four fewer fully funded students each year.

On the home front longer days and a sun higher in the sky did not compensate for a sense of frustration. Progress on the second phase of construction had been hampered by arguments over payments for the first phase; recruitment of additional faculty was slow; and admissions was moving erratically—something we had yet to become accustomed to. On the other hand, we were pleasantly surprised to receive lots of equipment from sections of Oxy that were being closed. There were handsome blue cabinets for the science labs, tons of glassware (some of which we would sell to provide dollars for other scientific equipment), and seven pickup trucks. The first conference on world religions was a great success. So also was the ingenious use of a stripped-down mobile home to accommodate the students who had been living in C-2, now to become the new science labs. The only problem was the absence of plumbing. We were still pioneering.

Project week, a standard feature in UWCs, began on March 25. The students headed in various directions, including a trek in Big Bend, Texas. In one sense it was the substitute for a spring vacation; in another sense it was an extension of service in new areas and directions. Finding faculty to accompany the projects was not as difficult as one might have assumed. Some 37 students remained on campus, including one group making a film in the Castle, site of the infamous movie of the 1970s called "The Evil." Tony Ray from California had to find a horse for the movie. He went to the local veterinarian and borrowed one which he then rode across town to the college. No one realized that he had never sat on a horse before. But ingenuity was a strong suit with the students, as was a born sense of salesmanship whenever prospective students visited with parents.

The snows persisted into the spring as each warm spell proved short-lived. We had had 263% more precipitation than normal, and it was bizarre indeed to see the sprinklers go on and cover the snow with lagoon water. In fact, it interfered with the faculty softball practice and made tennis on our new courts impossible. What a strange place New Mexico was proving to be!

Then the Army Corps of Engineers informed us that the ford across the Gallinas River, so essential for the heavier trucks, was insubstantial. Fortunately this did not slow down construction: the trucks just took the longer route to the west and back. With a professional manager, Jim West, on the premises, things went smoothly. It was noisy in the Old Stone Hotel as the second and third floors were ripped apart and debris cast from the windows. One day a crowbar entered the faculty lounge from the ceiling. We also had two dormitories to renovate, this time with one larger and one smaller apartment on the ground floor so as to increase the number of tutors available in the residence halls. And the science-math faculty were looking enviously at the remodeling in C-2: it would be pleasant to end the afternoon commute to Highlands University.

In April, the college held its first set of trial examinations. As with all the regular courses, success after two years of study depended on the final exams, administered simultaneously throughout the world and devised by faculty from around the world. Each student would be tested on English language and literature, a laboratory science, a second language, history or economics or social anthropology, mathematics, and generally either art or music. Later others would grade the exams. This procedure put pressure not only on the students but also on the faculty. It was formidable.

During this same month we went to London for the International Board meeting. The executive committee agreed that it would be appropriate to offer Hammer a seat on the board.

Then came the question of getting support from national committees for students to attend Montezuma. We received the least amount of help of all the UWCs: only 10.7% of our total tuition income came from national committees; and that figure included a special $150,000 from the U.S. Committee toward U.S. students studying overseas. This percentage was far below the 50% Hammer had expected. Happily we had received $118,000 from parents. These facts prompted Alec Peterson, who had followed the progress of the movement from its early days and had even taken a turn as chairman of the board, to say that the UWCs were living in a dream world: national committees could not and most likely would not find money for students at four colleges, let alone more. To reconstitute the committees was theoretically possible but impractical.

The discussion confirmed that the situation had grown worse for everyone. Adriatic, Atlantic, and Pearson all maintained that asking for parental contributions, an obvious source of tuition income, was embarrassing to them; and even though they would not interfere with our asking U.S. parents to pay, they did not wish the board to regard it as an acceptable practice. Although there was no happy resolution to the question of future support from national committees, at least it was apparent that the amount of gold residing in the United States for use by the UWC movement had been grossly exaggerated. That led to an inopportune observation: "We need $50,000,000 for international scholarships in London and $30,000,000 endowment for Montezuma if we are to con-

A meeting of the committee members of the United World Colleges: Jack Matthews, Gianfranco Bonetti, Michael Parsons, Armand Hammer, Thomas Symons, Kingman Brewster, and A.D.C. Peterson.

tinue to operate as the founders had envisioned." Of course, that could be said of virtually all the colleges; but Montezuma was still smarting from having hoped for so much and having received so little.

Another diverting topic was the future of the Venezuelan rural farm management project. It appeared to be on track even though it was short of funds and no one present at the meeting really understood its program, so utterly different from the IB schools's curricula. Discussion about a similar college in India received mixed reviews. No one was looking to a large expansion at this point in time; accordingly the board turned down the request for associate status from the Moshi school in Tanzania and St. Leonard's College in Australia.

While we were in London, we had a special meeting to discuss the relation between Montezuma and the U.S. Committee. McGill, Brewster, and I met with Symons, Sir James Whitaker from Atlantic College, Matthews and Gourlay. The question had become: who speaks for the United World Colleges in the USA? Everyone agreed that there should be one voice and that should be from Montezuma. As we sat in London, it was seductively easy to urge a common fund-raising effort, a subordination of the New York group to the Hammer College board, and a frank recognition that we could ill afford division among the supporters of the UWC cause, especially since, as McGill pointed out, Hammer was limited in what he could provide. Whether we could achieve these goals was quite another matter.

The entire discussion had left us with more questions about the international effort than answers. As Sir Ian Gourlay explained his role, he had been asked to be the chief staff officer, not an aggressive presiding officer. He was an advisor to a board who had little hands-on knowledge, met rarely and were not prepared to follow through on their own on any decisions taken at semi-annual meetings. As the colleges themselves were loosely associated (and the role of the head varied considerably), the future lay in the hands of a few individuals who might, or might not, rally the movement to decisive action. Even the mechanics of the services which the London office generously sought to perform were sometimes a bit muddled. There was little recognition of the political pressure which money might exert; or, conversely, the movement relied very heavily on the altruism, almost forgiveness, of those who might find a particular decision impossible to implement, such as providing scholarships to everyone. Meanwhile everyone strove to make the best of an ill-coordinated effort. The idealism of the mission sustained people who otherwise would have been forced to express dismay over the practical dilemmas.

As we all looked forward to the end of the first year, we realized that our returning students must have their extended essays ready when they returned—or so we hoped. For in the IB curriculum the 4,000-word essay is a major challenge, especially for those whose first language is not English. Along with the Theory of Knowledge course, which had begun under Maclehose's direction in January, these extra requirements became a bit daunting. The assignment of faculty supervisors was adding to the list of obligations teachers had at Montezuma. Everyone was looking forward to having additional people the following year to assign to such duties. In that recruitment of new staff, we were finding that the sciences and music were the most difficult. We had also decided that the service programs would do far better if we had a full-time supervisor. Where they all would live was uncertain and invoked extraordinarily vague language from the administration. But then there were those already in Montezuma who claimed that they had become familiar with inexact phrasing.

A meeting of the college's board in April was preceded, as had now become customary, by an evening gathering in Hammer's office to review the agenda to eliminate unpleasantries or surprises. Hammer clearly did not wish to hear about deficits or phase three of construction plans. Accordingly the discussion was muted and it began to trouble the chairman that we might not be meeting the normal legal requirements as set forth in our by-laws. Once again we were finding the absence of a charter unhelpful, and it was clear to McGill and me that the board members had a murky idea of their fiduciary role. But like many other matters we realized that we were still in the sorting-out stage. We were improvising until we could clarify our financial future. To us it was troublesome, moreover, that we did not always receive money in Montezuma from LA in time to make payroll. No one ever doubted the future of the enterprise; it was just that "in the meanwhile" uncertainties mounted.

The board met again in Los Angeles on May 18 to review expenditures to date, right on target at 75% of budget. We were worried, however, about the mounting expenditures charged against us from the U.S. Committee. We revisited the budget for the coming year. Some directors were skeptical of our ability to raise enough money to cover the deficits. Nevertheless, they agreed to proceed with four units of faculty housing for the fall. Following the meeting, Hammer asked us to send two students to attend the Occidental annual meeting to promote the college. Brenda Davis from the United States and Anna Leander from Sweden did the honors.

The board also created three committees: executive, finance, and development—primarily to handle business between full board meetings. Balloonist Maxie Anderson, then an Honorary Trustee, offered to put on a fund-raising dinner in the Castle in December, and the board approved fixing up the ballroom area for $100,000. Maxie's death in a ballooning accident in Europe that summer canceled such plans. It was the second such loss of a good friend of the college in little more than a year's time. But the need was obvious yet again as projections indicated that the college might have a deficit as large as two million since we expected only $123,000 in tuition income. The content of board meetings was becoming predictable: gloomy budgetary projections, high hopes for new money, and very little attention to programs. In a real sense this fiscal cloud distorted the picture, especially in light of the remarkable daily activity on the campus, for the college had quickly become a model institution attracting increasing attention in academic circles and leading to requests for visits. But the spring was too busy for that: next year the college would arrange for such visits.

An important tradition begun this year was the annual faculty-student softball game. It turned out to be a questionable decision since the faculty defense fell apart in the seventh inning, but it was a pleasant way to spend our last Sunday of the year together.

One thing was certain: the year would end on May 28 amidst tears and hugs. It was a fascinating confirmation of the first year's success; for the students were loath to part from their friends. They were not sure they would like it as much when the new students came: it was their home and they were the pioneers.

In reviewing the year as a faculty we concluded that we needed to distribute responsibilities among ourselves more equitably. We were proud of what had happened this year and even though the faculty trounced the staff in an error-prone game of softball, 31-12, everyone went about their summer business relieved and looking for a change of pace. And thus was introduced another instant tradition: the annual faculty-staff softball game and barbecue—with beer.

9: BROADLANDS & ALBUKIKI

For Lu and me a change of pace came in the form of another Broadlands in England. This time we could not be quite as optimistic about the return since we would be sharing the receipts with the *Mary Rose*, a Tudor warship which the Prince was raising from the bottom of the Portsmouth harbor. The U.S. Committee had done another superb job: the organization was impressive; the meals were excellent; and the side conversations were endless as we sought to cultivate new prospects. Almost 650 people attended the events. The ball took place on Saturday evening, June 4, at Broadlands, under a very large tent, "in the presence of Their Royal Highnesses The Prince and Princess of Wales." The next day there was another polo match at Windsor Park; and on Monday those interested in the raising of the *Mary Rose* went to Portsmouth.

What became apparent was that, in contrast to the 1982 gala, this one came after a successful first year of a United World College in the States: we could not be ignored nor could we be faulted. Whatever the committee felt, we also wondered whether the effort was worth the return—at best $175,000—compared to what we might do on our own. We were feeling our oats, I suppose; but it was also abundantly clear that relations between Los Angeles and New York, during the proceedings, were cool. Hammer's staff began muttering about better coordination, a reference to the fact that we did not know what other fund-raising the U.S. Committee might have in mind. We became persuaded that we should have all UWC development efforts under one office. We did not raise much additional money on the spot; and, even when we wrote each participant later, we received virtually no replies since, as one person candidly observed, "I came for a royal party; I've done my part; don't expect anything more."

While anxiety about future fund-raising resurfaced as a central concern at Broadlands this year, we also had many conversations with others like Sir Ian Gourlay, Tony Besse, and Sir James Whitaker about our scholarship policy and, of course, Hammer's intentions. No doubt we whined a bit about not getting more money from national committees; and, in London's eyes, it was sufficiently touchy that Robert Creighton, associate director of the International Office, wrote Bill McGill that summer after seeing our board minutes of May 18. Rightly he admitted that "UWC scholarship policy...must appear rather a muddle." His annotations confirmed that others expected family contributions. But then he tried to describe how the International Board welcomed parental contributions where possible but not if social and political factors made that unpopular—the waffle that would continue to cause friction and misunderstanding for years to come. Then the take-out was obvious: they would try to raise more money to avoid these situations. Even in 1983 we knew that this would not happen, and we reserved judgment on the scholarship issue. In another sense we had to admit, begrudgingly, that it was all part of that international understanding we supposedly guided young people to appreciate and uphold even when clearly some were less enlightened than we.

Meanwhile, after returning on June 10 to Montezuma, I had concluded that we did need better "coordination" in our admissions. Accordingly I addressed the problem in a letter to the U.S. Committee in late June. In some sense it was a review of what we had spent, including paying candidates's travel expenses for interviews. Our main concern was that the process was confusing since applicants sent their materials to Montezuma, then heard from a committee chairman in San Francisco, a financial review from Walla Walla, Washington, where a committee member lived, and acceptance from Montezuma, all in the name of a committee in New York City. Moreover, by now it was clear that we would have to provide the financial aid needed by U.S. students coming to AHUWC while the committee would support those going to other colleges. The bottom line was that there should be only one voice for UWC and one admissions office, Montezuma. We were grateful for all the committee had done, and was doing, but the situation had changed with the opening of the college. The letter was not well received, which was predictable; but the fact remained that we had to change procedures. One paragraph may be all this issue deserves in a history, but it provoked reams of commentary and worsened relations between the two constituencies in a manner that was regrettable even if unavoidable. It is also an illustration of how people, all dedicated to a noble cause, can quibble in an embarrassing fashion about procedures and personalities.

There is a persistent myth about the academic world when classes recess for the summer: the public assumes we all go camping and rest for three months. Not so. We had a busy schedule. We had to complete phase two of the construction, and that involved the science faculty. We had to wind up the recruitment of faculty and the admission of students. For we had learned that some countries like India could not complete selection before the end of July. Some countries failed to respond; therefore, changes occurred through August. Housekeeping was important as well. We needed inventories; we had to refine accounts; we needed to improve the infirmary, for we had learned that students bring or acquire exotic illnesses.

We also looked at the admissions scene following this second year of recruitment and decided we needed some professional assistance. Howie Muir, formerly director of admissions at Trinity College, came on board as a part-time assistant. By then we had also discovered another fact of life at a United World College: people like to visit, especially in the summer. "Let's go have lunch in Las Vegas and see what that United World College is all about," was a typical Santa Fean diversion. We counted over 2,000 such visitors before August. To handle this burden and to begin planning summer programs for the future—and to add some counseling skills to the staff, we hired Hilda Wales. The institution might be small but it was complex.

That was one of the themes at the board meeting on August 3rd, when the board approved, again, fixing up the east portion of the Castle for a fund-raising event in October commemorating the dedication and introducing new patrons to Montezuma. It would be possible to make the ballroom (actually the original dining area for guests), the lobby and the circular room on the east wing presentable, but we did not have sufficient funds to make them useful in cold weather. Otherwise, phase two had moved along well with the inevitable exception of equipment not arriving when needed. Nor would faculty housing be ready until September 1, an inconvenience but not a crisis. The sewage lagoon was more troublesome, and the betting was against our having all the fresh paint on the dorm walls in time. In one sense we had made astonishing progress over a short time; in another sense we were disappointed that all was not ready ten minutes ahead of time—partly because of our pride in the place and partly because Hammer always assumed the impossible was doable.

These were not the only challenges of August. The Immigration Service had devised a new form but did not distribute copies to us. Therefore, many of our new foreign students would have only 30-day visas, and we would have to do new forms for some 156 students shortly after their arrival. A similar problem arose for some of our foreign faculty. Three of the first-year faculty could not originally get more than one-year visas. We got extensions but then had problems getting the papers to them, especially in Nigeria. Two new foreign faculty could not get their paperwork until after school started. From all these experiences we learned, but we also now knew that changes were inevitable and unpredictable. At least this year we would have a student lounge area in the Campus Center, more classrooms in the Stone Hotel, and a spanking new science complex.

Now that we had veteran students, we asked the second-years to return on August 27 to prepare for handling the orientation period. A week later the new students began to arrive. One of them, Sanjay Manandhar from Kathmandu, Nepal, wrote about his impressions:

"The Royal Nepal Airlines jet stood on the tarmac with busy ground staff all around. The sky was indigo around the northwest . . . My parents were silent except for some small talk. I, on the other hand, was bubbling with excitement—there were new things to see in America. I had dreamt so much about it, and finally the moment had arrived . . . The plane taxied and took off south towards Phulchoki hill, over a chaotic pile of lower Mahabharat hills and over the plains of Terai and India . . .

"Approaching people at Kennedy airport was difficult to say the least. I thought the people were really rude. Some would not even talk to me; others ignored me entirely . . . Finally, a mobile bank changed my five dollar bill [for a phone call to my uncle in New York]. The person behind the teller looked so melancholy that I would not have been surprised if he said there had a been a death in the family that day. Upon seeing me, though, he was irked enough to change his mood from melancholy to irritation. I was wondering 'What I have done that he should be so rude to me'. . .

"The plane to Albuquerque took off around 9 p.m.. On the plane a woman next to me started talking to me. She asked me where I was going. 'Albukiki, to study in a place called Montezuma.' . . .

"The Albuquerque airport was deserted. No baggage and no people from the college. An airline representative helped me to call the college. Security answered. When I explained that I was a new student, they asked for my name.

'You're not on the list,' they said. 'Are you sure you're supposed to be here?'

A cold chill ran down my spine. I asked to speak to the only name I could recall from my conversations with Pradesh [a second-year Nepalese]. Marcel Roy was the most jovial person one could talk to at one in the morning. He discovered my last name had been spelled 'Kathmandu' . . . " [Sanjay stayed at a hotel and took the train the next day—all experiences that challenged both his understanding and his pocket book.]

"The train stopped at Las Vegas and I felt my journey had come to an end. People from the college greeted me and took me in their car. The air smelled different. People smelled different. The clothes looked fancy. Everything was far apart and spacious.

After a dip in the road, the familiar castle came into view. Only then did it hit me that the place I had sent letters, telexes to, and heard so much about, was a reality."

It had been a long first day for Sanjay and for many other foreign students reaching New Mexico and the college. We forget what an impact this first trip from home had upon these students and how varied, troubling, and yet exciting the initial days had been. For some it was routine; for others it was disconcerting as it had been for Sanjay.

10: A SECOND COMING

Orientation was staged differently this fall. After their physical examinations, the new students headed for Cimarron and the Philmont Ranch. We always believed that putting everyone into the wilderness immediately not only threw them together so that they became acquainted, but it also prevented remaining home alone in the dorm or drifting off to town. A dry spell helped with the success of this outdoor adventure, primarily conducted by second-year students. Certainly they were distracted by scaling the Tooth of Time, coping with tarps and cooking stoves, and assessing the accuracy of what their elders told them. When classes began on September 15, the college still could not locate eight newcomers from such countries as Ghana, Sierra Leone, and Indonesia. Eventually they made it. In this second year we had 65 countries represented in remote New Mexico.

The academic whirl began; students chose their afternoon service programs; wilderness training began on the rocks below the Castle; and the soccer squad anticipated a series of unofficial matches around the State. The new science center was more important than we had realized because so many foreign students were planning careers in engineering, medicine, and science teaching. It was clear that UWC graduates felt that they needed a solid professional preparation before they undertook service jobs in the public domain. How this trend would affect the future contribution of former students to the goals of the movement surfaced as a legitimate question for the various colleges to research. As the number of graduates from all UWCs would soon approach the 10,000 mark, this issue seemed especially pertinent.

The flush of excitement which the opening of a new year evoked did not allay the concerns in Los Angeles about the failure of the U.S. Committee to contribute more funds to the college. Hammer asked for a meeting in New York on September 16. Privately, before the others arrived, he remarked to McGill and me that, if the committee did not change its attitude, he would consider changing his will, which then provided for half of his estate to come to the college upon his death. That had been the agreement when I accepted the job originally. It was the only time he invoked that threat. At the meeting we explained what we wanted: the U.S. Committee should give priority to the college; they should think of helping to select students for Montezuma first and foremost; and they should increase the funding for American students, even if it meant limiting the numbers going to the other UWCs. They said they would think about it.

As October approached, second-year students realized that they must make plans for university admissions. That proved to be complicated, not only because they were interested in applying in many different countries, but also many expected to remain in this country and attend American universities. Financial assistance was critical. Fitting all this paperwork into the schedule was to become a major chore each fall. One event reminded students of their youth: James Roosevelt and his wife, Mary, came to the college. When this son of FDR spoke about his father and particularly the war years, the students were fascinated by this connection with a man and time of which they had very imprecise knowledge. We always hoped to have many distinguished speakers at the college, but the distance from each coast and then from the Albuquerque airport made this unlikely. Yet, when someone did arrive, the students responded magnificently. The first-term congressman from New Mexico, Bill Richardson, was flattened by the questions they asked him. Ten years later he knew how to deal with these sophisticated young people.

In response to everyone's concern about funding, McGill and Hammer arranged for Thomas Nickell, a prominent development officer with the University of Southern California, to study our situation and make recommendations. His conclusions were surprisingly simple and direct: either Hammer must provide for the future from his resources or the college must have a development office with a broader base of supporters. Much of the commentary was self-evident, but one surprise was his insisting that Santa Fe be the location of an office. He also opposed the campaign for $50,000,000 at the international level since it would cut into potential donors to this college. What Nickell did not indicate was where we would find the new supporters. When the board heard the report, they thought it would be better to begin by using the Los Angeles office to raise monies. (Hammer had established, and paid for, a college liaison office at Oxy headquarters to keep him informed and to handle our public relations.) The issue was to lie dormant for a few months in any event for by now Jim Pugash had left and the staff in Hammer's own office was being reorganized.

Meanwhile, the figures for the 1983-84 budget showed a total expenditure of $2,362,000 even though there had been cost savings of almost $100,000 since the first cut. That meant a deficit of over one million for the year. The pattern of expenses closely resembled that of most educational institutions; that is, personnel costs were 65%; then came maintenance and utilities; with only 5-10% at all susceptible to variation through cost reductions. Tuition income from committees, parents, and endowed scholarships would exceed one million but we had yet to lift the level of contributions to even $500,000. Another way of expressing the revenues was to note that of the possible total from tuition (if everyone paid 100%), we received only 18% from parents, 24% from committees and other colleges, and 16% covered by restricted scholarships. The balance of 41.5% came out of our operating funds—and this did not include what was an annual "scholarship" for each student of $5000—the difference between the total possible from tuition and the actual cost for each student. This was not unusual among the United World Colleges, but it vividly illustrated the absolute necessity of substantial endowment to cover the annual shortfalls.

All these dreary matters were pertinent to the considerations before the International Board this fall. Prior to the meeting the heads met to discuss the work of the national committees, so crucial to the admissions process. The review was tedious and confirmed what we knew; namely, that there was wide variation in the performance of committees and too wide a difference in the support they proffered to the individual colleges. Put bluntly, only five to ten committees functioned effectively. That made all the more remarkable the fact that we still got students from 70 countries. In Eastern Europe we were still working primarily with governments, and that was proving unpredictable. The heads also learned that the International Baccalaureate had a substantial deficit and clearly needed reorganization before it could consider curricular changes or continued expansion. After our second day of discussion we felt we had made limited progress and there was an obvious resentment at the London office for not justifying its existence, at least in our view. Thus began a decade of friction between the colleges and the International Office, which would have been more accentuated had it not been for Ian Gourlay's patience and his sympathy with our complaints.

One afternoon I met with our president, His Royal Highness The Prince of Wales, at Kensington Palace. We discussed how best to gain support for the UWCs in Nepal through the king or his brother. The Prince said that he would arrange for us to meet with the heir to the throne when we were in Kathmandu in December. We also talked about the interest expressed by Prince Sadruddin in appropriate technology. The president was interested in opening such a program in India. In fact, Prince Charles seemed more concerned about this kind of practical training than in the IB—which explained his continuing participation in the Intermediate Technology Group in London, affiliated with the largest private technical assistance program in the States, Volunteers in Technical Assistance (VITA). This concept would reappear often in discussions with the Prince. He also asked about relations among the constituents in the United States. I was oblique until he asked if there was a solution, to which I replied yes if everyone followed Montezuma's lead. He laughed and then agreed.

When the board met for dinner that evening, Prince Charles steered the conversation around to the Third World again. He wanted us to be more venturesome with agricultural programs; others wanted to hunker down until the finances were better; and a few spoke of future IB colleges. The paralysis which talks about expansion into the Third World produced spread to the next day's board meeting. Tony Besse brought up his international scholarship proposal again. Singapore made quite clear that there would be no fishing for such funds in their waters. Others concurred, but Besse contended that certainly the United States could help. Even though Hammer, Prince Sadruddin and Lord Carrington were all present, they chose to remain silent; and unfortunately Lord Carrington never came again, partly out of frustration and partly because of his NATO assignment. One other occurrence amazed everyone. When Luis Marcano indicated that the Venezuelan effort was short three million, Hammer offered to match $1 million if they raised $1 million. In view of our financial condition, McGill and I found this a bit irritating. As it turned out, the Venezuelan Committee would not accept Hammer's condition that he be Honorary Chairman of their board and meet regularly with the Venezuelan president, and no money went from Los Angeles to Simon Bolivar College.

The fall was hardly into October when the college staged an international day open house. Proceeds were divided between the Special Olympics and the Cystic Fibrosis Foundation—a practice that would endure for many years. Students had already organized a weekend on campus for youngsters afflicted with cystic fibrosis. The students dressed in their "native" costumes, which raised a question in the minds of U.S. students: what is our national costume? Most compelling of the presentations was a Balinese warrior dance by I. Gusti Raka Panji Tisna from Indonesia. Visitors were also enticed to join a chain dance led by Amadou Wane of Senegal. Probably the most important dividend was the endless conversation among students and visitors, be it on the Castle veranda with English tea or on the playing fields with games. The 2500 visitors taxed both parking and facilities.

A similarly festive occasion was held on October 20 when the board met and visitors were encouraged to return to commemorate the1982 dedication. Snow eliminated many visitors, but not the Oxy plane from Los Angeles which landed in Las Vegas despite the zero ceiling. We had dressed up the lobby and ballroom in the Castle. The luncheon tables filled the ballroom. Mark Larrimore, a U.S. student, was master of

Indonesian student Panji Tisna performs a Balinese dance at international day.

ceremonies for the festivities after lunch; and Hammer surprised everyone by dancing with students. This beguiling conviviality was not so visible at the board meeting later in the day. Wid Slick, the owner of the Plaza Hotel in Las Vegas, presented an offer to develop the Castle into a family summer retreat. The board turned down his offer, the

William McGill, chairman of the board, addresses guests at the college.

last one the college would receive for many years. The board also preferred not to act on Phase III of new construction until there was better financial news—and Phase III still remains unfinished.

The following day, brilliantly clear, there was a special luncheon at Patty (Mrs. Maxie) Anderson's home in Albuquerque. Students performed again at this cultivation event, dubbed the Fiesta del Valle at Hacienda Valle Grande. There in the Rio Grande valley with the Sandia mountains at our backs, everyone was optimistic about the future.

Then it was back to normal in Montezuma as students awaited a conference on justice. We had learned that the calendar needed periodic ventilation so that students would not become either worn down or depressed. This was more likely to be a problem in the second semester than during the fall when Thanksgiving and the prospect of the Christmas break buoyed students.

Lu and I went to the Himalayas to hike during the holidays and to meet with committee members in Nepal and India. As arranged by Prince Charles, Prince Gyandruk of Nepal received us and promised support of our efforts. In India there was a crisis since the one-man committee in Delhi could not function any longer. Therefore, it was no surprise when the committee moved to Bombay and future Indian students came from that region rather than the north. When we returned, we found that the Russian students had stayed home, officially because they missed "Mother Russia" so much. We never learned why this happened, but it reminded us of the unexpected problems an international school may face.

The appearance of flu, chicken pox, and increased grumbling about the load they as students were forced to carry led the faculty to review the pace and balance at the college. The schedule would be changed for the third year of operation, primarily to prevent the pile-up of major events. But one major event in February was a great success: a conference on tolerance. Once again the students handled much of the organizational details inevitable in a three-day discussion. The workshops went well. Few ever got to say everything they wanted about cultural differences but in the end most confronted their own intolerance. What was also apparent was that this second year brought more activity, and occasionally more problems, to the community. The Scandinavian Day, the first and only such severely regional "national" day, was surprisingly imaginative given the small number of available participants. A smorgasbord preceded the customary slide show of home scenes and then outdoor games in mid-winter. Henrik Hovland of Norway did not change from his costume of a sparkling white T-shirt, hiking pants, and boots, an outfit to which he adhered without exception during the entire two years.

In a quite different way music was gaining in popularity and quality the second year. John Edwards had come from Singapore. He had an astonishing amount of talent to draw upon, even though in admissions the college never specifically looked for a cellist or flutist. They just appeared in sufficient numbers to form a quartet, a good chorus—which in time was expanded to include people from the community—and to some few to give concerts. Gaurav Chopra had studied music in India before coming to Montezuma. He was prepared to perform on a guitar or a santoor, and later he would return home and become a successful professional musician. So also in art more and more students were displaying unusual talent. That added a wealth and diversity to the community that was important to everyone living in this rural area so far from major cultural events.

Toward the end of February the board of directors met again in Los Angeles. The meeting had been scheduled for February 8, but Hammer had the opportunity to attend the Olympics in Sarajevo, visit our student's parents there and attend Andropov's funeral in Moscow. Thus the meeting was deferred to the 17th. The night before McGill and I talked with Hammer. He told us he would cover the deficit for only one more year, and he thought we should defer any further construction. He also surprised us by indicating that, at Prince Charles' request, he had given $35,000 to the IB to "bail them out." At the meeting next day, in a procedure that would become familiar, all directors were re-elected for another year. There was talk of having a major person like President Reagan speak at graduation, which Hammer hoped would be a fund-raiser as well.

The board approved spending some money on the east part of the Castle so that it could be used for certain public events. It also agreed to repair the basketball court, attend to erosion around the faculty housing, and look favorably on a faculty-student renovation of the old casino next to the Castle (a project which did not occur because the State engineer condemned the foundation). In response to the Nickell report on a development office, the directors decided to ask Carolyn Walker and the LA office to see what it could do—and consider the appointment of a director of development. In part, this discussion was the obvious response to the budget projections for the next year, with a possible deficit of well over 1.5 million. And for the first time the question of recreational facilities, specifically a swimming pool, came before the board and Mrs. Hammer donated $200,000 for it, a sum which was later withdrawn to cover deficits. In a contrapuntal closing Chairman McGill reminded the board that, whatever else might be necessary, nothing was as important as the academic reputation of the school. That had been, and remained, the highest priority, to be tested in the spring and in prospective university acceptances. It was an appropriate observation both because of skepticism abroad and the internal debate about possible overemphasis on academics. The college had to establish itself very firmly as a superb academic institution.

Upon returning to Montezuma, we learned that Dr. and Mrs. Hammer would come to visit on February 22-23. One immediate result was an astonishing clean-up of the campus, including the dorms since I indicated that they would want to visit some of the rooms. Hammer addressed the students and reminisced about the Soviet Union in a thoroughly engaging fashion. We hoped that it would become an annual affair, but they never came back for more than a day at a time— primarily because of the effect of the high altitude on their health.

Surprisingly we had had a mild winter thus far, but March brought repeated snow squalls and those who went to the Grand Canyon during Project Week were surprised by the variable conditions. This year the number and variety of projects increased, including those who worked with the Dallas Community College in Texas and at some schools in Colorado Springs. As was predictable, those going to Mexico had problems with their visas, including a South African who discovered that she could not enter Mexico. In the end transportation was the main challenge.

Finally the snow stopped; students turned to university plans as the time to hear came nearer. The April returns were promising although some could not yet get the financial assistance that they would need. As we reflected on the results, we concluded that we would have to change procedures another year since it required so much of the time of the faculty and the dean. Too many foreign students, not knowing much about universities in North America, had not been as realistic as they should have been. This review coincided with a faculty-staff discussion of ways we could trim down fiscally.

Nearly two years of experience was providing some clues; but we soon discovered that there was not that much slack, even as we pared down the number of U.S. students we would support going to other UWCs. Once again looming behind the magnificent experience provided at the UWCs was the financial cost of supporting foreign students as more and more committees found it increasingly difficult to locate even airfare and pocket money.

One diversion in April was the 24-hour relay run around a soggy playing field to raise money for the victims of cyclone Domoina which had caused widespread damage in Swaziland. It also provided a chance for the community to come together, watch the posting of the miles run on the bulletin board in the cafeteria, and then find, to everyone's delight, that the students and townspeople had raised $3450. All such occasions confirmed the strong feeling everyone had about close relations with the citizens of Las Vegas who, in turn, took great pride in the college. The next race was to get ready for the first complete set of IB examinations and plan for the graduation to be held May 24, 1984.

That made the creation of Getaway families all the more important. During the second year the college had concluded that even further links with the community would be both pleasant and helpful. On the one hand, there had been great interest in Las Vegas about the students attending the college; on the other hand, among many foreign students there was a lively interest in finding out how Americans lived. There was a logic in trying to bring the two groups together by inviting townspeople to serve as homes where students could get away for a meal, a weekend, for conversation and a new and different relationship. It would be another means of addressing the issue of cultural differences. The idea of a home away from home caught on quickly. As Maria Jose Tort Canto from Uruguay remarked, "I thought it would be a good way to get to know Las Vegans better." The Vasquez family was puzzled, however, by the heavy load of work she carried. So also for Jiang Ning from the People's Republic of China: "At first I didn't realize how much my Getaway family would impact me [it is appalling how quickly foreign students pick up our less fortunate use of words], I just thought that we would probably have fun. I didn't think of the things I would learn about the U.S. and the people." And everyone had to adjust to the hugging impulse which, curiously, was certainly a feature of Montezuma life. This idea of Getaway families eventually spread to the other UWCs. Hilda Wales could feel proud of all the effort she had put into seeing the program succeed.

Before the examinations began, the college had selected a Vice-President for Development, Joseph F. Marsh, who had served as president of Concord College in West Virginia and Waynesburg College in Pennsylvania. Anthony Portago, a member of the board living in Santa Fe, would join him during the summer when the office was established on the third floor of the administration building. It would test the possibilities of finding new sources of funding.

The issue was of equal interest at the International Board discussions at the end of April. They were disappointed when we indicated it would take a couple of years before we could say whether there was substantial financial support available not only for Montezuma but also for the movement as a whole. In face of a tight situation in London for the next two years, such a message was sobering; but once again it illustrated the naive hope people continued to cherish about Hammer's generosity.

While in London the Education Committee of the International Board met with the heads. The first topic concerned the possible expansion of appropriate technology programs like that in Venezuela. Sir Alec Peterson particularly urged that we introduce that idea in a UWC in India. In a manner that was to become painful over the next few years, the movement divided over this issue. Most of the heads felt we should concentrate on what had been successful; namely, the IB schools. A few like Peterson argued that we should be doing more to help people in the Third World more directly. Not surprisingly, Swaziland maintained that the developing countries wanted a strong academic program to provide leadership. I maintained that there were other organizations better equipped and more experienced with rural problems than the UWCs. We never resolved the issue, and I often think of Luis Marcano's patience as we repeatedly buried and then resurrected his college in Venezuela.

At dinner at London's Atheneum Club that evening Prince Charles expressed his growing concern with the have-not nations in Africa and Asia and our seeming inability to help those in the non-western world. "It is time our students got their hands dirty," the President remarked. The sentiment was appealing; and, as I would continually discover, there were those all too ready to jump on the Prince's bandwagon. It mattered not that community service provided some opportunities to get the hands dirty; it matter even less that there were no funds to underwrite such new programs; it was an attractive thought that took minds away from the very real limitations we were experiencing with existing programs. But it did not get a warm reception in the United States.

The second topic was equally familiar: how to get more assistance from the national committees. Atlantic had felt the impact of the two new colleges in the form of declining funds from those few national committees providing their own students with bursary scholarships. It was not only the consequences for each college's budget that worried us; it was also the trend downward as inflation increased the burden on the institutions themselves. So far as the heads could determine, there was no strategy at the center to address the issue. In fact, the board meeting confirmed that nothing much would happen until either there was a substantial change in board membership or a stronger demand for leadership from London—something unlikely to happen since the colleges operated so autonomously, were so scattered, and were so willing to disparage the efforts of the International Office.

All these issues receded as May came and graduation was imminent. The board had become enthusiastic about doing something special for the occasion. A new board member and president of Management Three, Jerry Weintraub, volunteered to arrange for the Beach Boys to contribute a performance. That would introduce an interesting wrinkle into the preparations. We had decided early on to hold a formal graduation ceremony as part of the American experience for our students. Admittedly none of the other UWCs held such commencement exercises: they preferred to let the first-years leave as soon as they did their few examinations and then simply have a "leavers" dinner for the graduates. But before we could draw up plans for the grand event, the college had its first heavy rash of thefts. When simple appeals to community spirit failed to elicit the return of equipment, books, and the like, we undertook a search which located a modest amount of the stolen goods and one packet of marijuana. Since the UWC policy was very strict on drugs, we asked the person to leave; but, since clearly it was more an accident than a dispensary of drugs, the person was permitted to take the examinations off-campus. Another student found stealing money was denied participation in graduation. These were the minor episodes of backsliding that became inevitable, troublesome, and frustrating. And when they occurred, they riveted attention as firmly as any fiscal crisis.

The tempo picked up when the Beach Boys's Mike Love visited the campus with his troupe to review the conditions under which they would perform. During lunch at the house, no one ate the chicken salad that had been prepared but pulled out their tackle boxes filled with herb teas, vitamin pills, and dietary supplements. Then, to display their California style, each took a turn at the telephone so that not all would be seated at any one time. Then we walked the playing field, Love stripped to the waist and full of exclamations as students peered from the cafeteria at the Hollywood hype. Later some lucky few would join him for a dip in the hot springs. Even though we were trying to keep the concert quiet, the story leaked and then we had to disappoint the local folk by saying it was a closed event. In the end we invited 200 high school students from Las Vegas. The State Police and everyone else in the security business became involved: it was Hammer showtime.

Many of our students were not familiar with the Beach Boys since the group was formed when their parents were in school. Therefore, initially, faculty and parents were the most enthusiastic about the prospect of a concert; but it did not take long for the students to find out that the Beach Boys's sound was truly remarkable. It was loud as they tested their equipment during the faculty-student softball game. Two trailer trucks had hauled in the extensive array of equipment. Even though they donated the concert, the first stop on their 1984 World Tour, they did run up a striking bill at the Plaza Hotel in town, including imported organic juices, special bottled water, and no doubt other exotic items.

The tent went up on the playing field; the platform was placed on the north side where the dedication had taken place 18 months before; a stage for the Beach Boys had been erected at the southwest corner of the playing field so that the cables could easily reach a power source. The students who, as one person quipped, "lived in a petri dish at the end of a dirt road in the Rocky Mountains" were astonished.

May 24, 1984, was a beautiful day. A goodly number of distinguished guests, including His Majesty King Constantine of Greece, flew into Las Vegas, thus challenging the airport's supply of jet fuel. After a press conference in the campus center at which Hammer assured everyone that he planned to renovate the Castle, we held the commencement exercises. Sir Oliver Wright, the British Ambassador to the United States, was the speaker. The format worked well, especially when each student climbed the steps to receive from Hammer a certificate, just as each had received a matriculation certificate during the fall of the first year. The college was adept at creating instant traditions. The only hitch was that Hammer always declared to the audience that he was handing each student an IB diploma—which was not possible since these were not issued until August after the examinations had been corrected by the battery of examiners from around the world. As is generally true of all graduations, what was said was quickly forgotten. What was different was the tremendous emotional impact on everyone as the students walked across the platform beneath the 46 flags. No doubt the fact that these 95 students would always be the first graduates of Montezuma added to the sentimentality of the occasion when 800 guests applauded and wept.

Lunch followed in the large tent, whipped by the persistent winds of the day. Then came the big moment of the afternoon: the concert by the Beach Boys—or, as Hammer remarked, "The Beach Balls." Mike Love, Bruce Johnson, and Al Jardine joined with others in filling the Gallinas canyon with sound. They even played "Graduation Day" as a tribute to the students and parents. It was a loud success, capped by a student snake dance that wound through the audience to surround, and thus to honor, Dr. and Mrs. Hammer.

The afternoon ended with a brief board meeting. The financial news was typically both good and bad. The college continued its tradition of running under budget; summer programs would produce some income; and income from tuition would run over the half million mark for the next year. But participation in Social Security would cost the college an unanticipated $182,000. The board also urged the administration to discourage foreign students from trying to remain in American universities after graduation—an attempt in keeping with the guidelines of the UWC movement but in the

Armand Hammer chats with The Beach Boys, Al Jardine, Mike Love, and Bruce Johnson at the first graduation.

Armand Hammer, Martin Meyerson, HM King Constantine and British Ambassador Oliver Wright chat on commencement day 1984.

end a futile gesture. In practice the plans of the graduates depended on what financial aid they might receive and on the IB examination results they might achieve. A few had concluded that they would take a year off and do more community service before dedicating their time to career preparation.

The buses drew up in front of the dormitories. The suitcases and boxes piled up by the converted horse trailer, to be loaded for the airport. Presumably the rooms had been cleaned and all the left-behinds bagged for Amnesty International. Then the good-byes began. Marcelo from Brazil collapsed; Tony and Anny staggered; Mark was philosophical; and Jennifer was quiet. But it was impossible to get the buses loaded. Eventually the fleet left and the campus was distressingly quiet. The first graduation had ended. Hammer's dream had been fulfilled.

11: TIME TO REGROUP

The summer of 1984 provided a much-needed time to regroup and to reconsider. Foremost was how much summer activity we could develop, and then tolerate, in view of the need to clean, refurbish, and prepare for each fall. Fortunately the kinds of programs which liked the area, such as Elderhostel and the French School from the University of New Mexico, did not create much strain on our facilities. But we did not yet know how many different groups could move in and out on weekends, when we would need extra personnel, in a manner that would encourage them to come back another summer. The test of summer programs was not alone how much income they might generate but how much goodwill we might cultivate in this way. We felt comfortable but not complacent in this regard.

During this summer we also opened the development office in the Old Stone Hotel on July 9th. Joe Marsh began the unavoidably tedious process of organizing all relevant information, and Anthony Portago assisted him. The first task was to undertake a systematic search of foundations, corporations, and prospective individual donors. We had lists; we had directories, but we did not have a program through which to identify the most likely sources of new money. Closely related to this issue was the absence of a public relations program beyond what, from time to time, the Los Angeles office was permitted to try. The college was no longer the fascinating fresh story it had been; there were no visiting royalty; and attempts to arrange for an appearance on *The Today Show* had fizzled. We had begun to hear a familiar complaint: "The college is the best kept secret in America. No one knows what it is, who goes there, and even where it is." Clearly we needed to publicize the school more broadly if we were to garner new support. We spent the summer organizing the files, preparing approaches to likely foundations, and seeking outlets for stories on the college. Progress was slow, but we felt that we were at least entering a at least entering a new phase in the long-range quest for adequate funding.

Closely related to this program was the third and final Broadlands event in England. Once again the U.S. Committee had done an excellent job in arranging for the gala. And once again the Prince of Wales agreed to participate after insisting that proceeds be split with the *Mary Rose* effort. He also insisted that this was the last such affair he would support. Given that the three-day visit required immense work on the part of the organizers, everyone concurred in this decision. Moreover, there was some resistance, especially on the part of Atlantic College, to using English soil for a fund-raiser to benefit the Americans. Be that as it may, the affair would net, we hoped, some $200,000 which would go for scholarships.

It was June and it was England at its best. After a dinner and auction at Sutton Place in Surrey, on Friday, June 1st, there was the formal affair at Broadlands on Saturday evening. All went well until the charter bus which took some of us from London chose a route better suited for Portsmouth (where some would go on Monday to see the *Mary Rose)*; and even I recognized the error. Accordingly we were a bit late that evening, to the distress of Zsa Zsa Gabor. We had also learned on these buses that the attempt to provide hospitality was thoughtful but not always judicious, especially when the glassware took off on a sharp curve or the champagne glass was smaller than the opening in the decorous holder, to the dismay of at least a few guests. On Sunday there was the customary polo match in Windsor Park. For the first and only time Queen Elizabeth and Lady Diana were present to cheer on the Prince's team. Despite all the shuttling about, the glamour appealed to the patrons and the returns were promising.

However, amidst these festivities there was a proposal put forth by a member of the U.S. Committee, Marvin Frankel, that alarmed both the London office and Hammer. Frankel had been very instrumental in finding people to attend the Broadland events and felt that he could assist the committee and Prince Charles by coordinating all the charities for which the Prince had interest in raising money in the United States. The key sponsors would meet with the Prince once a year for dinner and a small board would oversee the distribution of funds in accordance with the Prince's wishes. Over tea in the ornate sitting room at Claridge's, in a corner away from the dowagers, Symons, Gourlay, and Brewster asked me to meet with them to discuss ways to frustrate the scheme. Matters worsened when at the Sutton Place dinner and auction, there was very little mention of either Hammer or the college even though Montezuma was the major recipient of this charity affair. Things simmered but did not boil over in England. Yet, surely there would be further discussion later among all parties, an unwelcome prospect.

On August 15, the board met in Los Angeles. The evening before McGill and I had met with Hammer to review the agenda. There was nothing ominous coming up; therefore, Hammer wanted to know what to do about the New York Committee. He wanted the Prince in his capacity as president of the UWCs to disband the committee. He had never liked the fact that the committee was a separately chartered organization in New York State, essentially untouchable, unless the international office chose to disenfranchise it. We concluded that a party in Montezuma in October might improve relations. The board agreed that we should hold an international day, include members from New York, and invite a number of potential donors.

Then the directors talked about the academic program at considerable length. Martin Meyerson, a director and president emeritus of the University of Pennsylvania, felt that we should attach an associate-of-arts degree program as a third-year option and as a safety play should the IB become unmanageable. It might ease the problem of future accreditation. I was asked to prepare a summary of this idea. It was at this meeting also that Hammer indicated that he wanted my title changed to President and the powers of that position so defined that this officer would be the legally responsible agent for the board. It was a move little understood by colleagues at the other UWCs. Fortunately Hammer did not say anything further about shipping some Arabian horses to the campus, an idea that he had broached in the spring.

The campus was enjoying some late summer rains and the most recent landscaping prospered. As the time for students to return approached, we did not know, yet again, how many new candidates would actually arrive—anywhere between 100 to 108. We had some slack since, for a variety of reasons, only 90 second-years would be back. On August 20 the veterans came back, resumed work on the Theory of Knowledge and prepared to welcome the newcomers. It was different than the year before: it was more relaxed and there was no sign of resentment at having others come.

Orientation at the Philmont Boy Scout camp in Cimarron, New Mexico, was not quite so dry, but it went smoothly. However, it was clear that now everyone wanted to play tennis as a sport and ski at Taos in the winter. A mathematics teacher, Peter Hamer-Hodges, was interested in helping with both activities. That led some faculty to question whether we were getting more affluent students than before, an issue that would resurface regularly. The fact that Prince Pavlos of Greece was a new student reinforced such questioning but, it could be argued, increased the diversity.

What we all agreed was that each year was a renewal with half of the students fresh, eager, apprehensive, and enthusiastic. There was no time or occasion for skepticism, indifference, or disillusionment. It was a tribute to those who designed the UWCs that they had struck on an approach that engendered such goodwill and hard work. As we all reviewed the IB examination results, we were pleased that we had done respectably well, better than Atlantic but not up to Pearson's results. But, of course, comparisons were not permitted; we could only aim to do better over the next few years to assure everyone that Montezuma was the best UWC.

Classes began on September 13 with only the Gaza Strip and Zambia unrepresented among the 67 countries. Of the 197 students 101 were girls and 96 boys. Bumptious and ambitious, the new arrivals appeared ready to wrestle leadership from the second-years. Certainly we had reason to feel that Montezuma was now recruiting better candidates than initially.

As this would be our second year at full strength, we decided that we would try to refine our various needs and thus to streamline our operations. But first we had to cope with heavy rains that flooded one dorm and carried away plantings up the hill. The sanitary system was acting up as well, and the quality of coal was once again unacceptable. These were the episodes that kept one humble. And no one could believe the snowfall on September 26.

October proved to be a busy month indeed. In anticipation of international day the students were busy trying out recipes in the kitchen and, without much forethought, asked the food manager to order 250 pounds of flour for bread and 2500 bananas for another dish. Luckily the menus were appropriately down-scaled. October 11 was "A Day of Celebration." The crowds came in school buses from the fairgrounds down Hot Springs Boulevard; and the students appeared in their best costumes. But, as one remarked, "They looked at my name tag and were too embarrassed to ask where Malaysia is." The visitors zeroed in on the food stands where, among other delicacies, were fried bananas along with fish and chips. Charlotte Brenner and Stephan Klasen from West Germany did a folk dance; Latin Americans put on various other popular dances; Naomi Hosada from Japan, the traditional fan dance; and local kids joined in break dancing.

Later in the month there was another, similar festive event, for the board members and friends of Hammer from Los Angeles. It began with a luncheon in the ballroom of the Castle. Hammer spoke briefly and repeated his hope that we could do away with nuclear weapons. He also remarked:

"We should treat nations the same as we do individuals. If they do something wrong, they should be punished . . . There is only one way we are going to survive on this planet, and that is to see that we live in peace, with friendship and goodwill among all people."

At this luncheon Patty Anderson presented the Maxie Anderson Scholarship to Paul Moore, a second-year student from Washington State. During a brief concert Suzanna Vervoordeldonk of the Netherlands and Fiona Caldwell of Great Britain performed solos and, to the surprise of everyone, Mr. and Mrs. Guilford Glazer announced that they would donate a harpsichord for future concerts. Clearly the day was successful.

Before returning home, the members of the board met to review the opening of a new year. Jayne Weintraub, also well-known as the popular singer of the fifties, Jayne Morgan, joined the board. Most important was the decision to enlarge the library by enclosing the adjacent courtyard. And, in anticipation of the 100th anniversary of the present Castle, Louise Courtelis, a member of the board from Miami who, along with her husband, Alec, had become active in planning the future of the college, proposed having a Las Vegas Night to raise funds for its restoration. Again a movie premier was

Charlotte Brenner (Germany) and Stephan Klasen (Germany) perform at one of the many celebrations held on the Montezuma campus.

presumably "in the works." The weather had closed down by then; and, although the Hammer plane departed in good order, the Courtelis's plane could not return from refueling in Santa Fe. Accordingly, they had an unexpected journey by car. It would not be the last time weather and the airport conspired to discourage airplane trips to Las Vegas.

A week later the search and rescue teams were alerted at 12:25 p.m. that a hunter was lost in the Elk Mountain region. Up there 14 inches of snow would make reconnaissance slow. In combination with St. John's College in Santa Fe, the college was ready to rotate teams every 30 hours. Two days later a helicopter spotted the man and he was rescued. In that year the UWC teams were summoned ten times to go look for missing or stranded individuals in the Pecos Wilderness area—striking testimony of the importance of this kind of training and service. Unlike the sea rescue for which the UWCs had become renowned, these searches involved long periods in the woods, across rugged terrain, with limited information about either the person(s) or location, the kind of exercise that requires discipline, stamina, and careful coordination.

Simultaneously, the college held a three-day conference on religion. Bishop Lancelot Fleming from England, the Queen's personal chaplain and formerly at Norwich Cathedral, was the keynote speaker. The emphasis was on "dialogue, not debate." In an institution where there are so many religious beliefs, some fervent and others casual, the topic provoked a predictably wide range of reactions, one of which was especially engaging: "I think some students aren't as closed-minded now. You aren't as wrong as you were, but they are as right as they ever were."

At the end of the month the United World College of the Adriatic held its formal dedication ceremonies, with His Royal Highness The Prince of Wales in attendance. For most of us it was our first visit to this UWC, founded the same year as Montezuma. Situated in the small seaside village of Duino, some twenty kilometers west of Trieste, in hilly countryside dominated by a Castle which, ironically, that college could not use as it had originally planned, the Adriatic College had experimented with providing most of its housing in homes in the small town, so as to become more a part of that community. But, however different the setting, as Chairman McGill remarked, "The students look just like those at Montezuma." However, in another respect, on this occasion at least, life was quite different; for wine flowed freely, the food never ended, and the cafe across the street from the administration building was a perpetual gathering spot for a cup of cappuccino and conversation. The festivities were impressive as were the formidable police escorts, sirens blaring, that accompanied the motorcades from site to site. The festivities culminated in a concert at the Verdi Theater in Trieste. To observe the support provided by the government of Italy was indeed most encouraging.

Not so encouraging was the discussion at the meeting of the International Board. Once again the issue of an international scholarship fund surfaced. We were criticized for not permitting more fund-raising in the United States for this purpose. Then the executive committee chairman indicated that Mr. Besse's scholarship committee would be collapsed into another committee, a move which revealed a lamentable clash of personalities and inevitably a delay in developing any central effort to raise money. When Prince Charles joined the meeting, he spoke strongly in favor of having parents pay, an unpopular suggestion in that setting. Beneath the surface was some growing resentment at the Anglophones. To add more fuel to the fire at this meeting was the issue of Venezuela. Now a *fait accompli,* Simon Bolivar was, as McGill noted, "a most tentative step across this educational frontier [from a force working for world peace to one] dealing with the educational needs of less developed countries." There is reason for "just a tinge of apprehension, for we must find new ways to maintain the UWC community in the face of larger diversities than we have ever known before."

On the lighter side, we had seen a dedication that bore little resemblance to ours two years earlier—except that, at the last moment, the Italians had rolled out new turf in front of the recently opened academic building and kindly mentioned they had learned this technique from their New Mexican colleagues. Otherwise, it was all quite different, from the meals in magnificent settings like Udine to gatherings down by the water in Duino. Sir Ranulph Twisleton-Wykeman Fiennes was now Hammer's representative in Europe; and we all wondered how long this famous explorer would last, especially when some of us unexpectedly found ourselves in a courtyard in Udine without transportation. Hammer had gone ahead and we were left to hitch a ride on a bus at midnight. Fiennes had gone around the world, pole to pole, in 1982, thanks to some help from Hammer, and was a close friend of Prince Charles

November and December in Montezuma were sufficiently punctuated by events and call-outs for search and rescue that we got through the period without too much evident depression. On one occasion our team saved a 65-year-old hunter by carrying him out on a litter for nine hours across rough terrain. No doubt the two national days that fall also helped buoy everyone's spirits: Commonwealth Day and European Leftovers were experiments in regrouping the students, and the latter marked the Hungarian version of the Blues Brothers, thanks in part to the newly popular emphasis on American jazz which the physics instructor, Bob Wade, had introduced. The Castle ballroom provided ample space and, with the heating system on, proved a good site for college meetings also. The only problem was scampering down the hill fast enough to be first in line for dinner. For the second time in three years the day of departure for the winter break was marked by a heavy snowstorm—15 inches. The customary messages about the meaning of the season were scratched in favor of an early departure for the airport, except for those few tackling the volcanoes in Mexico who would take a van to Mexico City.

The end of the calendar year of 1984 did not bring a resolution to either the financial deficits or our relations with the committee in New York City. We had revised our operating forecast and projected revenues of $1,537,603; but our expenses were going to run $2,798,438. What was now apparent was that we did not have enough restricted or endowed scholarships to cover the large gap between committee and parental contributions, and that trend had worsened with the new students, 51% of whom were supported directly by the college. I had concluded that we needed to have someone come and study our operations carefully to see what we might do over the long haul. Accordingly an experienced analyst of educational ventures, Matthew Cullen, came in January. His report was hardly buoyant, for he saw only two options: increased support from Hammer and the board for the period until Hammer's estate provided for additional endowment, or the acceptance of more full-paying students at the expense of the academic reputation the college had so carefully built. He did not think money-saving efforts like eliminating a few positions or mailing fewer brochures, etcetera, would make any difference.

Equally unpromising was the response from New York. We did not seem destined to work together easily, and certainly the absence of substantial success in the east in raising funds complicated the financial-aid picture. It was becoming clear that in the course of the next six months we would have to review all our options on these issues and consider how best to proceed. It was also becoming apparent that Los Angeles felt our new fund-raising office was not performing effectively enough. Prematurely, the conclusion was that it should move back to LA. What few appreciated was the amount of work required to find out which, if any, foundations would assist us, which corporations might consider a proposal, and where we might find new individual donors since board members did not respond to requests for their assistance in the search. A bit of the bloom was off the rose.

This winter brought some good skating and cross-country skiing. It was always a marvel to watch those unfamiliar with these sports launch forth with great confidence, only to return an hour later looking as if they had been frozen in the wilderness for a week. With sufficient ice, the students, led by Serge Pelletier from Canada, rashly challenged the faculty to a hockey game; the results were devastating as the sheer bulk of the six and only faculty players overwhelmed the two teams of student skaters. Lu was invited to become a substitute, but 15 seconds on the ice convinced her that only Shona Armstrong (also Canadian) looked unmenacing. Ted Reineke, technician for the sciences and transportation coordinator, tended goal in his jogging shoes. Cross-country grew in popularity with the beginners going around the perimeter of the soccer fields and the others venturing up Sebastian Canyon—to become well-known also for its May parties. Training for search and rescue included snowshoeing, something requiring more energy and a far different gait. For the downhill enthusiasts, Sipapu was convenient for the Wednesday afternoon special trips and on some weekends a van would go to Taos. The heavy snows prompted us to have three faculty members trained in avalanche detection and rescue.

No doubt the absence of any indoor recreational facilities drove more people to the slopes, even the tennis courts, than might have been the case had the long-promised pool ever been built. Another "sport" had gained notoriety: chess. Pir Maleki, an Iranian who had completed his doctorate in mathematics at Kansas, organized a team which did extraordinarily well, losing only to Los Alamos. There was most likely a connection between this success and our finishing among the top 15 schools in North America in the annual mathematics contest.

February brought another meeting of the board in Los Angeles. The board concluded that the development office should return to LA and that Myra Silverman should take over that assignment under Hammer's assistant and director of college relations there, Carolyn Walker. One bright note was a gift of two million dollars from Kemal Zeinal-Zade, a businessman operating out of Geneva who had long been associated with Hammer and Occidental. This was an excellent illustration of what Hammer could accomplish when he put his mind to it. The board recommended naming the science facility in honor of this donation. After some desultory discussion about a movie premiere, Hammer asked that the minutes record a request from the board that the head redefine his responsibilities so that this office could provide more involvement with the UWC movement, with long-range plans for the college, and for raising money. As McGill and I sat around afterwards, we could not resist commenting on the utter contrast between the upbeat, vibrant life in Montezuma and the dreary passivity of the board, quite prepared to grab at a quick fix or to reverse field. Some directors were truly committed but others had never even visited the campus. Yet, in fairness, most did not wish to interfere and left people in Montezuma to operate the college as they thought best. And many had been singularly generous.

These developments coincided with a request from London that colleges coordinate their requests for the Prince of Wales to visit or to assist in fund-raising through the central office. Certainly there was good reason to know who was asking whom to do what, but at the time the request appeared more like a way to protect royalty—or to anticipate a diminishing role by Prince Charles in helping the movement. Whatever the reason, the result was a lot of maneuvering, frequent transatlantic calls, and irritation from Los Angeles. Hammer had his own way of approaching Kensington Palace. With the announcement that the Prince and Princess would visit the States in November of 1985, the plot thickened.

More immediate was a growing concern about foreign faculty at the college. The government had announced new regulations concerning both the ability of those on temporary visas to remain in the country and the manner in which degrees would be counted. That affected both Maria Elena Maldonado in Spanish (a Uruguayan) and Olatunji Augustus in English as a second language (a Nigerian). The fact that neither had an advanced degree in the field in which each was teaching and the fact that we could keep them only if there were no Americans with equal experience qualified and willing to teach made the prospects so tentative that both elected to return home. At the same time John Edwards in music concluded that his family should return to England, their homeland which they had not seen for 12 years. Edwards had just organized Sunday afternoon concerts in the Castle Ballroom for the winter and spring. This decision was similar to that of Marcel Roy the year before when he and his family had returned to Montreal. Normally faculty turnover had been modest, but for the coming year we would need at least four replacements, including art.

This challenge was equaled by the lack of promising U.S. candidates for admissions. Although the number of applications had gone up, the number of well-qualified candidates, though sufficient for a class, had not increased. We had been hoping that we could continue to improve the quality of American students, especially if we had to admit more U.S. students who could pay at least some if not all the comprehensive fee. There was an obvious irony since our foreign inquiries had risen. National committees had become enthusiastic about the results at the college and we were receiving inquiries from individuals who, because they were not residing in the countries where they were born, sought special admission. Again, as we reviewed matters against another year, admissions would require special attention.

This spring also the North Central Association scheduled a review of our own self-study —a voluminous compilation of information in two volumes, no doubt more helpful for our archives than for their decision. Their decision on re-accreditation was very favorable, and we received an award of excellence as well. The State of New Mexico concurred in their findings and continued to provide us with state accreditation, a delightfully informal process which until 1990 was quite painless. One reason for such praise was the ever-improving acceptance rate at various universities. The examination results of our first graduates, compared with all candidates for the IB worldwide, were also very flattering. Where all schools combined earned 8% of the highest grade awarded, AHUWC earned 13.7%; and we had half as few candidates failing any examination as was true worldwide.

New to the campus this year were three Arabian horses, quickly named by the students Ted, Andrew (the dean), and Neil (Hunter in biology). The gift of Hammer and shipped from Florida by Alec Courtelis, they introduced a new community service: rising at 5:45 a.m. to shovel manure and break the ice on the water buckets. A corral had been hastily put together next to the maintenance building. The horses were young and training to ride them proved daunting for the twelve students who chose this as an activity. "Neil" was sent to pasture. They made their mark at graduation, nonetheless, when they rode on the president's front lawn to honor the Hammers. We did not keep the horses very long because the cost of feeding and caring (which was to have been borne by Hammer) got added to our budget.

Another major event in the early spring was the Freedom from Hunger March from the Roundhouse, as the State Capitol in Santa Fe is called, to Las Vegas—70 miles. Koome Mwiraria from Kenya was the spirit behind what was a formidable organizational problem. Blisters accompanied the walkers, especially by the time they reached the Plaza in Old Town Las Vegas Sunday afternoon, after two full days on the road. The $17,500 raised was donated to relief services in Africa. Two African students also introduced the campus first-hand this year to the struggle over apartheid in South Africa. Senti Thobejane and Tseke Morathi were political exiles going to school in Tanzania before they came to Montezuma. Once in Montezuma, they, like so many other students from troubled countries, provided personal accounts of life where peace and plenty seemed so distant. In another matter students distinguished themselves and honored the college by placing AHUWC ninth in the country for students of mathematics. Zsolt Bihary from Hungary got first in the Southwest region; Laszlo Boroczky, also from Hungary, was fourth; and Huang Qin from the People's Republic of China was seventh.

Students on the Old Pecos Trail, Santa Fe, at the start of the 70-mile Freedom from Hunger march.

In a sense these contributions had a bearing on a report which I was preparing for the board of directors about changing from a bridge institution (12th and 13th grades offering the IB) to a standard two-year college in the American tradition—or some combination of the two. The conclusion was not totally biased, but it did come down in favor of remaining an IB-based United World College. In a way that may have disappointed those who saw the need for the UWCs to try other routes, as was the case in Venezuela and might be in India. Yet, there was little question that its academic reputation would remain stronger as an IB school than another junior college. "Rich preparation, not thin duplication," was the recommendation of one outside advisor. Even the prospect of some federal money as a two-year American college did not seem sufficient reason to pursue the matter further.

Norman Dlamini and Dominic Tsabedze (Swaziland), Alex Khumalo (South Africa) and Changela Hoohlo (Lesotho) perform the Gum Boot, an African coal miners' dance. It was first introduced by Senti Thobejane and Tseke Morathi, refugee South African students living in Tanzania.

At the executive committee meeting at the end of April, the members urged the college to find more money from parents and to press for more full-paying students. It was a predictable and understandable request. More important was the decision to have a fund-raising event in Palm Beach, Florida, when the Prince and Princess would be coming to the States, even though the New York Committee had already held a dinner in February honoring the Countess Mountbatten of Burma. The development office in LA projected a return of $10,000,000—an overly optimistic figure but correctly indicative of the superb opportunity which the occasion would present. Later in the spring Mrs. Patricia Kluge agreed to serve as chairman of the event and Hammer announced that one million of the proceeds would go as endowment to the London operations. In point of fact, much earlier Hammer had proposed such a dinner be held in LA. Of the proceeds

50% would go to the College, 25% to the *Mary Rose* Trust, and 25% to a charity of the Prince's choosing. In March the venue changed to Palm Beach and Hammer promised the one million as an endowment for the International Office. Hammer intimated that such money would permit Prince Charles to step out of the UWC presidency whenever he wished without having to worry about raising more money. Reportedly this offer, generous and tempting, presented problems to some royal staff. Was Hammer buying the royal couple? Matters were still shaky when in late April the board, at the Honorary Chairman's suggestion, passed a resolution for the affair:

> "RESOLVED, that in recognition of the outstanding contributions of Dr. Hammer to the cause of world peace through support of the United World College movement, including the establishment of the United World College of the American West at Montezuma, New Mexico, which was accomplished at the request of the late Lord Louis Mountbatten, Earl of Burma and which firmly establishes the United World College movement in the United States, that Dr. Armand Hammer shall be honored by the Board of Directors of the AHUWC at a special Gala on 12 November 1985, in the presence of His Royal Highness The Prince of Wales, President of the International Board of the United World Colleges, and Her Highness the Princess of Wales."

Again the routines of spring took over as the second set of graduates prepared for their examinations. Like their predecessors they had learned far more than we could measure or they could realize. It remained a mystery, for instance, that they had managed to keep track of their schedules over two years, attend all the activities, ignore the reminders of the faculty about papers and the dean about extended essays, tolerate each others' idiosyncrasies, gain so much weight, and mature so spectacularly. Many had lost a bit of their initial idealism, but most had merely adjusted their outlooks to be both more sensitive and more realistic.

At graduation on May 25, 1985, the sixty-four flags whipped in the breeze, and 600 people were relieved at the sight of blue sky after a typical spring downpour. The tent was lavishly decorated; the reception for visitors, faculty, and staff at the Lockwoods's house preceded the luncheon. Then came the graduation exercises. The format was established: after Hammer's congratulations, Senator Pete Domenici, the senior senator from New Mexico, delivered the commencement address. But as would be true at each graduation, it was the parting of friends that captured front stage. As Roger Kenna's mother remarked, Roger had been reluctant to leave Vermont, but two years later he did not want to leave his closest friends from Africa and Latin America. Gaurav Chopra's parents from India were struck by how many friends their son had made, and how much he had done: "He is involved in everything!" Another illustration: the parents of Tamer Adel Abdel Gawad of Egypt had made a special effort to reach Las Vegas where, to their horror, there was no taxi at the airport to take them to the college. A faculty member remedied that problem, and they then told us that their son's extended essay on the administration of the Suez Canal had gone all the way to the Canal chairman who was deeply impressed. This year there were no Beach Boys, and the celebration closed with the departure of the buses for the airport.

Armand Hammer, Senator Pete Domenici, and Ted Lockwood talk before the start of the 1985 graduation exercises.

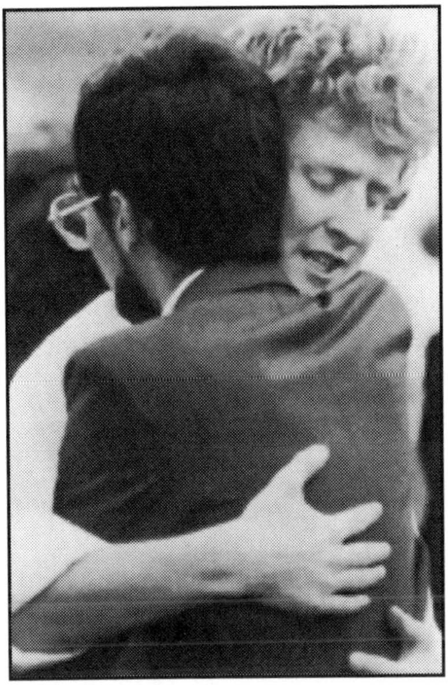

Typical of the farewells after graduation: Lindsay Pahs (Colorado) and Gaurav Chopra (India) embrace.

The brief board meeting that same day had its moments of optimism: the Hoover Trust, donated by Mr. and Mrs. Cecil Jordan, ranchers in California, had been transferred to the college, and that meant $413,000 more in endowed scholarship funds. The business manager, Al Romero, reported that the next budget would rise only 3.5%. Then Hammer explained the one million donation proposed for the International Office from the Gala as the condition for the royal visit. Nothing had happened on the movie premier. In recognition of his very significant contribution, Kemal Zeinal-Zade was elected to the board along with Mrs. Cecil (Sandra Hoover) Jordan.

After the students had departed (or most of them, at least), the faculty met for two days to review yet another year's experience. There was pride in having completed three years with obvious success, but there was concern about the future as well. Would we begin to suffer from institutional sclerosis? Could we find more efficient ways to operate and thus help to address that nagging question of financial stability? Could we improve our admissions procedures? And, on the simpler side, could we prevent the escalation of national days into competitions for the biggest and longest? On that issue we were to be disappointed.

12: A MEETING IN WALES

After a short recess, we geared for an active summer with various groups using our facilities for generally a week at a time. We hoped to realize a profit of $75,000; but, as we always learned in explaining summer programs, it was not only the dollars received from participants that counted, it was our ability to defray some of the cost of people who would otherwise be less fully occupied or laid off that counted—not to mention the public relations value of having so many visitors on campus during a time when it looked its best.

However academically benighted such administrative views might have been, summer programs did help the college. Our only other concern was the limited time in mid-August provided to maintenance to clean, paint, and refurbish the dormitories.

From June 18 to June 21 the International Council of the United World Colleges met at Atlantic College in Wales. Although most of us were housed on campus, a few were relegated to Cardiff, some 45 minutes east, including the Los Angeles contingent. It had been more than five years since such a gathering, the tenth since the founding of the movement. Fifty national chairpersons came to share their concerns, to hear about recent changes, and to review particularly admissions and scholarship policies. The Prince of Wales gave the opening address at Bradenstoke Hall in St. Donat's Castle. Such sessions were both necessary and frustrating: necessary to reinvigorate the national committees and frustrating in the show-and-tell atmosphere that prevented realistic consideration of issues facing the movement. There was comic relief prior to the opening. Hammer and his staff drove up in three large Rolls-Royces rented in London; the Prince arrived in a single small sedan, having flown into a nearby military airport.

The International Board met and reelected Tom Symons as its chairman although there was a sprinkling of votes for Kingman Brewster and Sir Michael Parsons. Thus was patched over an obvious awkwardness about this key position which some wanted offered to an outsider who would shake things up as opposed to postponing the redressment by staying within the board. Hammer diverted attention again by reaffirming that he would contribute one million from the fall gala as an endowment for the international office. In side conversations members were less complimentary; some were even fearful that Hammer might try to become chairman of the International Board and run the UWCs like Occidental subsidiaries. What some forgot was that his gift was about the only major contribution during the decade. A good dinner in the Cardiff civic center, with all its engaging formalities, assuaged feelings and provided local color. Hammer liked these occasions and was quite impressed with Atlantic College. Once, while awaiting a telephone call in the head's office, he coughed and asked for water. Everyone lunged for glasses and spigots; he turned and smiled at Lu and said, "See how they jump." Andrew Stuart, the Principal of Atlantic College, was suitably impressed.

Not so impressive was the opening of the Council sessions. The Prince reminisced about his life under Lord Mountbatten and praised Hammer for his generosity. (These comments contrast strangely with the views included in Jonathan Dimbleby's book where also there appears an account of strained relations between the Palace and Hammer.) At the end of the session the Prince strolled over to where Hammer, McGill and I were standing. He handed a letter to Hammer and asked his reaction. Marvin Frankel from the U.S. Committee had written directly to Kensington Palace to ask for another Broadlands in the spring of 1986, half of the proceeds to go to Atlantic College and half to provide the U.S. Committee with the means to be independent of Montezuma. We were stunned. After the earlier effort in June of 1984 which had led to an unfavorable response for Frankel, no one could believe that he would try another end-run. We brought Tom Symons and Sir Ian Gourlay into the conversation as the Prince went to a luncheon. It was suggested that McGill and I meet with the executive committee of the International Board that evening. For this to happen at such an event was distressing indeed, especially as members of the U.S. Committee were in attendance.

During a break that afternoon, Hammer took McGill and me for a stroll—an unusual practice for him—and insisted that we get rid of the U.S. Committee. Then he went back to Cardiff, only to call later to find out what we had accomplished. The only immediate result we could claim was the decision of the U.S. Committee members to leave the conference and return home. When probed on the issue by Symons and Brewster, the committee members attending the Council meeting became indignant and would have nothing further to do with Hammer and left. They planned a meeting of the committee in New York the next week, and Hammer told McGill to be there "to eliminate the committee."

It was true that this episode in so charming a venue was upsetting, but it did provide a diversion from some rather tiresome discussion about the role of leadership in the movement. This was reminiscent of the seventies: former UWC students wanted to look at their own problems and not carry the burden of leadership in the world at large. Personality adjustment in a shrinking world was their concern, not the public service which had been featured so long in the UWC literature. Despite typical Welsh rainstorms, some of which came horizontally off the Bristol Channel, we worked in a game of tennis on the Atlantic College courts, the surface perforated so as to permit easy drainage. Once the conference was over, and the stars had departed, the heads and their wives went off to the Brecon Beacons for hiking, talk, and fun.

We stayed in a small inn and, again in spite of the dark and brooding skies, we went on a hike distinguished by Kathleen Watson's fall which resulted in a broken wrist. All the heads conferred, stared, sought splints, and clearly demonstrated their lack of wilderness training before Anne Macoun from Pearson College took matters in hand and stabilized the injury. We reassembled for drinks and dinner after Kathleen, wife of the head of Singapore, David Watson, returned from the local hospital sporting a cast. Our English colleagues showed their skill at darts and magic tricks, but none could decide how best to reorganize the international office so that we could achieve more cohesion among the parts. All had expressed concern about who would succeed Ian Gourlay as director general: some wanted David Sutcliffe to leave Duino and assume the role; others thought it should be a North American since we were so indifferent to tradition and prone to prompt moves. What was decided was that the heads and spouses should meet more often in places remote from cities like London.

Meanwhile Hammer had called from the States in the middle of the night to ask that I accompany McGill to the meeting in New York of the U.S. Committee. "You make sure that Bill dissolves the committee!" were the instructions. Again such a call was testimony to everyone that Hammer could track down his employees at any time anywhere in the world—even if it meant Andrew Stuart had to traipse around campus at three in the morning to locate his American associate. Despite the great concern of the executive committee when they conferred with McGill and me, I had an uneasy feeling that neither the International Board nor the London office was prepared to discontinue the committee even though they were worried about how all this might affect Hammer's support. For us the issue was becoming distasteful.

The meeting in New York was preceded by a conversation among four of us: Phyllis Farley, Marvin Frankel, Bill McGill, and myself. Frankel had concluded that the reaction to his proposal was sufficiently harsh that he stepped down as co-chairman and indicated that he would not try to raise money for the UWCs. Everyone agreed that it might be propitious to create a new coordinating body. There was even talk over the breakfast table of dissolving the committee; and Farley and Frankel both resigned from the college's board. The only question was how to convince the committee as a whole.

McGill stressed that we had all known that there must be an improvement in relations among Los Angeles, Montezuma, and New York. Yet, the U.S. Committee had not proposed anything concrete. Merger seemed out of the question. Therefore, he proposed the formation of a new non-profit organization to replace the present structure. The idea had had the tentative endorsement of the UWC executive committee. He recognized that some committee members were probably unaware of the Frankel proposal to Prince Charles or of the other plans. Too often, he observed bluntly, the committee cited admissions concerns as the root of the problem whereas the key issue was the lack of genuine commitment by the committee to the Montezuma college. He was correct in this assessment. Some members hid behind the claim that the college was too partisan, and only the committee could retain objectivity about what was appropriate in admissions and for the UWC movement. But we had been accustomed to the disingenuous arguments on admission. We then reminded them that repeatedly they had failed to inform us of their fund-raising plans and that, in light of their lack of support, we saw dissolution as the only alternative. McGill and I left the room so that they might talk among themselves. We sensed that for some this confrontation was a shock.

When we returned, the committee expressed its sympathy and pledged to meet again soon to provide an answer. But obviously not everyone was of the same mind and some were angry at what they saw as another Hammer power-play. Certainly the creation of a new body, to be called "Friends of the United World Colleges in the United States," nominated by the chairman and the president of the Montezuma board and lacking any authority but designed to attract donors, had limited appeal. Since the issue was largely emotional, any logical solution had little chance of success: we could only hope a sense of realism might lead to an acceptance of the new approach once the committee could figure out how to disburse its assets and discontinue its separate identity as a 501 C3 organization incorporated under the laws of the State of New York.

During the following month, there were many conversations among the various parties, including London. Kingman Brewster had long known the senior members of the U.S. Committee; he was equally aware of our dilemma; therefore, he offered his good offices to seek a solution. He especially wanted to salvage something from the situation without yielding entirely to Hammer's insistence on one common body for the U.S.. Some were merely hoping to gain time. The international executive committee even suggested that the U.S. Committee appeal to the International Board in November, a move which would have infuriated Hammer. Ian Gourlay and Tom Symons were also spending an inordinate amount of time on trying to meet our demands for surgery by dispensing salves to all the complainers.

Matters were further complicated by the fact that Hammer had undergone an operation which had proved sufficiently serious that we could not discuss matters with him directly until August. Hammer had also lost his brother, Victor, during this same summer. We convened an executive committee meeting in Los Angeles on August 7. Hammer had concluded by then that we should have a new chairman of the board, Arthur Krim, a New Yorker, Chairman of Orion Pictures and a well-known fund-raiser for the Democratic party. Ostensibly this move would not only improve our efforts in fund-raising but it would also permit a fresh approach to the New York situation. Ironically, McGill had done precisely what Hammer had wanted in June; but by August that was no longer satisfactory. (This resignation was not only badly handled but was unnecessary. Ironically, Krim had been chairman of the board at Columbia Univesity when McGill was president and each had a high regard for the other.) Presumably we would simply await the disappearance of the U.S. Committee. Any hope of strong action was beginning to erode away.

Meanwhile Brewster and Symons both felt that matters were quite unsatisfactory, and everyone should try to avoid an unattractive, unproductive, unhappy discussion in London in November. Accordingly the phone calls resumed, and I spent an extraordinary amount of time on this issue on the assumption that something had to change or the whole UWC situation in this country would deteriorate seriously. It was the old game: if Hammer did not get his way, he might pull out; or if he did get his way, some felt that the movement would have sold its soul for the promised one million.

Our August 7th executive committee session proposed a merger of the two bodies, to be pursued later in the month. That did not appeal to London. Symons felt that Los Angeles refused to recognize the contribution which the U.S. Committee had made since its creation in 1967; Brewster persisted in proposing a new organization as a tactical compromise. U.S. Committee members were talking with members of the International Board about their grievances. Hammer had written the Prince about the merger idea (by making all U.S. Committee members also members of the Montezuma board in exchange for their discontinuing the New York operation), and the UWC president had supported this notion.

By the second week in August Brewster had concluded that his idea of a new organization would not work and that, instead, everyone should move toward a merger but one that would avoid the committee's being suicided. That would mean U.S. Committee members formally recognizing the role of the college; no one could seek funds in this country without approval from Montezuma; and admissions would be coordinated by Montezuma. In effect, the U.S. Committee would become a committee of the AHUWCAW board, no longer independent and primarily raising money for U.S. students to attend all UWCs, not just overseas. Legally it would retain its separate identity.

At dinner in Toronto later in August, Brewster, Gourlay, Symons and I agreed to this approach which we would try to sell to the U.S. Committee on August 23. The committee endorsed it with cool enthusiasm. As I sat there, I was relieved that we had made some progress but I had no illusions that we had solved the problem. Hammer responded by wanting clarification on each agreement, which I provided; and we finally came to an amicable settlement which each party interpreted as it wished and London found acceptable if baffling. The agreement had hardly been worth the effort. A radical solution would have been better in the long run; but curiously it may not have mattered all that much anyway; for those who wanted to help with UWC projects would do so and those who wanted some other gratification would withdraw over time. The ruffled feathers would eventually lie down, but it would take much longer to re-establish any sense of trust among the leading participants.

13: THE PALM BEACH GALA

It was with much relief that we returned to the campus to find life looking normal as the second-year students poured in on August 26, ready to enlighten the newcomers who were contending with bears and bites at Philmont. We also had to remind them not to pet the very tame deer which roamed through the campsites since they carried the fleas which could cause the plague, something which the State of New Mexico kept as quiet as possible.

The Philmont visit was remarkable also because a skunk had wandered into one of the tents reserved for girls. They screamed; then they tried to entice it out by calling "Pepe Depew" and offering bread. Finally the last girl made a dash for it; the skunk sauntered out causing no problem but eliciting the observation: "I just knew sooner or later it would throw its quills at me."

The faculty had concluded that it would be better for second-years not involved directly in orientation to come after the first-years. We had also begun a week earlier this year so that we could more easily provide all the requisite science labs and language training sessions, including special tutoring for those who found English incomprehensible. We had learned by now that some few could not handle the academic requirements without the extra tutoring in English. Some UWC heads regarded a working knowledge of English as unnecessary, but we felt that we had to insist on this requirement, and assist as needed, not only because some U.S. embassies would not permit those without a knowledge of English to attend but also because the chance of success on the IB was marginal for those linguistically handicapped.

Two articles about the college appeared in the early fall and helped bring our programs to a wider audience: John Ehrlichman, then a resident of Santa Fe, wrote a kindly piece for *Parade* magazine and Joe Marsh's description of the college ran in *The Rotarian.*

We had tried, with the help of the Los Angeles office, to place more articles but our success had been modest indeed. More inquiries as a result of these articles argued strongly for more public relations. The November Gala in Palm Beach might help.

But before that came a meeting of the board in Los Angeles on September 11, 1985. Ian Gourlay joined the meeting since Hammer felt that members might wish his comments on the merger with the U.S. Committee. We had invited all U.S. Committee members to decide whether to be honorary trustees or active directors. We asked those joining the board to come to the meeting. David Harnett and George Franklin decided to join us. In discussions with them beforehand, they both dissented from my interpretation of how admissions would work. Meanwhile the evening before Hammer concluded that Franklin and Harnett should sign a paper agreeing to Montezuma's primacy. They balked; the board talked about it; then they joined the meeting, and it all turned out rather shabbily. It was both embarrassing and discouraging.

The meeting did confirm one most important matter: the creation of a $20,000,000 endowment by Occidental Petroleum on behalf of the college as a tribute to Armand Hammer. Earlier in the year Gil Glazer (a board member), Bill McGill, and I had seen such an endowment as the most probable long-range solution to the vexing financial issue we faced. Thanks to support from Dr. Ray Irani, Oxy's chief operating officer under Hammer and now a board member, the idea was accepted. At this meeting it was announced that $10,000,000 would be set aside in a special trust for the college and the balance would be completed in donations of 2.5 million dollars each year. It was the culmination of a long period of cultivation by McGill and me of the Oxy officers and board members. It offered the relief we had long sought and made the college less dependent on Hammer's estate for the endowed funds necessary to cover the annual deficits. To make matters even more promising, Mrs. Hammer pledged one million dollars.

In a summary prepared for the fiscal year ending August 31, 1985, we reported that we had saved $74,000 in operations, produced a net income of $69,000 in summer programs, and had added $2.5 million to the fund balances, thanks to the Zeinal-Zade and Hoover-Jordan gifts. Our total budget had run $2,723,867, or $13,619 per student—another way of showing what our tuition levels would need to be to cover all our expenses. But in reality, of course, we could neither charge the requisite level of tuition nor collect it. But parents, national committees and scholarship assignments did put us over the one million dollar mark in tuition income. Our deficit was $1,260,837, a figure we could conceivably cover once the Hammer Trust was fully funded. That trust did have restrictions; namely, that it could be used only for the normal expenses of the college, not for capital improvements, and was available only so long as the college bore the Hammer name, was the only UWC in the States, and had accreditation. What would have shocked many who had estimated the cost of starting the college in the first place was the number listed under the plant fund representing the value of all buildings: $11,674,950, a figure which included also all equipment, capital improvements, and the residual value of the property. It was vastly different from anything that Sir Desmond Hoare, sitting by the Bristol Channel in the 1960s, would have ever predicted; but such costs were to be common for prominent international schools in the last quarter of the century—truly an impressive investment in world peace and cooperation through learning.

The fund-raising had, on balance, gone well, and the list of benefactors was reassuring. It certainly helped provide the faculty and staff with fresh confidence in the future of the institution. After all the wrangling during the summer, things seemed most promising. Then one September evening after dinner the telephone rang. Hammer wanted to know if I could fly to Palm Beach that night. His staff had run into opposition in Palm Beach over the November gala. The John Birch Society was after the Russian sympathizer while others wanted a big cut of the proceeds in return for granting a permit. The city council had voted it down 4-1, with the mayor also likely to oppose it.

At six in the morning I was standing on the runway at the Santa Fe airport ready for an Occidental jet to take me directly to Palm Beach to try to salvage the situation. When I was briefed by Oxy staff, it was apparent that one problem was that no one knew anything about the charity involved—to most it was just another Hammer deal to show off royalty. The press had not helped either since they knew nothing about the college and were quite prepared to attack Hammer as well. I talked with the Mayor, the British Embassy and council members. Alec Courtelis had come up from Miami and, as a staunch member of the board with valuable connections in Florida, he assisted in dismounting the opposition. An offer to contribute $75,000 for local charities also softened some views At the evening council meeting, the vote changed to 4-1 in favor.

Now all that had to be done was to replace Patricia Kluge as the chairman since the London press had uncovered that in her young days in London Mrs. Kluge had allegedly been involved in some inappropriate magazine promotions. Fortunately, in answer to Hammer's demand we find another person, I was able to persuade Mrs. Milton Petrie to serve as chairman. As it turned out, Mrs. Kluge was too busy with a large reception-dinner in Virginia at precisely the same time. How close we came to seeing the entire grand event go down the drain is a moot question; but clearly the college's mission made the difference in the face of the extraordinary conservatism of the local government in Palm Beach.

With that crisis behind us, the serious planning began. An emergency meeting of the board on October 9th in Los Angeles concentrated on finding more people to attend at a cost of $10,000 per couple—or $25,000 for a seat at the front table where the dignitaries would eat. Everyone had an assignment to press hard on friends and neighbors. In the end more than 60 benefactors contributed $25,000 each and 150 couples became patrons at $10,000.

In the meanwhile the aspen were turning, the fall term was fully and well-launched, and another major event was planned. During late October three days were devoted to a peace conference on campus. It coincided not only with the annual observance of United Nations Day but also with the meeting between President Reagan and Mikhail Gorbachev as they sought to reduce the Cold War tensions. The purpose was to focus on the possible sources of conflict worldwide and then to seek ways to resolve them.

A game called "Fire Breaks" permitted students to take on the roles of the superpowers. Everything from Star Wars to the role of international law entered into the discussion. Out of the workshops and late-night conversations came a conviction that we must attack each roadblock to peace one by one. For to someone from Southern Africa, the nuclear threat was hardly as important as apartheid in preventing better understanding among peoples. And to those from developing nations attacking hunger and poverty was more urgent than a space platform. What also emerged was a thought that we as an institution should begin to find ways of addressing conflicts systematically and not just from time to time through a meeting.

During these three years students had sought to develop their own newspaper, *The Phoenix*. Some issues had been sophomoric, but recently it had tackled some significant campus concerns in a balanced fashion. This would not always be the case and eventually it made the error of printing materials that skirted being libelous—confidential evaluations among other things. This brought to a head the traditional problems of responsibility and ultimate ownership. Regrettably, in the face of pressure from the administration, it folded. But for the mid-eighties it was an interesting journalistic effort. Americans had also pushed for a yearbook. The first one offended Hammer because it showed a picture of four young men on a hike, pausing for relief. Fortunately "Dear Abby" rose to the defense of the publication. Otherwise, Los Angeles published *Kaleidoscope* three times a year to inform the outside world of the more interesting developments on campus.

It was during this month that we realized how great our potential liability could be. One of the vans which was taking a load of students to El Paso turned over when it hit a patch of "black ice" near Artesia, New Mexico. Miraculously there were only minor injuries even though all the students were thrown from the van. Everyone realized how lucky we had been in view of the fact that our vehicles covered well over 200,000 miles a year.

Out in Los Angeles a crisis-mentality prevailed with respect to Palm Beach. Admittedly it was a mammoth planning operation, but we had learned how differently they approached matters than we. However capable the staff, and that they were, they felt under constant pressure. Only Rick Jacobs, the new assistant to Dr. Hammer and a witty, efficient adviser genuinely interested in our project, appeared unmoved by the flurry of memos and the flight from the 7th to the 16th floor on Wilshire Boulevard. I always thought Oxy staff envied us our New Mexican pace and considered judgment, possible only because we were far enough away that not even the fax machine worked that reliably.

In late October there was another meeting of the International Board in London. Both Hammer and Krim attended what was a comparatively calm meeting. Nonetheless, it was to prove momentous since there would be a new chairman elected. Hammer was backing Sir Michael Parsons whose business acumen he liked and who had served well as deputy chairman. The evening before Hammer had called me to his room at Claridge's to review the votes. He was worried that Kingman Brewster might be elected. I said it looked very close indeed and might well depend on the vote of the present chair. To Hammer our inability to influence the outcome was frustrating; he was not accustomed to having matters taken out of his hands. That annoyance was even more evident the next day when Brewster won. I sensed that the vote may have been more against another "Brit" than for Brewster. Be that as it may, my greater worry was Brewster's health. Lu and I had sensed even in 1982 that he was not well—certainly not the person whom I had known at Yale.

The heads had met as an education committee to review admissions quotas, for such they were when we agreed on the number each of us would seek from each country. We were not happy with some countries like Pakistan where we felt that the selection process was not as meritorious as it should be. In other countries like Ghana we found it virtually impossible to get information back and forth. We hoped that the newly formed Network of former UWC students would assist more frequently in the selection process since they knew what it took to do well at a UWC. It had been a puzzlement to the North Americans why there was still so little support from former students. Admittedly the new institutions would have to wait a while, but Atlantic and Pearson had graduated a considerable number. In response, the central office had invested more money and effort in strengthening the alumni association, and chosen from that association were three network directors, one of whom always attended international board meetings.

When the heads met by themselves, a step which some UWC chairmen regarded as tantamount to insubordination, we went over the same ground we had covered in June in Wales. What could we do about the central office? Sympathetic to Gourlay's predicament, we nonetheless concluded that we needed a sense of direction and strong leadership from London if the movement was going to prosper. To some degree it was wishful thinking and to some degree it ignored the fact that, however much we worked well together, we were a federation and not a closely coordinated "company," despite the legal title. We thought that we should try something and proposed to meet with the new chairman at the IB meeting in Paris in February. Perhaps most important was the mood of our discussion: we felt the need to mobilize our resources and get on with new business, somehow to break the drift we all sensed was pervasive. As it happened, this concern did not go away over the next five years.

When we returned from a London that had been surprisingly clear and comfortable, we prepared for Palm Beach. Fortunately, Andrew Maclehose as dean was becoming accustomed to running the college in my absence; and this he did well indeed even though it was not what he preferred. In fact, along with some faculty there was an uneasiness about the amount of time I spent on these other matters away from Montezuma. Other UWC heads received similar criticism. Clearly no one had foreseen how complex some issues could become, how politically complicated an innocent question of scholarship support could become, and how much time heads would need to spend finding new sources of support. And it was precisely this donor preoccupation that Palm Beach presumably would solve, for the moment at least.

At The Breakers, the famous Palm Beach hotel where the main events would take place, everyone was flying around with last-minute assignments on the morning of November 12. Mine was to talk with Bob Hope, the Master of Ceremonies for the dinner. Hope wanted to know where he would stand, how he could see his notes, and which place he would occupy at the head table. That was the hitch: the head table was already so long that it stretched the entire length of the ballroom, and those who had paid $25,000 for a seat there might well conclude that it was far preferable to be at one of the round tables from which you could see all the rich and famous.

Hope did not like his left anchor position. We had arrived two nights before since the planning committee had arranged for a black-tie reception and dinner at the Norton Gallery of Art and had hung the Armand Hammer Collection known as "Five Centuries of Masterpieces." It was truly an impressive collection for which its owner was properly renowned. The guests intrigued the press and public as they arrived in their cars at the Gallery: Ted Turner and his wife, Jane Fonda; U.S. Senator Paula Hawkins and her husband, Walter; Gregory and Veronique Peck; and the Perot family. As a prelude to the main events the next day, it was a striking start.

Under somewhat cloudy skies on the 12th, people assembled in the lobby at 11:30 a.m. to mount the limousines for the polo match in West Palm Beach. Mickey and Minnie Mouse greeted the guests: it was like combining Disney Land and Windsor Park. The local Palm Beach team won, defeating the Prince of Wales's team. The Princess of Wales presented the cup while her husband watched and she gave him a kiss for his valiant effort. Then everyone experienced a typical Florida late-afternoon traffic jam. We avoided it by leaving before the final chukker.

The hotel lobby was lined with cameras and those eating in the regular dining room brought their salmon fillets to the corridor as well. The guests ran the gauntlet in true Hollywood style. Those who had paid the maximum went to the Magnolia Room for a special reception with the royal guests and the Hammers. In the Venetian Ballroom having been checked by security, dinner was served at a decorously later hour than planned on the timetable. "Coupe Diana," a chocolate shell filled with raspberries and whipped cream, was the dessert. Since the dinner was to honor Hammer's efforts for international peace, he gave the opening speech after a warm introduction by Merv Griffin in which

The Palm Beach Gala: Joan Collins, Bob Hope, Armand Hammer and Prince Charles, November 1985.

the entertainer referred to him as the "Wizard of Oxy." His theme was familiar: "It will be the young people someday who will bring peace to the world."

The Prince of Wales departed from his formal text and, surprisingly for him, used the device of rhetorical questions to make his points:

> "How does anyone expect anything to get done in life unless there is some effort to educate people's characters as well as their minds? How are we to have any hope of balanced and civilized leadership in the future unless there are some people who have learned about service to others, about compassion, about understanding, as far as is humanly possible, the other man's religion, the other man's customs and his history; about courage to stand up for things that are noble and for things that are true? . . . How on earth do they expect us to get anything done without money? . . .
>
> I find that I become increasingly fed up with hearing absolute nonsense

> talked about the United World Colleges. I keep hearing disparaging descriptions of it—that it's a pet project of my great-uncle. I also get tired of hearing United World Colleges being rather dismissed as an elitist educational experiment. And to cap it all there have unhelpful comments over the months about the actual business of fund-raising."

He thanked Hammer for his generous support and asked others to do likewise. In many ways it was his most effective speech on behalf of the UWCs and regrettably it was the last occasion on which he spoke so fervently. The media gave wide coverage to his remarks and there is no question that this was a success both financially and in terms of public relations. The evening closed with Bob Hope and Victor Borge entertaining the 400 guests, who subsequently tried to squeeze on to the dance floor to get as close as possible to the royal couple who were doing more than the fox trot. All the guests received a Francis Hammer Rose done in porcelain and contributed by Helen Boehm—and a tribute book on behalf of Hammer.

The next morning as we were having breakfast with the Gourlays, Hammer came by to give a check for one million dollars to Sir Ian. There was only one problem in the midst of that grand and gracious moment: the check was drawn on the college. I later suggested to Gourlay that he refrain from cashing it until we had enough in the bank to cover it. We did not yet know what the college would receive, something between two and four million, but it was amply clear that this had been one of most spectacular fund-raising events in the history of American education. It also turned out to be the essential bridge in our financing for the next three years; for it provided money for the scholarships that were not covered otherwise. In the history of the United World Colleges it would remain one of a kind.

14: EVALUATION TIME

Certainly this year had vastly improved our financial prospects. The next task was to review our accounting procedures. The creation of a separate Armand Hammer Trust under its own board and administered elsewhere needed clarification so that the budget could reflect whatever contribution it made to the income side. Invested initially in Occidental bonds, there was the further possibility of conflict of interest, no matter how restrained the trustees Arthur Groman and Morrie Moss. In addition, there were funds like the Zeinal-Zade money residing in a quasi-endowment fund supervised through Occidental Petroleum. In effect, there were two centers handling the funds of the college; and the board of directors had responsibility, in truth, for only the monies directly monitored by the business office. And even there the directors did not bother to inquire about how the funds were invested. With the addition of the Palm Beach revenues, it was clear that we should await an audit until later and then hope that we could arrive at appropriate procedures. As the person who made the final budgetary decisions, I was always troubled by this assumption that it was all right for Oxy's chief financial officer alone to make investment decisions for us.

The fall term came to a quiet close on December 20. We had decided to run as late as possible so that we might try giving examinations two weeks before the end of the term. Although it made it possible to get the reports done earlier in a more informative way, especially about academic progress, students did not concentrate much on their studies during the final two weeks before vacation. The faculty felt that this year's graduating class might not be as strong as the two previous classes even though university acceptances to date might suggest otherwise. In talking with other heads there may well be a kind of cyclical pattern to academic performance. That pattern may reflect the degree of involvement in other activities rather than anything else—or even the degree of camaraderie among the students. To distinguish this holiday the snows had held off, the roads were clear, and new students questioned whether we really did get snow.

The board had met in Los Angeles on December 18, 1985. Six members of the U.S. Committee joined the discussion, and it seemed that at least some of the grievances on both sides would be softened. We increased the number of directors authorized to 40 and expanded the honorary board to accommodate the majority of U.S. Committee members. A lively discussion on the three-year program led to the decision that we had best remain a two-year IB school exclusively. The announcement of Ryoichi Saskawa's gift of $500,000 to endow the campus center and Emma Getz's endowment of the president's house for $250,000 provided some budget relief.

The success of Palm Beach convinced many directors that we were now in a position to look to long-range development. That coincided curiously with the discontinuation of the development officer in the Los Angeles office. Myra Silverman had been transferred to handle a cancer campaign Hammer was launching; and then, without consultation, Hammer had moved to fill the vacuum with David Harnett, a member of the U.S. Committee and prominent in admissions work. The appointment lasted 72 hours, and again we would be without any help in fund-raising in 1986 beyond that which the staff in Los Angeles could provide as they worked on other college business for Hammer. These moves did not improve relations between LA and Montezuma.

To study more carefully the overall position of the United World Colleges and the current financial posture of Montezuma, J. Burchenal Ault, former head of St. John's College in Santa Fe and a fund-raiser in that city, agreed to analyze the missions and budgets of all UWCs and report on what he would consider as possible steps that we might collectively take to assure a stronger movement. We both thought that, after Palm Beach, it would be wise to use the Prince's obvious attraction to raise even more monies for the colleges. That hope was temporarily dashed when London vetoed a dinner in Houston to coincide with Prince Charles's visit to that city in February.

The report opened with an appropriate tribute to Hammer's generosity and the astonishing accomplishments of the first four years. As the report examined the financial health of the institution, it felt that a balanced operating budget was within our grasp by 1990, thanks largely to the new endowment funds and recent donations. The report then reviewed the physical plant needs, and concluded that it might require some ten million dollars of capital expenditure over ten years. By the early nineties an endowment of $30 million should be in place to overcome any future imbalances. Having rather optimistically portrayed the position of Montezuma, Ault took a look at the other UWCs. Everyone needed more resources and that posed a threat to AHUWCAW since the United States is the most promising source of international endowment monies. In one chart the bottom line was $110 million that needed to be raised over time to assure all the UWCs adequate endowment. Since the scholarship fund so frequently proposed by Antonin

Besse was $50 million, this conclusion did not seem surprising and over 15 years did not seem out of reach. Therefore, the report closed with a series of suggestions as to how that might be accomplished, provided the London office was reorganized to concentrate on this fund-raising effort. However daunting the figures, the idea was hardly new. I sent the report as part of the materials to be reviewed for our February board meeting in Los Angeles.

Hammer called late one evening to denounce the report and order me to tell each director not to read it. He was angry in a manner I had not heard before. I said I would write each director —knowing full well that now they would read a report they would probably have stuffed into a briefcase unread. Hammer did not specify what he found objectionable. Perhaps he did not wish others to know, as surely they did, that the college still needed more support, or that the UWC movement was not as well-financed as their achievements might suggest. Or it may simply have been a fear that others might swarm all over sources in this country that he wanted reserved for Montezuma. In any case it was both a misreading of the report and a misinterpretation that led to many awkwardnesses over the years. Curiously, Hammer sent Morrie Moss, one of our generous directors, a successful investment manager in Memphis and a trustee of the Armand Hammer endowment, a copy. Moss's reply reminded Hammer that this kind of analysis was what was needed to appreciate the overall picture, one that Moss found neither so forbidding nor so disheartening that the report should be suppressed.

Now that the college had many more revenues to draw upon, Los Angeles decided that it wanted more financial information on a monthly basis, organized in a corporate format even though as a non-profit institution we followed traditional accrual accounting. With the large accounts under LA supervision (the figures for which we did not receive in regular reports from them), it was increasingly difficult to know just what our balances were. Therefore we assembled a finance committee meeting on February 18, in Los Angeles. The intent was admirable: to maximize our revenues, to simplify our investments, and to arrive at a common accounting procedure which would carry over into the annual budgeting process. When the board met the next day, we explained how we would group our assets in two accounts, one for endowment and one for operations. A step forward, it did not however address the fundamental question of who had responsibility for the college's funds. It was strange indeed to have to request periodic transfers from California of $150,000 to operate an institution in New Mexico. The most obvious consequence was paperwork, especially from Montezuma to Los Angeles. Final figures from Palm Beach were available. Receipts were over $4 million, of which the College would receive $2,571,302. London had cashed the million-dollar check in the meanwhile.

At this same meeting the report from the North Central Association confirmed our accreditation for another seven years. The self-study prepared by the faculty provided 500 pages of details; their report contained 42 pages largely of commendations. But there were some pertinent suggestions. They urged the administration and faculty to develop more handbooks on policies rather than leave it to memory. In the academic area they felt we should offer more options and provide more computers. The library should have more professional help, they argued; and under student life they recommended a trained nurse be on campus and new infirmary facilities be planned. And, to the delight of those on campus, they urged us to build some indoor recreational facilities. But by this time it was apparent that, no matter how many dollars might be set aside for the swimming pool, it would always yield to the pressure of the annual deficit.

Obviously in this history it may be perplexing to the reader that the scene continually shifts among Los Angeles, London, and Montezuma. To those on campus what happened at meetings elsewhere held little meaning until it was translated into salaries, equipment, or new policies. Yet, the future of the college was always intimately connected with the prosperity of the movement, potentially with decisions in Los Angeles by either the board or Hammer, and with the outside funding that might or might not become available. To tell the story of the campus would be a different narrative, perhaps more entertaining but misleading in trying to understand how a new institution was born and raised. Yet, although the dominant themes of this essay are finances, relations with the various UWC constituencies, and the adjustments made in Montezuma to improve upon the basic design of a United World College, the ultimate story is what happens over time to those young people who come through the college, go on to universities, and then make their individual contributions to the world. That is a story that must wait until a later decade.

Meanwhile, the students had decided that this year's conference should focus on the issue of hunger. The Ethiopian famine had brought the problem to the front. Recognition that perhaps half of the world's population suffers from malnutrition lent even more piquancy to the topic. For three days outside speakers augmented the materials prepared by the students who had voted to eat only rice for three days prior to the conference. Accordingly everyone was hungry as they learned of the complexity of the issue involving politics, economics, availability of resources other than food, and public awareness. As always the hope was that from this discussion the students would acquire a better grasp of the issue of hunger, that they would find ways personally to address the problem, and that they would carry the concern with them as they continued their university studies.

The maturity of the students had begun to win faculty support for some modifications in the guidelines governing conduct in the residence halls. They decided to permit limited interdorm visiting after the evening safety check. The experiment was extended into the next year.

Not so sanguine was the faculty reading of project week plans this spring. More and more students seemed destined to do maritime research on the Mexican beaches. No doubt many second-years did feel the need to relax one final time before the prospect of examinations overwhelmed them, but it was clear the recommendations would change in 1987.

During this comparatively open winter, we began to study the future of two buildings: the old theater on the west side of the campus and the casino next to the Castle. Neither structure had firm foundations; the interiors were unstable; and they did present a liability. While the engineer was checking out these buildings, we had him inspect the trusses over the ballroom in the Castle. We discovered fractures and a failed panel joint, as well as fatigue in the floor joists of the ballroom. The cumulative effect of these findings was to begin some long-range planning for the facilities; and in the case of the Castle, to rethink its uses during this anniversary year.

For it was on August 16, 1886 that the third Santa Fe Railroad Hotel had opened its doors atop the promontory to the north of the Gallinas River. The two previous hotels had burned to the ground. Before the Railroad acquired the property, the area had reportedly been the site of peaceful conversations between the pueblo Indians and those of the plains. In 1841 Julian and Anthony Donaldson received a grant from the Mexican authorities, then in control of New Mexico. Their effort to make a commercial operation failed and they sold the site to the U.S. Army for a hospital since the hot springs appeared to have restorative values. In those days the temperature was some 130 degrees.

During the Civil War the army found so little use for the property that it turned it over to O. H. Woodworth who tried to convert the hospital into a hotel called The Adobe where rumor has it that Billy The Kid spent a night. In 1879 the Stone Hotel was built. When this structure (now home for offices, classrooms and the library) opened in February of 1880, the Denver paper noted that "The list of killed and wounded has not yet been published." The Santa Fe Railroad bought the land because they were running a spur to the ice ponds to the west of the property. After fire consumed the first structure, architects Burnham and Root from Chicago designed the present Queen Anne style hotel which in January of 1884 burned, leaving only some of the stone framing. Again the railway rebuilt the hotel, which contained some 243 rooms. Near the hot springs they had also erected a bathhouse capable of handling 500 people each day. Fred Harvey was in charge of the restaurant which offered an extraordinary fare of green turtle soup, pheasant and other eastern delicacies, fare that would never be repeated in Montezuma. But it was not possible for the owners to make ends meet, and the opening of the El Tovar on the rim of the Grand Canyon spelled the doom of this Victorian resort. Even a fourth attempt in 1895 fizzled despite the addition of gambling in a newly built casino adjacent to the main building.

Eventually the property was donated to the Y.M.C.A., but they had no use for its 100,000 square feet. They passed it on to the Southern Baptist Convention which established The Montezuma Baptist College in 1922. Even though it imported football players from Houston, it could not survive the Great Depression. The Catholic Church purchased it in 1937 to start a seminary for the Jesuits being forced out of Mexico. They redid much of the interior of the Castle, adding structural posts in the ballroom that eventually contributed to the failure of the main trusses, designed like a railroad bridge to carry the weight of the upper stories by a series of diagonal beams.

During the late fifties and early sixties the seminary was flourishing and felt justified in adding some cement-block buildings in the lower field to accommodate the seminarians. In 1972 the Church held an auction to sell off as much as they could, packed up, and returned to Mexico. There is little doubt that it was during this time, with new roads, that the Montezuma Castle, as it was affectionately called, became the State's best known reminder of the Victorian era during which the railroad had transformed the territory into the 47th state. What we also discovered was that Las Vegans had a rich memory of the events at the Seminary and especially of the Italianate gardens. They would tell of the young Mexicans starting at dawn and running up Hermit's Peak for lunch and back for supper. What we saw in 1981 after almost ten years of utter neglect were damaged buildings, single-cell dorms, and a Castle whose interior was in poor repair and populated by some 2000 bats.

Artist R.C. Gorman presents a commemorative poster, *Earth Mother,* to Ted Lockwood and Kay Applegate, chairperson of the committee organizing the 100th anniversary of the rebuilding of the famous Montezuma Castle.

Thanks to our Los Angeles office and Beverly Silvera in particular, we decided to have an anniversary celebration on August 16, 1986. We hoped that the event would attract the media and the moneyed interests. With luck we might even raise enough funds to refurbish the famous building. Accordingly we began plans for the summer.

During April we held the first spring international day on campus. It was to become a regular feature every other year, so that all students would have the opportunity to offer programs to visitors, primarily from the immediate region. It was a great success with 2000 guests, exhibits, special dishes, dances, and conversations. The proceeds went to the local chapter of Big Brothers/Big Sisters and towards Colombian volcano relief. On the east coast the U.S. Committee held a dinner at the Cosmopolitan Club to raise scholarship funds. Lady Mountbatten spoke on behalf of the movement. Something around $40,000 was contributed. And on the other coast Hammer had arranged for Malcolm Forbes to be the commencement speaker.

Spring brought its fearsome concentration on examinations and some of the normal follies. The resident tutors had become discouraged by the lack of respect for the newly liberal guidelines. Therefore, we concluded that we should make a concerted effort with the next new class to rebuild consensus for the guidelines. The first two years had been easier; now we were learning that the newer students neither had the same commitment to the community nor apparently as conservative a background as we had found true originally. Some ascribed this shift to the rising affluence of the student body, something which was sensed but not necessarily provable.

In comparing notes with other boarding institutions, we were obliged to recognize that these young people had never known hardship as had older generations, that their expectations were quite different as well. Of course, there were the obvious exceptions in the student body; for some did come from very underprivileged backgrounds and knew the horrors of displacement, war, and hunger. In a sense the distance between them and a student from Copenhagen or Los Angeles only complicated the issue. In the midst of so much idealism, disciplinary problems would remain an unfortunate burr.

As we looked at the applications for the new class entering the coming fall, we found far more girls than boys coming for the first time. With 105 in the new class, we scrambled to consider new arrangements for housing them. Simultaneously we were pleasantly surprised by the university plans of the graduating students: Harvard, Bryn Mawr, Chicago, MIT, Oxford— no one could have asked for more impressive confirmation of the high regard accorded the program and the people in Montezuma.

Graduation came and our new fire engine brought from Pasadena, California, as a gift of some of Hammer's staff stood proudly in front of the administration building. The volunteer students in their yellow slickers posed with Hammer alongside the well-polished 1957 Seagraves pumper. It seemed like a good idea at the time it was delivered since there was no nearby volunteer fire station. However, there was a limitation to its

The gift of a fire engine required a firefighting team, pictured here with Chief Norman Meredith in plaid shirt in foreground, supervisors Harold Santillanes, Jesus Dimas, and Les Defthelson.

usefulness since we had no heated garage and the water in the tank would freeze during the winter. Fortunately the Albuquerque fire department had given us new hoses when those that came with the truck had burst when first used. Training was spectacular, but nothing compared with the ride which Harold Santillanes from Security had when one day he brought the truck from its parking space near the Castle down the hill. The brakes failed; he just missed the Security station and the lagoon and finally ran it into a bank going uphill into Pine Forest. Its career on campus came to an end when the Gallinas Canyon volunteer fire department offered to repair it if we would donate it to them. That was an even better idea.

The commencement exercises for 1986 faced a washout when a horrendous downpour struck during lunch under the big top, making all the playing field area mushy green grass. Lightning made many insecure as they wondered if the forty-foot poles were grounded. Others worried about the locale for the ceremonies. Amazingly the whole commencement program, including provision for the chorus, was moved to the Castle ballroom, including a perilously narrow platform, in 35 minutes. Somehow that lent a more relaxed atmosphere. It also led to a longer ceremony.

When I introduced Hammer, I mentioned his recent return from the Soviet Union after delivering aid to the victims of the Chernobyl nuclear disaster. Thereupon, to the delight of the audience, he departed from his customary brief remarks and told of his visit, adding: "We now can see vividly that the world cannot readily cope with a serious nuclear power accident, much less a thermonuclear war." When Malcolm Forbes, the well-known editor of *Forbes* magazine, philanthropist and motorcyclist, rose to give his speech, he opened with a poke at Hammer: "I think he mentioned every famous person but God, and no doubt he has his links with Him too." He added: "You're a part of history right here, because there are very few places in the world where a graduating class can meet the founder, listen to the founder and inaugurate a hall that's never been used for such an occasion on a campus that is new but will go on in perpetuity." The balance of his remarks sounded more like an invitation to do whatever they thought would be fun than to improve the human condition. Students applauded wildly.

Then Forbes received the first and only honorary degree ever awarded by the college— one in international entrepreneurship. (Later his secretary called to ask more about the hood and degree since it would hang on Forbes's wall alongside 40 other honorary degress. We could only vouch for its uniqueness.) For the first time a graduating student, Margaret Drent from Canada, made remarks on behalf of the class. Arthur Groman from the board had encouraged us to introduce this custom, and thereafter audiences found the brief student messages more compelling than those of the special guests. Certainly Margaret acquitted herself admirably. And, as was becoming customary also, the students sang "Innsbruck, I Now Must Leave Thee" at the close. The whole affair ended in tears as parents, students, faculty, and guests prepared to depart.

Before Forbes departed, we had hoped that he might agree to a handsome gift. But Hammer intervened: he did not want anyone to approach the famous and wealthy financier for reasons that no one could fathom. It was the last time we invited such a personality for commencement. Among the others leaving campus that day, probably ten percent were students taking a year off before entering university. There had been a rising discussion of third-year options and a growing feeling for some it would be a wonderful time to do more community service.

For instance, Helen Rowlands from the United Kingdom worked in Mexico for the *Asociacion Sonorense de los Amigos* doing everything from helping people manage their bee hives to being an electrician; two others went to the Philippines as school interns; and five were planning to travel to Peru on a work project upcountry. Finding the information students needed about such opportunities was complicated but later one of our graduates, Mark Hodde, would compile just such a directory. Even Prince Charles took notice of this possibility when during the summer he spoke of mobilizing the ex-student network to tackle specific projects. This fit nicely with the first questionnaire ever to be distributed from the London office to former students worldwide.

Chairman Arthur Krim introduces the graduation speaker for 1986, Malcolm Forbes,

We needed to know more about what kind of volunteer work they were doing, such as our own graduates from India who were teaching reading and writing to orphans living in slums along the Queen's Necklace in the Bay of Bombay. The potential was immense. Finally, departing this year were two original staff members; Lucy Cruz who had been in charge of building the library collection and Charles Hanson, the first economics instructor and later our first contestant on the popular quiz show, Jeopardy!. The place was getting older and departures like these would be more frequent in the future.

Over the years in admission the college had enjoyed the help of the Hugh O'Brian Youth Foundation (HOBY). We had been allowed to use the list of HOBY Youth Ambassadors, all very capable young high school leaders with objectives similar to those at the UWCs. Not surprisingly, many U.S. candidates came from that pool, like Tony Leach from Detroit who had just graduated and who in turn had convinced Timothy Long's mother to let her son attend AHUWC. Many were the paths by which students reached New Mexico.

Traditional at this time of year was a board meeting to confirm the budget for the upcoming fiscal year. In anticipation, the finance committee had met in Los Angeles to review our resources. The accounts were in better shape; projections were more secure;

and although our situation had improved considerably, there was still no way to cover the annual imbalances. We faced a deficit for the coming year of $742,800. Once again, it was apparent that we needed another $10 million endowment to close the gap. Through stringent economies we had held the overall budget increase to 1.4% despite salary raises of over 4%; and we remained under the magical figure of $3 million.

In other financial actions, I had convinced the board that the trust should no longer invest in Occidental securities because there must be a Chinese Wall between the corporation and the nonprofit college. Eventually the portfolio was changed to government-backed securities yielding 9%. At this point we were receiving 75% of the annual interest in the trust, the balance being reinvested. We would review this policy and later move to 85% and in 1991 to 100% being available toward operating expenses. Would that we had been able to invest the funds in a manner comparable to university endowments and thus see it grow in total value. On the other hand, most colleges and universities did not have as large an endowment per student.

Finally, at the meeting Alec Courtelis, who had become the most active board member and vice-chairman, reported that neither the casino nor the theater were worth trying to save and, therefore, should be demolished—which was done just before Christmas when the news would have minimal coverage. We had learned of the sensitivities of the local historical society about the Castle and older buildings on campus and tried to respect those legitimate feelings as far as practicable. Simultaneously we were awaiting a report from the U.S. Parks Commission on possible ways to restore the hot springs. Hammer hoped we could make them commercial and turn a profit. Others had inquired about leasing the springs for similar reasons; but no one had the $75,000 ready for the investment. Security was trying to keep the place tidy; students had done some work on the pipes and clean-up; but essentially there was no way to assure it would remain uncontaminated. Serious town users helped, but the casual visitor and night parties combined to trash the springs repeatedly.

In June the International Board met in London; but its new chairman, Kingman Brewster, had been struck with a heart problem that precluded his presiding on the occasion. Business went smoothly. There had been increasingly strong interest in Japan, China, and India to form United World Colleges, but it was unclear as to where any would find the requisite funds and when anything might happen. What had become clear, nonetheless, was the decision to open the Simon Bolivar UWC in Venezuela this August. Not yet officially a member of the UWC movement and subject to many reservations by those who felt such a departure into terminal rural farm management programs was unwise, the college still enjoyed the support of Prince Charles and the Venezuelan government. When it would become a UWC remained an open question, but its chairman and president, Luis Marcano, appeared at all meetings and seemed undaunted.

During that summer of 1986 we realized that we had completed four academic years at Montezuma even if it seemed but yesterday we had been staring at the dust bowl that now featured regular soccer matches as part of the community service program. The results had been most encouraging, except for that year's graduates. We had a record high of 16 failures, seven of whom came from the United States. But others had done spectacularly well; clearly UWC graduates still commanded the top scores worldwide.

The highlight of the summer was our first reunion for the 400 graduates of The Armand Hammer United World College on August 14th, 1986. Some 60, many of whom were graduates of other UWCs, came with their friends and families to get sunburned, to talk, to see the class D movie "The Evil." which had been filmed in 1973 in the Castle, and to talk some more. Many undertook community service projects; others tackled Hermit's Peak which had become such a famous destination for all UWCers at Montezuma. A barbecue loaded with spicy New Mexican dishes and a campfire ended the first day. On the next day conversation moved to the future of the UWCs. Everyone wanted to do more "networking," something much more likely with the advances in e-mail and Internet. Lu was busy trying to get up-to-date on addresses and to locate lost graduates. On Sunday, amidst volleyball, tennis, and soccer the United World College Alumni Scholarship Fund was established by those attending and by faculty donations. At the same time, we concluded that we should wait until the first graduating class had been out for ten years before holding the next reunion.

As we prepared for our fifth academic year, the State of New Mexico began to repair state route 65 across the river from the campus. Things were changing, and all traffic headed up the canyon would go through the campus on blacktop roads; and the soccer field would finally have a fence on its south side along the roadway.

Sitting on the wall along the dining room that August, we sensed that the first phase of the college's history was drawing to a close. The routines necessary to operate were falling into place. The steady flow of new students was assured; the recruitment of new faculty was beginning to occur more frequently; and the staff was beginning to wonder what changes might be worthwhile considering. We had not completely solved some of those standard questions before a residential college, like the proper mix of freedom and responsibility, compassion for others, and sensitivity to the cultural differences so obviously represented on campus. We had done much, but we could not relax. Just as we could not forget raising more money, repainting buildings, or replacing broken steam lines. Now the challenge would be to improve operations, to expand our horizons, and to reconsider the mission we had so willingly accepted.

15: A NIGHT AT LAS VEGAS

The end of August, 1986, marked the beginning of another academic year. We had changed our minds again and brought the old-timers in a few days early to prepare orientation for 111 new students, most of whom arrived on the 22nd. We were pleased that we now had 70 countries represented, but we did worry about the disparity in class size which was occurring from one year to the next. Orientation at Philmont was successful despite cooler weather and more rain— and bears who had come out of the high mountains, where it had been so dry during the summer, to find better berries. No doubt one new student summed up this experience for all who had gone through the four days in the wilderness: "It was great at Philmont; I'll never forget it; and thank goodness I am back in Montezuma!"

The second-year students expressed their determination to improve conditions, and the new students joined in this mini-crusade. For the first time we were trying faculty exchanges as a way to bring some new faces to campus and to provide our own instructors with a change of scenery. Nat Mann (mathematics) and his wife, Dottie, went to the International School in Geneva and Arthur and Julie Robinson came in their place. South Africans Andi and Daphne Kumalo from Atlantic College, with their two young sons, exchanged seats with Bruce Ives (economics) and his wife, Susan. The new librarian, Dorothy Meredith, had come during the summer to reorganize the collection and to analyze our needs which, to many faculty, were quite extensive; and her English husband, Norman, an engineer, soon was helping with the electronic equipment.

The only setback was the fact that one physics teacher, Umesh Pandey, could not get his visa in India to return to the States. Otherwise we had reached the point where we could feel that the daily schedule, beginning with classes at 7:50 a.m., was well in place and we might even be able to turn to matters long deferred because of our inexperience.

But such was not to be the case. The celebration of Las Vegas Night on September 27 would require much preparation. Then two days later Hammer and friends planned to visit for international day.

Seven hundred people came to Las Vegas Night, all contributing to the restoration of the Castle. Beverly Silvera had made all the arrangements, including yet another tent for the playing fields; but this time the winds were too formidable and everything was moved into the Castle, appropriately enough since it was the designated charity. The main feature was the gaming in the Castle ballroom. "Millions" of dollars exchanged hands in blackjack and roulette while some took turns in the "dream machine" after having purchased the fake money. There were the usual drawings and prizes donated by merchants in the State.

At the end of the night the event had raised $116,000 toward the restoration of the Castle, presumably just the beginning of the effort to bring back this historical building into active use. Plaques were placed on the wall of the ballroom to honor major donors to this fund; but no future event managed to stimulate comparable interest and support. Eventually the donations were used to finance various studies made of the structure and of its possible conversion. But, when the fireworks went off at the conclusion of Las Vegas Night, with rockets grazing the Castle rooftops, everyone cheered and hoped and went home happy.

Sharing a table at Las Vegas night: Wid Slick, Ted Lockwood, Anthony Portago, and Lu Lockwood.

Two days later Armand Hammer and others came from Los Angeles for the third annual international day. The students, as always, listened attentively to Hammer, not only as the man who knew Lenin, but as a person who still played his part on the world scene, having just engineered the release of Nicholas Daniloff. On this occasion he announced that the Soviet Union had agreed to send two students and a teacher this year. (After 1984 no more Soviet students had been permitted to come to Montezuma.) He then told of his success in bringing Dr. Robert Gale, a bone marrow transplant specialist, to help the victims of the Chernobyl disaster. Hammer subsequently arranged for Gale to talk with the students about both that experience and the devastation a nuclear explosion can cause. A concert followed, featuring the new harpsichord played by Agnieszka Ziemba of Poland and two violinists, Jiang Tong of China and Laurie Wood of the United States. Hammer and many of the guests joined in the traditional African dance which closed the student entertainment. The event had attracted a good number of friends from Los Angeles and thus raised our prospects of further support from the west coast.

At international day, Hammer talks with Yvonne Akpalu (Ghana), Joseph Poku (Ghana), Alex Khumalo (South Africa) and Priscilla Maloney DeCastro (Panama),

By now another feature of the Montezuma experience had been fixed on the fall calendar: southwest studies. Designed specifically for the first-years to acquaint them with this region of the country, the program had expanded. Prior to the five-day expeditions in the fall, the faculty prepared a series of lectures on various aspects of the region, from politics to geology to the cultures in the area. These were not always the most popular of exercises, but the faculty felt that we should make some effort to remind people of the history of the southwest.

Laurie Wood (USA) on violin, Agnieszka Ziemba (Poland) playing the new harpsichord donated by Dianne and Guilford Glazer, and Jiang Tong (China) on violin.

The break in the regular schedule that permitted trips to the Grand Canyon or Carlsbad Caverns was better received. For those of us who went to the Grand Canyon that October of 1986 it was a challenge to organize and then to keep track of 55 students whose camping skills and hiking abilities varied widely. Some camped along the Colorado River at 2,400 feet above sea level while others stayed on the rim at 7,000 feet, with day hikes. The weather was considerably colder at the top than down below. Carl St. Remy from the Bahamas wondered if he would ever be warm again: his solution was to gather as much dead firewood as possible, very much in the same spirit that the visiting faculty who had come along to see one of the great wonders of the world did; for Kumalo searched the forest for a mammoth stump which he thrust on the fire—and drove everyone away with the heat. Lu and I took one group on the 17-mile hike down and up the Bright Angel Trail in one day; others went part of the way—always enthralled with the tremendous formations in their many hues of red and orange. "Awesome" was the favorite adjective.

Southwest studies in the snow at the Grand Canyon.

Other first-year students worked with a local school in Trementina, New Mexico, where there are only eight children remaining in this ghost town. At the Carlsbad Caverns, the students helped with removing the inevitable graffiti. The serious cavers went through the entire maze, another one of those experiences to share with people back home. In some ways sharing, even years later, their impressions of the countryside may well enhance others' perceptions of the world that is out there to be seen.

In keeping with these breaks from the intense everyday academic life on campus, the college tried an academic festival day in November by canceling classes. Some students caught up on their work; some went to visit the museums in Santa Fe; others just talked and ate the day away. Always a favorite topic at faculty meetings, pace was an important element in the life of a UWC, and each campus had devised its own solutions to the strain of the IB curriculum, the community service commitment, and the demands of residential living. For the two considerably older new Russian students, who had arrived shortly after Hammer's announcement, it was proving a difficult experience, especially as they were as uncertain as we of just what the Soviet instructor, Victor Saposnikov, was supposed to do. Victor, as everyone called him, did not know math, which was the field we understood a Russian instructor would offer, could only teach Russian, for which there were few takers, and try to work up enthusiasm for rugby. Our students suspected he might be a government informer. Victor could not bring his wife and child, however; only the second year did his wife come—but the child was kept home to assure their return. In short, this experiment neither improved international understanding nor helped the program; but it was entertaining. Periodically, students would voice the hope that the president would declare one of his surprise "free" days.

On a different front, the board of directors concurred with Chairman Krim's conclusion that we must mount a development campaign, using the Los Angeles staff to organize it. Alec Courtelis agreed to head up the campaign, but both of us knew from looking around the table that not many would wish to work on such a campaign or increase their own level of giving. Like the International Board, our directors assumed naively that it was sufficient to announce a fund-raising campaign without providing for professional assistance or increasing their own level of giving. Most of those associated with Hammer and Occidental quite rightly felt that they had done their part; now it was time for others to carry some of the burden. We were treading water; and it had also become obvious that the college relations office in Los Angeles was not in a position to run a campaign. Courtelis then explained to the board that the Castle showed some signs of further deterioration. Accordingly the board authorized a study to be done, primarily during the summer of 1987.

The International Board met in London on October 31. It was an uninspiring session with a small attendance. The usual topics surfaced and the discussion on fund-raising led nowhere. Some members were concerned about the expense of holding the next meeting in Swaziland to commemorate the 25th anniversary of the founding of Atlantic College; but it was agreed, finally, that Waterford had been ignored too long and was entitled to this public notice and support. It was also clear at this meeting that the U.S. Committee had lost favor and many persons wanted it to turn over all its business to Montezuma. Curiously enough, there was an argument for doing just that since the committee had accepted Hammer's offer to run its business out of the Occidental Office on the Avenue of the Americas in New York City to save money. But then Oxy announced it was closing its office there at the end of the year. In November the international education committee met with Chairman Brewster and reviewed a long list of questions, a practice the heads hoped would continue annually, even though it did not result in any action.

All was quiet during the holidays after school closed on December 17th. When the faculty met in January of 1987, they agreed that it had been a better year thus far; they also concluded that the vacation was too long. The difficulty of placing students who could not go home for the holidays was proving harder each year, and it was becoming a cost to the college. During January Lu and I continued a tradition started earlier at the college—that of having fireside chats at the house for both classes. We found that not only was the dietary supplement in the evening attractive, but also the opportunity to ask about all sorts of things, particularly rumors.

The campus had always been a fertile breeding ground for gossip, ranging from a visit by Gorbachev to using Security to patrol the dorm halls at night. In this vein our two Soviet students, Yuri Leontjuk and Igor Morgachev, had a chance to check out one rumor when Lu picked them up hitch-hiking. Was it true that I actually knew Kerensky? To their astonishment the answer was "yes" for in 1947 I had been his host at Trinity College. Curiously, when I once asked Hammer about the Russian leader in the 1917 Revolution, Hammer displayed no interest. He did express interest, however, in buying Georgia O'Keeffe's home in Abiquiu and, as was happening more frequently, he asked me to find out how he could purchase it. Six months later he dropped that project.

The appearance of snow and the hardening of the ice up the canyon lifted student spirits and provided some important training opportunities for those entering the Mount Taylor Winter Quadrathlon in Grants, New Mexico. This year the College would enter 11 teams, including 33 students, a former student and five faculty members, in the 50-mile competition. First came cycling, then running, then cross-country skiing, and finally snowshoeing to the top of the mountain—5,000 feet higher than the starting point—and then reversing the process back to the finish line. Weather could and did make conditions brutal, and eight competitors this year withdrew because of hypothermia. But that did not prevent some impressive performances by UWC students. Jenny Pickell (USA), Shona Armstrong (Canada), Taru Virtanen (Finland) and Magda Merali (Portugal) won the women's competition and finished ahead of all the college's men's and mixed teams with a time of 4:52:44. For an institution that did not sponsor any athletic competition these results were remarkable. And it proved to be fitting preparation for the kind of rescue operation teams from AHUWC performed two weeks later when they assisted the evacuation of four people from the Duran Creek Mining Camp, trapped by the heavy snowfalls.

Mountain search and rescue had become quite sophisticated by this time. Joe Nold, director of the wilderness training program, had devised a training scheme that introduced all students to certain basic survival skills and then allowed the students to decide whether they wished to learn more advanced techniques such as winter mountaineering and advanced first aid. Much of the value of such training lay in developing a team rapport. Second-year students provided the leadership and the faculty stayed at base camp with the radios. Experience had shown that understanding individuals was as important as technical skills in the success of rescue missions, coming with increasing frequency. I often thought back to Prince Charles's worry that we would not be able to match the sea rescue program or challenge students effectively enough. To the contrary, our MSAR was proving far more demanding than water rescues and, to the faculty's consternation, involving far longer periods away from campus.

The winter term was progressing well. Latin American National Day (L.A.N.D. for Freedom was the slogan) was a great distraction even if gastronomically ominous. The Human Rights Conference February 4-6 was as good as the conference on world religions held in December, an event marked by an outstanding presentation of Islam—a topic which evoked strong feelings but also excellent speakers. We were concerned whether we could mount two such conferences within two months of each other; but the organizers and the students in particular rose to each occasion. These events in the Castle were threatened, however, by the condition of the trusses over the ballroom floor. Over the holidays we had examined the interior of the Castle and done a preliminary review of the masonry. We would have to do something come summer since both wood and stone, not to mention the window frames, were deteriorating more rapidly than we had assumed.

It was most unwelcome news for a board which still had to worry about making ends meet. The Armand Hammer Trust had grown to over $15,000,000, which, when combined with other assets, gave us, on paper at least, an institution with over $30 million in assets. By now, thanks to Palm Beach and some modest contributions, we were carrying a cash balance of two million dollars in reserve. We knew that this was a most important nest egg. We had hopes of coming close to matching income against expenses, and I had set as our target holding at least one million in reserves until we could enlarge the overall endowment sufficiently to cover our shortfalls.

Direct tuition money was still sluggish, but the return on restricted funds was approaching one million annually. During this fiscal year we had exceeded three million dollars in expenses for the first time. On a per student cost basis, we had increased 18% over five years, a figure considerably less than inflation during the Reagan years. What was curious if not always comforting was that the distribution of those expenses across the various accounts had not changed dramatically despite our attempts to cut costs in management and maintenance. We knew we would return to all these considerations at a later date.

A new issue had arisen: AIDS. The UWC movement had been discussing the possible consequences for the colleges and had expressed the hope that we might arrive at a common policy. Initially, Pearson, Atlantic, and Adriatic had proposed testing all students prior to admission. Singapore would leave the issue to government policy—which, in that case, declared AIDS illegal. Obviously in this country it was a highly charged issue, and the weight of opinion was against invading the privacy of individuals by requiring blood tests. That did not deter the London office from pushing us to join in a common policy of obligatory testing. Neither Krim nor I had any interest in agreeing to testing; but we did feel that the situation required our attempting to describe a policy. But we could not be optimistic as to its effect since in most medical matters the records we received from certain countries were unhelpful—and these were precisely those countries where AIDS reportedly was most prevalent.

We concluded that we had to step up our discussions with students on sexual relations and drugs; that we would provide guidance to anyone with HIV-postive; that we would leave to the individual student or staff member any announcement of that person's infection; and that we would alert all parents as to our policy. Eventually we also offered anonymous blood tests. In the other colleges they were discovering that they could insist on tests for admission but could not be privy to that information and that any attempt to exclude someone with HIV-positive might lead to incredible legal entanglement. The world at large was floundering in its effort to address this epidemic, so redolent with moral issues. We sensed but could not prove that one consequence of the public discussion about AIDS was a slackening of promiscuous behavior on campus.

The snows continued as each weekend brought a new fall. It made planning for project week seem almost unrealistic: would we ever dig out to go south? We decided to shift the emphasis from being time off to involvement in volunteer projects. Nold and Lawrence Tharp in economics had located some remote villages in northern Mexico where our students could assist in bringing art and music as well as work on construction of school facilities. Everyone could improve their Spanish. Other projects included working with the Dallas Community College and learning some archaeology in Lincoln County, New Mexico. Some would continue with the outdoor expeditions to remote areas of Arizona and Colorado. The budget had remained at $150 per student for everything. We felt we had successfully veered away from allowing project week to become just another vacation.

During this same month of March, 1987, the International Board met at Mbabane, Swaziland, home of the United World College of Southern Africa. Unhappily neither Hammer nor Krim felt able to attend even though the Prince of Wales would be there. The college sits high on a hill above the capital city. We immediately noticed an anomaly: Swaziland reflected all the tensions which its neighbor South Africa expressed with respect to apartheid but made a good income by providing gambling to white South Africans on weekends.

Not surprisingly, the dominant issue on campus was apartheid, symbolized by the fact that liberal South Africans had founded the college as a non-racial school where black students from this area of Africa could obtain a strong education, expect to go to university, and subsequently provide the needed leadership for the countries in Africa. In that sense Waterford kamHlaba's mission was more closely allied with the original goals of the UWC movement than any; yet, it had always been seen as almost second-best. Everyone hoped this meeting would dispel that notion. Certainly Richard Eyeington, head of the college, and his wife, Enid, made everyone feel very comfortable in a land not that easy to reach yet so beautiful to behold.

The board meeting was poorly attended but significant in its agenda. Sir Michael Parsons, at Chairman Brewster's behest, laid out the unpromising financial condition of the International Office. Even with Hammer's endowment, the office did not have enough money to last more than two years unless the colleges increased their annual subsidy. Although no one picked up the ball, the issue would not go away. Also on the agenda was the reorganization of the board and the creation of an Educational Policy Council.

The previous fall Brewster and I had talked about this plan when we and the Aults had visited University College at Oxford, where he was the Vice-Chancellor, a most unusual honor for an American. It was the chairman's way of recognizing the need to seek more advice from the heads of the colleges in a manner that would be independent of board deliberations. As for the board itself, Brewster proposed shrinking the membership so that the dominant voices would be those of the college chairmen and so that it could function like an executive board and take action more efficiently. He hoped such a board would also have access to funding sources, a hope not fulfilled. From our perspective we sensed that the movement might finally acquire a keener business sense, a new energy for solving its problems, and provide a larger role for the heads in restructuring the central operations.

The festivities went off very well despite some horrendous thunderstorms, and everyone there sensed yet again that the United World College movement was indeed the finest international educational effort ever launched. Maybe being so far from home, people recognized more keenly the sweep of our programs. Lu and I visited parents both in Swaziland and Zimbabwe, a country where the national committee appeared to be too much the plaything of its chairman. We appreciated firsthand what we only understood remotely before; namely, the tremendous challenges facing a candidate for admission in these areas of Africa. There was a total absence of the normal support system for aspiring young people; politics and bureaucracy could act quixotically; embassies were indifferent; and money was scarce. We went home feeling strongly that we must maintain our scholarship aid in the developing world where the returns of a strong educational program were so obviously needed.

While pondering next year's admission picture, Lu and I concluded that we would have to use every available bed and anticipate housing 210 students. That way we could get out of the yo-yo phenomenon of 110 one year and 90 the next, a situation which only complicated how we approached national committees. Thus far the response had been sufficiently strong that we had no worries. It had always amused Lu that Hammer would be concerned about whether we would fill the school while we were worried about whether we would have the money from him to support the students we invited!

Recruiting faculty was proving harder than in the past. Some families were increasingly disappointed in the local school situation; others were not thrilled by the size and quality of our housing. Spring finally arrived and we decided to hold the traditional dinners for graduating students before the examination period. We wondered if the lilacs would bloom at commencement time, and we hoped the year would close smoothly.

It did not. During the examination period in May someone broke into Dean Maclehose's office, forced open the drawer in his desk that contained the key for the locked cabinet in which the IB examinations were stored, and stole a copy of the mathematics test. As all the second-year students were taking mathematics in the Castle ballroom at the time, we told them that they could not leave until we had solved the crime. First we asked them to record confidentially what they knew, if anything, about the theft. No one did anything despite the very real prospect that the IB Examiners Board in Geneva might disqualify everyone at Montezuma because of this breach of security. Maclehose and I then interviewed every student individually in another room to see if we could detect anything. Four students claimed to have seen someone in the dean's office. That was all.

We were not getting far; we recommended a search of rooms. The students agreed. That search uncovered an exam hidden under the mattress of a girl who immediately denied having been involved and claimed someone had framed her. She did admit that she had used a phone in the librarian's office that same night. We knew that among the five students admitting some involvement there had to be an answer; therefore, the dean and I continued the interviews throughout the night and the next morning.

The next day the girl confessed and was sent home immediately. The other four had interrupted her during the theft and then they all agreed to maintain silence and cover for each other. We denied the four compatriots the right to participate in the graduation and they had to remain off campus once the exams were completed. They were stunned; for some perverted reason they thought of themselves as heroes. Again, since discipline was not a problem, such an incident shocked everyone to such a degree that its inclusion here is a necessary element in the early history of the college.

During all this time we were in constant communication with Geneva to make certain our examinations would be accepted. We were permitted to finish the schedule of tests, but we obviously had to find another way in which to keep exams more secure. For the time being they were stored in our house—I'd like to say under the mattress, but there were too many of them. It was a sad prelude to commencement.

Other events intervened: we had as a house guest Professor Pat Young from Houston, an IB examiner, who introduced us to the British mystery writers. Claudine and Alan McHenry from the Lounsbery Foundation, which had supported us with important small grants, visited the campus. A group of students came to see my stamp collection, always a proven way to improve student-administrative relations. And then Hammer called to ask us to select ten students for the Michael Jackson Radio Show in Los Angeles on May 20. An Oxy jet picked them up; they stayed for the annual Oxy corporate meeting which coincided with his 89th birthday celebration; and then they returned to Montezuma.

Commencement came. On May 22 we held a reception for parents in the Castle, the last such occasion in that location. The rains began that night but by mid-morning the sun was out again. Abigail Van Buren, aka Dear Abby, as graduation speaker astonished and pleased the students by quoting from their personal letters in response to her request for information about life at the college; and Hammer was jovial. The Honorable Garrey Carruthers, the first governor of New Mexico to join us since 1982, brought official greetings.

Abigail Van Buren addresses the graduations of 1987 as Armand Hammer and Ted Lockwood listen.

Among other guests were film celebrities Ted Mann and Rhonda Fleming; and author Irving Stone and his wife Jean. Maria Elena Maldonado handed the diplomas to Hammer, the college's way of recognizing the service of a departing teacher. In spite of the tension the week before, the day was a wonderful reminder of the meaning of two years at Montezuma; or, as Armando Villegas-Jimenez (Mexico) remarked: "I have realized you are not like me, but you are someone special. I have shown something of myself and you have given me hope . . . Our lives at this place have ended. And today we will cry and say goodbye . . . I will never forget you."

And the lilacs had bloomed just in time. When Hammer spotted a vase full of them in the library as he was leaving, he asked a staff member to bring them along, vase and all, for transport to Los Angeles.

We were also saying good-bye to Andrew Maclehose as Dean of Studies. He would remain to teach a year, but he who had warned so often about burnout among the faculty and staff was its first "victim." There was no question that he had been indispensable in assuring that the academic program and service activities were organized properly from the start. His blunt ways had endeared him to the students who respected his integrity and fairness, even if they did not always catch what he said, particularly at the end of a sentence. What they did not know was that he was also very kind and gentle when it came to disciplining those who had erred. Never quite able to concur in the way things are done in the United States, he and his family had come to admire the area, to play their role conspicuously in the community, and to spread the word about Montezuma. His decision had come so late that we chose to ask one of the biology teachers, Neil Hunter, to step in as dean until we would decide whether to search for an outsider or not. Hunter would remain in the post for three years and do a commendable job while we tried to sort out how best to proceed.

At the board meeting held during graduation at Montezuma on May 23, those few who could attend argued for more fee-paying students since it was clear that any substantial fund-raising would take time. Fortunately Baron de Nora donated $500,000. We had reached a point where we had to change the quota required to make a meeting official, down to one-sixth of the membership. It was not a good sign; but it was encouraging that Courtelis was now playing a central role in the plans of the college. And it was he who told the board that the maintenance needs of the campus had not been addressed

The author Irving Stone and Rhonda Fleming Mann at the 1987 commencement luncheon under the big top.

adequately. To Hammer's dismay he also stated that the Castle would need nearly $200,000 before it was safe. He proposed that a very full and careful study be made during the summer of what he called "a structural nightmare." We would all become increasingly familiar with the Castle.

But more immediate was another Hammer birthday party in Los Angeles, with Merv Griffin as the Master of Ceremonies and Dinah Shore, another famous singer of the sixties, as the featured artist. Then we were off to Washington for a World Wildlife dinner given by Mr. and Mrs. Russell Train and featuring as special guest, Prince Gyandruk from Nepal. It was something of an old-home-week gathering since I was a member of the advisory committee to the King Mahindra Trust and Annapurna Sanctuary project.

Once back in Montezuma we faced a busy summer. Desert High II nutritionists, Elderhostel, Special Olympics, and the Trinity Forum all used the lower campus to full capacity. A study of the Castle dominated the upper campus. We no longer permitted groups to use the building or for tours to be conducted inside until we had a much better notion of just what problems we were facing. We also recognized it was both costly and ineffective to continue to apply band-aids where major surgery was called for. We had both interior and exterior damage to fix. Three engineers had studied the structural faults. In the ballroom at least one truss had failed and was driving the wall out. As the studies went forward, we began to realize that habit, not nails and bolts, was holding some of the east wing upright. Another view was that nothing dramatic was likely to occur since it had been there 100 years. We brought in an architect, Fran Scott from Kentucky, and a leading contractor, Stan Davis from Santa Fe. We worked up figures of what minimally we might do; the architect designed simple modifications that could accompany the basic repairs if we went forward with sufficient renovation to permit the use of the building by the college. We met with Courtelis frequently in Miami; for we felt that either we had to fix it up or put it in mothballs until someone wanted to buy or lease it.

Having crawled through the entire 100,000 square feet and having devised possible configurations that would improve the college's facilities, with the help of Francis Stanley, a distinguished Santa Fe architect who had become the architectural adviser to the school, I was convinced that we could not do much unless we invested something like five million dollars, a figure which would cover furnishings as well. As these conversations progressed, Hammer became increasingly concerned and, for example, in the middle of the night (2 a.m.) of August 21 called to talk with me about the Castle.

Courtelis was persuaded that we had to make a pitch soon if we were going to accomplish anything toward the restoration. These were moments when we dreamt of having apartments and a coffee shop and recreational facilities as well as excellent library space, an infirmary and student rooms to permit reducing the size of the student population housed down below. But until that magical moment, we had to face the fact that we would be obliged to use the dining room once again for shows, exams, and meetings.

The climax came on September 16th when Courtelis, Irani, and I met with Hammer in Los Angeles. We had prepared charts and floor plans for using 65% of the Castle for a variety of purposes. We had a bill prepared for five million dollars; but we had concluded that we would not render it unless Hammer was prepared to pay for it. In view of our scholarship needs, we were hesitant to press the issue since we could not realistically estimate how much additional expense heating and maintaining the building would cost.

We met in Hammer's handsome office. He listened and asked for alternatives. We had a fall-back plan of spending $1,400,000 for an auditorium and arts center, and an addition to the science facility. Hammer was still undecided. Then he said: "Let's call John Kluge. He's in Los Angeles now." From our end of the conversation it appeared that Kluge had a cold; Hammer said he would bring him some Russian pills to cure it; and we would be over shortly. In the limousine, he joked and said he would ask John to pay for the Castle. We went to Kluge's room at the Beverly Wilshire.

I had the charts and Courtelis and I were prepared to make the big pitch. Hammer opened by remarking: "John, we are delighted you have pledged one million dollars over the next ten years." Kluge replied: " Well, until the next merger talks are completed, I am not in great shape." "We have a better idea," Hammer interrupted. "We will forgive you the pledge if you will agree to underwrite the John and Patricia Kluge Auditorium. It will only cost you $400,000 more." Courtelis and I sat stunned. Not only did this end any immediate plans to restore the Castle; we had lost one million in endowment. But, as others would try to placate us, we had gained funds with which to build the new facility.

Back at the hotel, Courtelis and I concluded that Hammer would never renovate the Castle. We had learned yet again that Hammer was not going out on any limb—in his tree or his friends's. We would be better off giving it to the State or finding someone who would accept it in exchange for renovating it for some compatible use. From modest euphoria we had crashed to despair over the Castle.

The decision also meant getting someone to work on plans for the new multi-use facility; for we certainly needed to cram as much as possible into the structure. We sensed a need to hurry especially when the stock market began to fall in October. We asked Francis Stanley to go to work, while on campus we debated where to put the structure since it was clear no one wanted it anywhere convenient. While all this was going on, the board met in Los Angeles to hear the good news about the excellent IB exam results we had just received. They were delighted to learn that we would get $900,000 from the Hammer Trust; they were not so thrilled to learn that we still had our customary imbalance. Immediately the cry for more full-paying students went up, but Morrie Moss quieted it by commenting in his succinct manner: "The solution lies in more contributions, not in expecting more from parents and committees." The other diversion was a record enrollment of 212, with 15 more boys than girls.

16: A STORM IS BREWING

When the faculty had reassembled and new students arrived in late August of 1987, there was considerable buoyancy despite the absence of the Castle. Even when I reported on the failure of our Los Angeles mission, everyone turned their attention to the planning of the new facility rather than being despondent about the Castle. During the first meeting on community service in the fall, when traditionally the new students are baffled by the barrage of options, Tejal Shah (India) glowed when he heard that there was a young person from India in town who could not speak anything but Gujarati. He had his service program: to teach the newly arrived Las Vegan English, and to help the young man adjust to a scene quite different from his homeland. Tejal's compatriot from India, Mudit Tyagi, had also made a name for himself by declaring to a visiting lecturer on the Far East that he might well become prime minister of his country later in life. Many thought it likely, but Mudit would finish university and teach at Montezuma for two years before entering politics.

On September 19 we celebrated the second Las Vegas Night, this time in a tent on the playing fields. It raised some more money, but it had become clear that we would never attract through such events sufficient funds to restore the Castle. At the end of the month we went to Los Angeles for a dinner Hammer arranged for the King and Queen of Spain, whom he had hoped to bring to the campus. Since their nephew, Prince Pavlos, was at the college, they wanted to know more about Montezuma. It was then that I concluded that Queen Sofia would be a possible successor to Prince Charles if we had to stick with royalty. London concurred, but nothing ever happened.

Another international day on October 11 was a great success with 1400 guests. We had discovered how easy it was for the campus store, run by a faculty wife, Betty Hamer-Hodges, to sell tee shirts and memorabilia. And by this time Hilda Wales and other staff members had become very adept at helping the students organize such programs. On the other hand, it had become more difficult to find faculty to act as advisers to the customary national days. They had become more ambitious and less tasteful—which was perhaps a reflection of what was happening on American television, so often the inspiration for the skits. Despite the crowded housing conditions among the students, the first term went smoothly.

Meanwhile concern over the functioning of the international movement was growing. When the heads met in London in late October, everyone expressed dismay over the decline in scholarship support available from the national committees. What became apparent as well was the variation among the colleges with respect to covering airfare and pocket money. We agreed that someone had to take a firm grip on working with the committees and with arriving at some common practices. But it was clear the next day that the international board was in no position to do so.

Kingman Brewster was not well and could not exert much influence. The Prince of Wales had not been available for quite some months, and everything was looking a bit dreary. The deputy vice-chairman, Leonard Mayer of Mexico City, took the initiative to poll the members as to whether Brewster should be asked to step down. I balked, but Gourlay said he could not stop the move. Since Hammer and Krim seldom went to these meetings, I filled in for them, a practice which caused problems for some other board members simply because heads were not expected to sit with voting powers and, as happened later, attend special executive committee meetings. When I informed Hammer about the course of events, he firmly opposed Mayer. It would become messier before any solution would be forthcoming.

While in London, we were asked to join a group of prospective donors visiting Atlantic College. Thus on October 27 we found ourselves guests on the Orient Express bound for Bridgend in a torrential downpour which persisted after we reached South Glamorgan in Wales. The Prince was there; all went impressively; but around the edges circulated the latest rumor to the effect that the Prince and Princess were living apart. Certainly it was a feature in the tabloid press and led us to speculate on his future service.

When I reported to Hammer what had transpired at the fall meeting, he immediately interrupted and began expressing his displeasure with the U.S. Committee because he had learned that we were carrying the entire expenses of the admissions effort. We knew then we would have to redefine the approach, keep matters quiet for the immediate future, and try to cut back on the costs of supporting U.S. students.

Fortunately, the students were raising all our expectations because they not only seemed more talented than their predecessors but also more responsive to such items as extended essays, deadlines, even life in the residence halls. Thus encouraged, the resident tutors decided to include student representatives from each house in the weekly meetings which had been a feature of campus life from the beginning. Whether it was how to improve housebank or student plans for the holidays or the placement of informative medical information in the bathrooms, there were always topics to review. It was also heartening to discover that, whatever we were experiencing in dormitory living, it was most likely reflected on another UWC campus. And whenever I compared notes with preparatory school friends, I learned how fortunate we were.

The concert which closed the fall term was held this year in Highland University's Ilfeld Auditorium and may well have been our "finest hour."

Not so encouraging was the prospective situation among faculty. We would be losing Darrell Axtell, our first instructor in chemistry, and we would need a new person in the difficult position of teaching English as a Second Language. We were having green card problems in both physics and economics. Andrew Maclehose had accepted the position of founding a new school in Darwin, Australia. That meant locating a person who could combine instruction in Theory of Knowledge with handling part of the load in physics.

But behind the inevitable changes in personnel was a growing disappointment among some faculty about salaries, housing, and their prospects for the future. When the college opened in 1982, I had substituted for the normal tenure granted teachers in most schools and universities a five-year rolling contract after a probationary period of two to four years. That meant that satisfactory teaching and community contribution by a faculty member led to having a minimum of four years in which to find a new position should an annual review prove wanting. Some faculty thought that the review process was not formal enough. Others thought that our levels of compensation were too low; but the reports which I prepared from nationwide statistics demonstrated that, to the contrary, our scales were quite generous. No doubt they were reflecting the cumulative effect of working in this kind of institution where so much had to be done by so few.

They were not immune to the uncertainty which had always plagued our financial planning. They had hoped to see some recreational facilities constructed, along with more faculty housing of higher quality. Even though they were now excited about the new Creative and Performing Arts Center, they wanted to challenge almost every topic which arose in our monthly meetings. The change in deans had not helped; but they preferred to work with someone they had known for years than face the prospect of someone new from the outside. In that I concurred, at least for the immediate future.

Just before the holidays we had a conference on science and technology, but it suffered an early termination as temperatures plummeted and predictions of snow required the buses to leave earlier than planned on December 16. The predictions were correct; for when we held our customary Christmas party for faculty and staff, the snow began and continued through the holidays for a very white celebration.

As we began 1988, guests arrived in goodly numbers. A Czech correspondent, Bohuslav Snajder, came and stayed two weeks; then 22 young Soviets appeared under the guidance of eight adults, all somewhat dismayed. And Hammer called to ask me to help Bill Cosby with his plans on starting a special high school for talented Black youngsters. It was all related to Hammer's appearance on the Cosby Show January 21. Then came two shocks to our fund-raising hopes. First, Hammer announced he would build a $30-million art museum behind the Occidental Petroleum building in Los Angeles to house his collection. I could not convince him that it would be much more significant a contribution to the world if he housed his art in a renovated Castle in northern New Mexico where so little art was available and the cost would be modest. But then we were not conversant with the various maneuvers which others have claimed were taking place in LA those days. Second, he announced he would raise $500 million for cancer research if the U.S. government would match it. He obviously had other things he wanted to accomplish in the next few years.

At the college we decided to explore a new issue in the conference held January 27-29: north-south relations in each hemisphere. Ever since the school had opened, people had been aware of the views which students from the southern hemisphere held about the affluence of the northerners. A number of topics came under this broad umbrella, like terrorism and appropriate technology; and in the final session there was a workshop on managing conflict. Merle Lefkoff, a consultant in Santa Fe, was beginning a series of seminars in conflict resolution, a program which seemed quite promising as a way to approach international issues on the one hand and campus controversies on the other. Thanks to grants from The Harry Frank Guggenheim Foundation and the Kellogg Foundation, the college developed a basic program in conflict resolution which was implemented at all UWCs. Increasingly we felt that the colleges had to construct new approaches, reaching beyond the IB, if the UWCs were to retain a distinctiveness among international schools. It would take a long time before such innovations were accepted.

In February the board of directors met in Los Angeles. The main concern remained how to increase the endowment so that, in turn, we could eliminate the annual deficit. The conversation was lively, including intriguing proposals for the Castle which, Courtelis had indicated, would be mothballed. It was emblematic of the problem we continually faced on the board: despite genuine interest and goodwill there were few who could or would make a major commitment of either time or money.

A gala originally planned for London in 1988 had been canceled. Neither Courtelis nor I had had much success with new prospects or with trying to reinvigorate those who had given in 1982 in London. There was concern, but kind sentiments did not lessen the pressure on the administration to hold down costs and quietly prepare to tighten the belt—and for the president to hit the road for new funds.

Ironically, both north-south hemispheric relations and finances were featured at the IB heads conference in Geneva in February. Many IB schools in places like Africa and Ceylon could no longer afford the high fees for membership and for administering the examinations. Simultaneously the IB was trying to raise funds to cover the cost of so many new schools applying for permission plus the ever-increasing cost of administering examinations.

In a sense success might well undo the IB. Its director, Roger Peel, formerly head of languages at Middlebury College in Vermont, was valiantly trying to streamline operations while reassuring the UWCs in particular that the quality of the IB would remain intact. As matters turned out, the IB managed to turn the corner from where it had been in 1984 and emerge much healthier for the nineties. We had come close to collapse in the IB, an event which would have had profound consequences for the UWC movement. The UWC heads also met with Ian Gourlay to talk once again about the ineffectiveness of the center. We even proposed ways in which the movement could be decentralized. But fumbling around seemed to have become the order of the day.

Therefore, when the IB meeting ended on Thursday, Lu and I were relieved to steal away for a short vacation of skiing at Zermatt. We checked into our hotel, bought our lift tickets for the ten days, and went up to the top. Conditions were not that good, but the town was charming. At dinner that first night, February 26, the proprietress scurried into the dining room to say I had a long-distance call. It was Hammer phoning from his plane somewhere in the world. Without many preliminaries, he said he looked forward to seeing us on Monday, February 29, in Montezuma. The Soviets were coming to do a special television program in anticipation of his 90th birthday when Soviet TV would do a commemorative program. The phone went dead. We concluded that we had no choice.

We packed that night, recaptured what money we could, caught the train to Geneva the next morning in what was the traditional mad weekend exchange of billets, and tried to figure out how we would make it home in time. Sunday we flew to Albuquerque on the last flight in, had a few hours sleep in Montezuma, and tried to be cheerful on Monday. Hammer never asked about our trip and he never apologized for the inconvenience. Although our first reaction had been irritation, we decided we had learned from this typical Hammer experience. Therefore, once the cameras and Hammer had departed, we went to Colorado to ski in what proved to be superb snow. The only "cost" was to call Brewster in London in the morning since he was concerned about Hammer's role in the upcoming choice of a new chairman—and then in the late afternoon to call Hammer in LA to get his thinking about next steps at the international level. For when he had been in Montezuma, he had expressed his dissatisfaction with the Prince's inactivity and with the London office. A storm was in the making.

17: A 90TH BIRTHDAY

The storm broke on March 9th when Hammer called from his plane to ask me to leave for London the next day to join him for the discussions on the chairmanship. Rick Jacobs and I met with him. Before the nominating committee for the International Board would meet, Hammer began maneuvering. He had me fetch Galen Weston, chairman of the Pearson College board and a good friend of Prince Charles. Weston would not agree to be the next chairman. The three of us conferred, and Weston wanted me to stand. I declined. Hammer then asked Jacobs and me to let it be known that he would be willing to stand and that he would find the money necessary to put the movement on a sound financial basis. I suggested that most likely he would not get enough votes, which was probably accurate but which did not deter Hammer. He wanted to play on the international scene and any comments from me about worrying first about Montezuma's fiscal good health were irrelevant and unwelcome. Finally he agreed to hold off on his campaign for the chairmanship after I went down the board list and indicated whom they would prefer. He decided that he and Weston would run the movement by taking over responsibility for raising money for the London office.

But what to do next? Brewster called me from Oxford and asked me to come up to meet Sir Albert Sloman, a distinguished British academic leader whom he thought would take on the chairmanship. Hammer said: "Go, find out all you can, and arrange for Sloman to have breakfast with us here tomorrow morning. Take my car." So off to Oxford in a Rolls Royce for lunch at University College. As always it seemed like a different world. Brewster was obviously failing, but unfailing in being a genial host. We all talked, and Sloman agreed to come to London.

That next morning Sloman and I met with Hammer in his suite at Claridge's and ate breakfast. I did not think Hammer would like him and I expected him to badger Sloman about raising money, which Sir Albert firmly countered by saying he could not and would not become a development officer. But evidently Hammer had concluded he and Weston could run the show, that Sloman would be agreeable, and such a move would frustrate other candidates like Leonard Mayer from Mexico, still deputy chairman.

After the interview, Hammer then told me to attend the nominating committee meeting which Sir Shridath Ramphal was chairing at his office as Secretary General of the Commonwealth. It was another session dominated by the absent Hammer; for everyone wanted to know what the world traveler would do. They were not prepared to go against him, but were fretful. When I said he thought Sloman would do, they still worried—and almost recommended that Hammer be nominated for the chairmanship even though he would be defeated. I said that was unwise, but we had better find a good consolation prize. Ramphal wondered if he could be given a special title. Remembering that Lord Mountbatten had received some symbolic title, I asked about that. We all concurred that we should try out the title of International Life Patron, and I was instructed to inform Hammer. In trying to soften matters further, Ramphal offered invitations for Hammer and me to attend the Queen's reception that evening at Lansdowne House.

Walking back to Claridge's I wondered how I managed to get in the middle of all these conversations, the net effect of which was distressingly minor. Hammer was pleased with the solution; we got ready for the reception; and he and I went. One of the games his staff played whenever I was in London with Hammer was to jockey me into the task of entertaining Hammer so that understandably they could get some relief. It was my night. As Hammer and I stood around awaiting the reception, he managed to devour many an hors d'oeuvre. Fortunately the Westons came also; for everyone else came from one of the Commonwealth countries and were totally puzzled by our appearance since we had nothing to offer their struggling nations. When the Queen and Prince Philip appeared, we took our place in line.

The Queen may have recognized Hammer, but when she asked why we were there, there was silence until I decided to fill the gap: "We represent a colony that successfully revolted a long time ago." Happily it evoked considerable laughter as others glanced down the line at Mutt and Jeff standing there in conversation with the monarch. We went back to Claridge's for dinner at the table specifically reserved for Hammer the 60 years he had been staying at the hotel. He asked me to fetch the others, only some of whom were still unwisely at the hotel. We were told what to order; then Hammer fell asleep; but I was warned not to say anything interesting or provocative since he might be only cat-napping. Later we all settled down for a nice sleep when, now wide awake at one in the morning, Hammer asked Rick and me to come to his suite. (It may be germane to add that Hammer always made sure we had adjoining rooms so that we could assist at a moment's notice, which happened on this occasion when Hammer slipped and fell in his bathtub.)

"Prepare a letter to the Prince explaining all these developments so that we can take it to the Palace tonight. Then tomorrow we'll call him."

We hooked up Rick's computer and printer. They would not work. We went downstairs for another adapter. Then the computer blew. We went down for a typewriter. Around three in the morning we finished the letter, took it to Hammer, who was bathing, and he signed it. We took his car and handed the letter to the guard at Buckingham Palace. The guard looked puzzled, but Jacobs reassured him that the Prince was panting for the communication.

That the president of the UWC International Council was not impatiently awaiting the latest Hammer communication became clear when we tried to reach him by phone. Eventually we did, testimony to Hammer's leverage; the Prince was cool to the Mountbatten title, uneasy about Sloman, and more concerned about his skiing trip to Klosters. Yet, he did not insist on undoing everything. We had gotten beyond a very sticky point. Now the main concern was whether Hammer, somewhat thwarted at the international level, would turn around and withdraw from the Montezuma scene. But Hammer seemed content with his association with Weston and with the fact that the two of them would dominate discussions in the executive committee, newly formed in keeping with the Swaziland decision and empowered to act on behalf of the entire Board.

Hammer hoped, nonetheless, to see Prince Charles shortly and try to set a date for a 1989 gala in England. When he found the Prince was already skiing in Switzerland, he suggested we fly over and see him. Before that could happen, we learned that the Prince had been involved in a tragic ski accident at Klosters when an avalanche killed a close friend. As I listened to a later telephone exchange with the Prince, I became persuaded that he may well have lost some of his enthusiasm for Hammer's projects but that he was too clever to disengage from any possible future donations. In retrospect, it is clear that we skirted near to a rupture among the various parties, and the ambiguous resolution may have been the only feasible way out of the increasingly unstable situation at the center.

All these arrangements were confirmed when the International Board met in April. But prior to that customary meeting in London, Lu and I went to Duino at the request of David Sutcliffe to join in a presentation to the Italian government. Italy was considering sponsoring science programs for the Third World, and Sutcliffe saw this as a possible contribution from the United World Colleges. Nothing much came of this proposal, but the development of a science center in Trieste did rebound to the advantage of the Adriatic College.

When we all gathered in London on April 21, we learned more about a new Bulgarian interest in founding a UWC on the Black Sea. There were mixed feelings despite Jack

Matthews's enthusiasm for finally breaking through into Eastern Europe. Otherwise, the board welcomed Hammer and Weston trying to raise the money others had so conspicuously failed to do. The Norwegians announced that they planned to open their college in 1992. Their plans and proposed steps were a model in meeting the requirements of the board, unlike, as the Norwegians were prone to note, Venezuela in the past or India in the future. Then the Italians surprised people by saying that there was a possibility of a second UWC in the southern region of that country. This meeting was the last conducted by Kingman Brewster.

But before we left London, Hammer decided to take us all to see an unsuccessful play entitled "Ziegfield" at the Palladium because he had known Flo Ziegfield and his wife Billie Burke. At dinner that night at Le Jardin des Gourmets, he ordered for all of us, and then decided to leave quickly for his meeting with Galen Weston at 12:30 a.m. We had not finished our desserts; but Jacobs told Lu that experience had taught him in these circumstances to scoop up some chocolates and carry them back to the room. Sir Ranulph Fiennes was left to settle the bill with a very upset French restaurateur.

It had been a busy end to the winter. In New Mexico the main topic was the design of the Creative and Fine Arts Center. There were still those who wished it to be moved to another location so that we would not invade the area between the science building and the residence halls; but we had discovered once again how our rugged terrain limited the choices, especially if we were to keep the playing fields inviolate. The basic layout would provide for a large auditorium in the center, with a raised stage. The main floor, capable of seating 450 people, would remain flat so that the same space could be used for examinations, indoor recreation possibly, art exhibits, and dances. To the west of it was an open area designed primarily for art exhibits and receptions but also available as additional lounge space and television viewing. TV had always been a question: some thought it indispensable for keeping students informed in an area where the newspapers seldom covered international happenings; others pointed out that, more often than not, students would watch the soaps, the popular evening shows, or videos into the night. By augmenting our capability with a second area of television, the campus center might be a more sociable spot in which to congregate.

On the two wings of the building would be a new complex of three rooms for art and special spaces for music instruction and practice. There was no question that the college would be getting substantial space for its investment, and Stan Davis of Davis and Associates Construction Company promised no overruns. Delightfully that proved to be the case. Not so happily resolved, as it turned out, was the cooling of the auditorium for the warmer months. In keeping with New Mexican practices, evaporative coolers were installed; but their operation defied proper planning for events during summer. Hammer was pleased with the plans for the new building and indicated that henceforth graduation ceremonies would be held in the auditorium.

Hammer was about to celebrate his 90th birthday. We had attended his 88th in Los Angeles when the motif had been the eighty-eight keys of the piano. His 89th had been staged May 21st in the Grand Ballroom of the Beverly Wilshire Hotel. On that occasion the theme was "scenes from the past." Merv Griffin was the master of ceremonies; Placido Domingo and Dinah Shore sang, as well as Jayne Morgan Weintraub. And, of course, his good friend, Mstislav Rostropovitch performed on the cello. Hammer and Rostropovitch had always attended each other's birthdays. Those affairs had been both pleasant and entertaining even though they occurred just before graduation each year. At one Jimmy Stewart plaintively bent my ear about what it meant to be a "has-been" in Hollywood, especially if your hearing had failed as had his. At another, Placido Domingo expressed great interest in the college and promised to come for a visit. As so often had happened, people would assure us that they would come, only to find Montezuma remote or the offer forgotten even when reminded. We could have filled the ballroom with such guests. For the 90th Hammer had grandiose plans. At the 1987 graduation he had begun to lay the groundwork.

"Rick, get on the phone to Yehudi! After that get Isaac!" Someone had the temerity of asking, "Yehudi who?" Thus were arranged the players for the Bach double violin concerto at the Kennedy Center in Washington, D.C. Again his old friend, Mstislav Rostropovitch, would conduct the National Symphony Orchestra. The invitations presented a certain problem, however, since not everyone invited to attend the concert could be provided with dinner. Fortunately we did not have to face the jam-up at Watergate where a special dinner was served. At the concert Lady Bird Johnson sat with Hammer in the presidential box. In addition to the performance by Menuhin and Stern, Dame Kiri Te Kanawa sang Mozart. After the concert we went to a reception upstairs.

Hammer always liked to have famous musicians join in his celebrations. Isaac Stern performed at the 89th birthday party in Los Angeles.

Placido Domingo and Dinah Shore also sang at Hammer's party.

Maestro Mstislav Rostropovich never missed Hammer's birthdays.

What was especially poignant was the almost total lack of concern for Frances Hammer. She had remarked to Lu the previous year, "I am tired of traveling 300,000 miles every year. Even with our own drinking water and electric blanket, it is just too hard work. Armand can travel on his own." Others were to claim later that domestic relations had become strained. Yet, she had come to Washington, looking tired and uninterested in the swarming at the reception. But, we found her still interested in the college and willing to come the next week to graduation.

Our annual event had been postponed to permit Hammer to celebrate his birthday in the east and still hand out diplomas to the graduates. We were worried because there was a three-day gap between the end of the IB examinations and the festivities; but, for once, our worries were gratuitous and the students merely prolonged their tearful goodbyes, so much so that all the yearbooks had been autographed with appropriate messages well in advance of the bus leaving for the airport. On the Friday evening before commencement we invited parents to a reception in the back yard of the president's house. We had informed the students that such a meeting with parents only was necessary so that we could tell them the truth about their offspring. Some actually believed us. It worked very well indeed, and more parents came to this graduation than ever before. One family had been on the bus for three grueling days from Mexico. The Benders had flown in from Lublin, Poland, to see their son Iwo graduate as a *doyjaly chloviek (*mature man). Nevertheless, that still evoked some commentary about providing scholarships to students whose parents could afford travel half way around the world. More seriously, it seemed both a proper courtesy to them and perhaps the most effective way to begin an association of parents to assist the college. Annual letters from the college had produced but a desultory response. The evening ended with the Blue Moon Cafe in the cafeteria: students presented various skits, many gently poking fun at faculty and staff, and the customary loud music.

Saturday morning was sunny and bright. The tent had not blown down; the flowers were in place; and the graduation platform was set where the new auditorium would soon be erected. The visitors from Los Angeles arrived at eleven, including house majority whip, Congressman Tony Coelho from California, whom Hammer had asked to give the graduation speech. William Sarnoff, chairman of Warner Publishing, and Luciano Benetton, president of the Benetton Company, were among the guests who had orange juice and Perrier under the tent on the back lawn. Then we held the customary press conference in the Sasakawa Center, a rather mild version in deference to Hammer's 90 years and his plan to join President Reagan at the summit meeting with Gorbachev the next day to sign the recently ratified nuclear arms agreement.

Lunch was ready when we crossed the lawn to the tent, and the clouds began to move in. With 900 guests present we knew that we could not move the ceremony to the Castle if it rained. And that it did. Accordingly we made alternative arrangements under the canvas amid a steady downpour. Fortunately once Coelho had delivered some uninspired remarks and departed, the rain relented and everyone could hear the names being called for the students to receive their certificates. In many ways this class of 1988 had the most spirit of any even if their academic achievements were more modest; it was also to be the largest ever to graduate, 109 students from 62 countries. Jennifer Curry from South Dakota had been selected as the student speaker. As usual, we all had ambivalent feelings: glad to see them leave after their two years but sorry to lose some of the most attractive individuals we had known. A gigantic birthday cake, Hammer's favorite carrot cake based on a recipe from LA and baked by our own chef, Sadie Martinez, commemorated the occasion. Then he received a shovel for breaking ground for the new building. Given the delays and Hammer's plans, there was no board meeting that afternoon as people headed in various directions. Another year had ended successfully.

18: NEW FACILITIES

In late June, 1988, the bulldozers appeared and we began construction of the first new facility. Delays had been inevitable: the schematics took longer; the bids to subcontractors were slow going out and coming back; and the permits required more time than anticipated. We were operating on New Mexican time; but, as happened, we could not have excavated the ground during early June because of heavy rains. Moreover, we had to bring in engineered dirt to replace the local turf so that it could be compacted properly before the foundations were poured. We were also adding two large classrooms to the east of the science building. There was a sense of progress despite the budgetary tightness which continued.

That situation was apparent at the board meeting in July. When Occidental Petroleum made its final installment on the $20 million endowment, Ray Irani underscored the precarious state of the finances. In part it was to request the college to reduce its costs and in part to remind Hammer that talking about a movie premiere was not solving the problem. At a meeting of the finance committee just prior to the full board session, Hammer had responded to these same observations by asking for a $500,000 reduction in the budget. That was impossible and all we could offer was to cut out $50,000 from a revised budget. Others proposed that we limit ourselves to taking only 50% of the new students with any financial aid. One member proposed that Hammer use his influence to get the movement to ask parents everywhere to contribute to tuition as much as they could afford. It was familiar ground and did not address the immediate problem we had faced before and now faced yet again: continuing shortfalls.

In addition, we were forced to take out a promissory note to pay for the construction until Kluge made his contribution at the completion of the project, an inconvenience that added some thirty thousand to the bill. Again this cranky subject distorted the entire discussion at the meeting. As a counterploy I had always made a practice of telling some stories about happy occurrences on campus, and in this instance informing them that students from four different countries would be attending Dartmouth in the fall. Those ramblings did not improve the tone; and even Martin Meyerson, always so complimentary of the effort at Montezuma, suggested we look to more foreign students who could pay since the U.S. dollar was sufficiently weakened that many people overseas regarded American education as a bargain. No one offered to contribute more funds; it was left to the college to solve the problem.

The donor of the new auditorium, John Kluge, is sharing dinner with Mrs. Milton Petrie and Armand Hammer.

Then, as people were about to rise and go to another splendid luncheon down the hall on the 16th floor, Hammer announced that everything was set for another gala in England in August of 1989, the proceeds of which would go to the International Office. There would be 100 couples from the United States and 100 from Canada. No one bought any tickets: only later would the twist be put on board members. And no one realized that these plans to use the Prince next year severely diminished any prospect of his return to the States for a benefit on behalf of AHUWCAW. But the discussion had made it clear that we would have to tighten still further our expenditures and make concessions to the board's legitimate concern about deficits.

At the meeting we had transacted one curious piece of business: we got approval for the sale of some small parcels of land to permit widening the highway across the Gallinas River. We also changed banks in Las Vegas, another detail requiring formal board approval. I also reported that the U.S. Department of Labor was becoming increasingly uncooperative with respect to visas for foreign teachers. We were told that we could no longer require higher qualifications than would prevail in a secondary school. We had never advertised for teachers knowing six languages and having climbing experience in the Himalayas; but we were warned about saying that familiarity with the International Baccalaureate or training overseas would be welcome. For some foreign faculty already in Montezuma, this meant the beginning of longer preparation for permanent residency, even renewals. For many years Arthur Groman's legal firm in Los Angeles, Mitchell, Silverberg, and Knupp had provided *pro bono* assistance in filing petitions. Now we had to hire specialists in Albuquerque to pursue these requests, at best a tiresome and uncertain process.

On the world scene, there were some changes this summer. First, the International Executive Committee had to consider a request for a Bulgarian UWC on the shores of the Black Sea. Our Canadian colleagues were strongly in favor of this move. Hammer was uncharacteristically ambivalent. As a friend of President Zukov and a member of the Lubyana Foundation which was proposing the conversion of a summer arts camp into a permanent UWC, Hammer was in favor of the project despite the poor repute of the government in Bulgaria. On the other hand, he knew that there was strong opposition to this kind of association with the Communists. The issue had occasionally come to the floor of board meetings, and some senior directors had opposed any kind of collaboration with communist countries, even though they accepted a close tie between the Adriatic College and its neighbor, Yugoslavia. At this point no one knew how Prince Charles might react. As was so often the case, no one in the London office sought to ascertain HRH's position in advance, a practice that only underscored the failure to take full advantage of his notoriety and prestige—or its possible consequences for the movement.

In the end, Prince Charles was prevailed upon to hold a dinner meeting in October at Highgrove House to discuss the matter. Once in London, Hammer commissioned Fiennes to fetch a helicopter; and the three of us flew up to Gloucestershire and landed among the royal sheep near the house. The executive committee and a few others were there, including Kingman Brewster. After dinner Prince Charles asked Hammer his views. Deftly Hammer asked me to explain our position (whatever that was supposed to be). I merely stated my own opinion that it would not work: there was no money; the political situation was uncongenial; and we had other priorities. Hammer was off the hook. The Canadians unwisely pressed the case for recognition. The Prince became passionate in his opposition—which then permitted others to join his side, the main argument being the oppressive nature of the government. The evening ended with a long drive back in a car since helicopters could not fly after 10 p.m., while Hammer slept.

Sir Albert Sloman had become the new chairman and he was forced to focus on the deficits at the center. Although he was pleased that Hammer and Weston were taking the initiative by planning a fund-raiser for the summer of 1989, as chairman Sloman was faced with asking the colleges to increase their contribution. That was the opening gun of a three year battle over these levies. In other respects, Sloman managed to infuse some new energy into the office and the affairs of the movement while quietly noting that the situation described to him a year earlier was hardly what he had found when he sat down with the staff at London House. One issue appeared to have been settled, finally: the admission of Simon Bolivar to full status in the UWC movement even though it was not yet able to contribute any monies to the central office.

With a familiarity that was hardly beguiling, we knew that the beginning of our seventh year did not find us able to look to a future when issues other than finances would dominate the agenda. Yes, we had a good endowment, but there had been a steady decline in contributions from national committees, an apparent limit to what we could expect from parental contributions, and a fall-off in annual giving. We pledged ourselves to review all this prior to the next year, both at home and abroad.

Summer programs had been somewhat curtailed by the construction of the arts center; but by the time the new students arrived, there was a sense of progress and it did not rain at Philmont. Admittedly some new faculty were late arriving, and the new Soviet students maintained their record intact by arriving a few weeks later. Among the newcomers there were more boys than girls, contrary to the experience at other UWCs. Maybe the John Wayne image of the West influenced applicants. Registration went smoothly. As usual, the sign-up for activities and services was a massive assault on the dining room, with students racing around to be certain they got their preferences and then faculty approval for their choices. We did not have enough room for potential tennis players Hamer-Hodges informed me. Pir Maleki's chess team looked strong again. The committee preparing for a conference on world religions had matters well in hand for the three-day event in late September. In short, life was normal at the entrance to the Gallinas Canyon.

And normal too was a faculty concern that we had packed too much into the opening months. No doubt one reason for that concern was a flurry of searches that pulled students away from their studies and extended essays. To some there was another, more important worry: a rise in the clandestine use of alcohol and rather more intimate behavior than resident tutors had seen before. New students seemed more brazen—or our age was showing. The college responded as it always did whenever an issue seemed to reach a certain level of complexity: we talked and talked about how to get a better handle on unbecoming behavior. We had had enough unfortunate episodes that we felt little sympathy for a flagrant disregard of the guidelines, but we were also obliged to acknowledge that new students did not have our memories of episodes for the most part inaccurately preserved in the myths passed on from one class to the next. Meetings with student representatives did seem to reduce the pressure and to improve the understanding.

In October Ranulph Fiennes and his wife, Virginia, visited the campus to deliver a lecture on the Transglobe expedition—and to hike in the Sangre de Cristo mountains. His penchant for living dangerously intrigued the hardier souls among the students. It was one of the many, quite fascinating events of this fall of 1988. A conference on world religions at the end of September led to intense discussion covering Buddhist beliefs, matrifocal culture, liberation theology, and traditional church positions. It was little wonder that later we had yet another conversation about academic pressure. Students wanted less pressure so that they could enjoy more activities and longer service programs. The faculty quite properly insisted that without strong academic results, the students could not achieve their goals. The problem lay in assessing relative importance. Again, to some

When Ranulph Fiennes and his wife, Virginia, visited the campus, it was inevitable that they would join students and Ted Lockwood on a climb into the Sangre de Cristo mountains.

the tension was creative; to others, the tension was unbearable. In the end the faculty rearranged the schedule to open more "free" time during which students could catch up on their studies or learn the art of using leisure productively.

For years Lu and I had tried diversions at the house for students. The fireside chats had worked well. We had also introduced "snacks and slides" since pictures of the campus before it was restored evoked a lot of laughs. The matriculation dinners as well as the second-year dinners had confirmed the fact that everyone had at least one presentable costume and did enjoy the occasional formal gathering. Resident-tutor dinners permitted more relaxed conversations about campus matters just as the dinners for new faculty helped clarify, to some degree, the mysterious processes by which the college operated. I also had the opportunity from time to time of teaching history in Ivan Mustain's classes, especially those topics Ivan did not particularly enjoy.

Typically in the fall students worked with youngsters on a soccer program as part of community service.

The fall ended with a few snow flurries. Only when the first-year students went to the Grand Canyon at Thanksgiving time did they encounter snow and cold so severe that one night they had to take shelter in the local high school gymnasium. As the usual departures occurred, there did not seem to be as many tears, a product of the strong leadership which the second-years were providing. And a group of second-years were planning to go to Mexico over the holidays to do a construction project in the area where hurricanes had done so much damage. The 12 students from ten countries raised $1500 to help and then contributed their own labor in Matamoros—another tribute to the UWC ethos of helping others less fortunate. The other diversion during the late fall was watching the progress on the Kluge Auditorium. It was large! The classroom addition to the science building was also proceeding apace; and the hope was for occupancy in February. There were some musings over the clock on the face of the auditorium. For an institution that never used bells and had few clocks visible, to some it had seemed an appropriate decorative addition.

In January, 1989, I wrote to the board that our first new buildings were near completion and that some adjustments to our maintenance building would finally meet OSHA requirements. Since the board had authorized Courtelis and me to seek the sale of the Castle, I reported that it would not only require time to find the market but that it would also require us to review the implications of such a sale. In working with Wid Slick in Las Vegas on seeking inquiries, we concluded that we should be prepared for a number of alternatives. Some might wish only to lease the land under the Castle and parking lot; others might wish some land and additional buildings such as the faculty houses to be part of any deal. That would necessitate relocating such buildings and constructing new tennis courts. Originally we had set the price on the Castle at $50,000 plus settlement fees as we could not imagine anyone renovating the building and paying a substantial fee to the college. However, if someone wanted the other buildings on the upper campus and some ten acres of property, we felt that the sale price should be at least $550,000.

However often we tried to encourage the board to think about such issues, it was to no avail and we did our long-range planning among ourselves. That entailed the risk that we might make assumptions the board would later find unacceptable. Hammer did not want to think ahead; he just wanted a solution now. In this same letter I had to forewarn the directors that we had to make some changes in the residence halls to improve the heating and electrical systems, and to replace the old windows. There was no avoiding such issues, but we always felt that Hammer and his friends were uninterested in these management problems so typical for any institution and especially one which was aging rapidly.

All these concerns came before the board on February 15, 1989 in Los Angeles. Some interesting announcements opened the meeting; namely, the appointment of Alec Courtelis as vice-chairman and the announcement that, despite all the misgivings, the Simon Bolivar College of Agriculture in Venezuela was now officially a United World College and would graduate its first class this coming summer. Hong Kong had also indicated that it hoped to open a UWC in 1990.

The board was intrigued by the new program in conflict resolution at the college. Earlier in February we had arranged to assemble representatives from the Nicaraguan government, the Contras, and former U.S. ambassadors to meet in Montezuma to explore ways to solve the long battle among factions in that country. Dr. Merle Lefkoff served as the facilitator for this second-level diplomacy—which, in this instance, proved very productive.

The financial report was familiar. The trust had $22 million, thanks to further contributions we had raised totaling over two million; but the one and a half million income from the trust would cover only 50% of the expenses; money from tuition and national committees would cover another 22%; the remainder would have to be met through donations. With the decline in unrestricted and restricted gifts in recent years, the deficit of some $675,00 could become a further drain on reserves ($1,830,000). Ray Irani reminded the directors that the only long-term solution was the addition of at least $10,000,000 to the endowment. In light of these considerations, the college had limited its increases for the coming year to 3%. The directors accepted these figures and also expressed no qualms about trying to sell the Castle. Almost overlooked in the day's proceedings was Hammer's absence, one of the few times when he could not attend.

The new auditorium opened officially on February 10, 1989. Immediately everyone commented: "How did we get along without this facility?" Certainly art and music were relieved to be out of their very limited spaces in the administration building. The dining room would no longer have to be transformed, through duct tape and flimsy boards, into a theater. The inaugural event at the Kluge Center was a very successful student show in March to raise money for UNICEF. Later in the spring Sir Albert Sloman, chairman of the International Board, visited and addressed everyone from the podium of the new stage. There was a certain pride in showing off what was for the moment the best UWC auditorium. Sloman also used the occasion to review with me the many issues looming in London. The finances of the central office were in disarray. Their deficit of 120,000 English pounds was even more depressing than ours. Success at the August gala would be crucial. Gourlay had indicated he would leave his position shortly; the Prince of Wales was pressing for the movement to concentrate on rural issues and shake off its elitist image. Obviously with all the changes pending, the UWC movement was in its own slow way approaching a crossroads: the problem was that the signposts were unclear.

At Montezuma student behavior had once again preempted the stage. There was an automobile accident in the middle of the night, involving four students and alcohol. The driver was seriously injured. Lengthy discussions led to the decision that the driver should be given medical leave with the understanding that he could not return, a more considerate sentence than some wished. The others were all on probation and required to do community service by both the college and the city of Las Vegas.

In reviewing all these issues with legal counsel as an institution must nowadays inevitably do, we concluded that we had to reduce our exposure by providing locks on each dormitory door, clarify the guidelines, and re-emphasize state and local law. It was a reminder that even such a place as AHUWCAW was not immune. In fact, as we talked, we wondered whether we had been wrong in once thinking that the UWCs could serve as models where these kinds of transgressions did not occur and seldom was heard the argument that "boys will be boys."

We did find some relief and entertainment in the State's plan to reconstruct New Mexico State Road 65 on the south side of the Gallinas. To widen that road and to provide a cantilevered section above the river banks, the State would pave and widen the road through the campus and on up the north side of the Gallinas. Running all traffic through our grounds led to their erecting a discreet fence along the playing fields and changing some of the security provisions. Our famous ford on the east side would be rebuilt, but not until we had reenacted a version of the Milagro Beanfield War, when a neighbor regarded the improvements as an infringement perpetrated by that international billionaire from Los Angeles.

Among other spring news was the selection of Michael Stern, a U.S. second-year student, as a finalist in the 48th annual Westinghouse Science Talent Search. His winning entry had the beguiling title: Chemical Chaos: Experimental Mathematics and Non-Linear Dynamics in the Belousov-Zhabotinskii Reaction. Michael explained it as an attempt to show that there is order in chaos. Repeatedly the college had sent winners to the Science Olympiad, to the dismay of other high schools. In a quite different manner eight students had distinguished themselves during the project week by working with the New York City Outward Bound Center in a program addressed at the homeless in the South Bronx. A far cry from Montezuma, the streets were littered with box dwellers whom the students tried to get involved in recreation and to whom they distributed hundreds of sandwiches. It was a searing introduction to the immense problem of urban living among the poor.

Examinations and graduation came to a campus excited by the events in Tiananmen Square in Beijing. There was a surprising amount of goodwill as the second-year students turned over responsibility to the first-years who, in turn, were determined to remedy the ills of the past and assure a better year ahead. The 1989 commencement speaker was the U. S. Senator from Alaska, Ted Stevens who, perforce, addressed the implications of the Exxon Valdes oil spill. He acquitted himself impressively with a brief speech. Hammer withstood the unanticipated heat of the auditorium very well indeed. (It proved to be the warmest day in May on record.) As a twist in the ceremony he gave each graduate not only the college's certificate but also a "prescription for life"—a hand-penned message on his own medical prescription tablet from the early 1920's: "Seek opportunities to inform yourself and help bring peace to this world." Juana Sotomayor from Ecuador was the student graduation speaker, and she echoed a sentiment we had heard so often that it now seems axiomatic for those students whose homelands are poor and unstable: "I must confess that I didn't like my country until I came here. But it's mine . . . I must use what I have learned here to change those systems we criticize."

The day did not end when the Los Angeles plane left on the old runway at the Las Vegas airport because the Courtelis's plane chose the newly finished, longer runway, only to discover that their plane sank into the tarmac. Even after a wrecker had ingeniously retrieved the plane from the hole, it could not take off until it had been checked over thoroughly. Eventually another plane took Alec and Louise Courtelis to Santa Fe and home to Miami. What was miraculous was the fact that, in landing, the plane did not hit this same soft spot, the product of improper construction.

As we reviewed the year during the next two days after graduation, we concluded that we must improve our sensitivity to students who need counseling in their social life. Despite the spring's difficulties, the resident tutors were optimistic about our ability to sharpen student perceptions and improve conditions in the dorms, especially since we would be installing new windows, new carpets, and new lights. Perhaps the impending wedding of two faculty, Bob Wade in physics from Adams, Massachusetts, and Arvindra Sant in English from the Punjab in India, gave everyone a boost. Dear Abby had already sent Arvindra a copy of her book on how to plan a wedding.

19: A FINAL GALA

Only too quickly did the summer programs begin. They coincided with deep concern in Los Angeles over the London gala scheduled for August. It was proving a challenge to find couples who would invest $25,000 to fly on the Concorde for three strenuous days in England to benefit the International Office. No doubt the suit launched by disgruntled Occidental stockholders against Hammer for his use of corporate funds on behalf of what stockholders regarded as personal charities, the new museum and the college, added to the sense of unease on Wilshire Boulevard. We had no idea how this would affect any future financing, but it was an embarrassment.

Offsetting this kind of news was a reunion to be held at Montezuma. Thirty of our own graduates returned along with another 30 who were graduates of the other UWCs. Although much of the time was spent in the inevitable comparisons of then and now, and here and there, the main topic was the environment. When the future of the UWC movement was on the agenda, there was a surprising amount of opposition to any further expansion—a position which other graduates would set forth over the next few years in answer to the possibility of new colleges. A softball game and a climb up Hermit's Peak added a bit of nostalgia to an occasion which re-emphasized the bonds which students feel toward their UWC colleges. Despite its obvious success, we concluded that we would wait until our first graduates had been out ten years before beginning biennial reunions.

In July the board met in Los Angeles. Alec Courtelis, who had been handling more and more of the corporate business of the college, was elected chairman. The college reported another year of staying within its budget. Happily there had been some dollars left over from the construction of the auditorium which paid for the dorm repairs. Otherwise the slimly attended meeting was deceptively quiet: people were waiting to see what would happen.

The American-Canadian gala did take place in August 1989, and in the end the London office received $500,000 from Hammer and a similar amount, to be spread out over five years in accordance with Canadian law, from Galen Weston. England was dry

The Prince and Princess and Armand Hammer await guests at Highgrove House in England, August 1989.

and warm. The visit to Highgrove House by bus went extremely well and featured for the last time a joint appearance of the Prince and Princess of Wales. Highgrove is the Prince's private home in Gloucestershire, 347 acres of fields and gardens which, despite the drought, were quite green. Once again Prince Charles surprised me by asking where Lu was. When I replied that she could not come because her father was seriously ill, the next evening, in yet another reception line, he asked me what I had heard from her. There had been no staff prompting.

Prince Charles and Ted Lockwood discuss affairs at Highgrove House.

Unhappily his speech at Blenheim Palace that evening was a disappointment; for he chose to dwell on the need to help the poor rural farmers of the world. Not once did he mention either of the two colleges which had organized the event; not once did he discuss the movement and its accomplishments. Nevertheless, the gala was a success and did bring some new friends and supporters for the college. It was the last such event on the grand scale, however. To those few who were carrying the responsibility of sustaining the colleges around the world, it was a wearisome task—and it had become clear that the president would no longer devote much attention and energy to the colleges, especially those offering the IB. All of these factors made the choice of a new director general ever more significant.

Ray Irani, Hammer's associate and then successor at Occidental Petroleum, chats with Princess Diana at Highgrove House.

The college reopened on August 22, 1989. For the first time we organized orientation around Montezuma, in the nearby mountains, both to save money and to provide a bit more academic emphasis to what had been primarily a wilderness experience. It also permitted us to introduce new students to community service in Las Vegas before they were asked to choose their fall activity. Prior to the opening the faculty had met in a workshop to improve their advisory skills, yet another effort to address changing student attitudes and habits. Behind these concerns was a strong feeling among the faculty that, with the cutback in the housing stipend, we needed to improve salaries and add more housing. Although these concerns were standard annual exercises, the housing situation in particular had been a legitimate worry. As an institution we needed to have faculty on campus in as great a number as possible; but not all faculty living on campus felt the responsibility which formally resident tutors had to shoulder. But by now we had concluded that those who elected to live off campus should not receive a housing stipend. Even with faculty help, we could not find a solution satisfactory to all parties.

What was a surprise was a new calendar in which we held our first national day in September, then a pre-Thanksgiving holiday in mid-October for southwest studies, permitting a warmer introduction to the Grand Canyon, and an Anti-Apartheid march from Santa Fe to Las Vegas. That march did not arouse the same public response as did a walk for hunger even though events in South Africa were front-page news. Yet, the march did bring students together; and, as one faculty member remarked, "The first five to six miles we walk for fun. The remainder we walk for our beliefs."

The semester came to a close uneventfully. Students dispersed, and we went on skeletal staffing for the holidays. On December 16, 1989, we received the sad news that Frances Hammer had died. Not only had she been a charter board member and generous donor, but she had also been a good personal friend to us and to the college. It was not a surprise given her age, but it was a harbinger of changes we knew were inevitable however unwelcome. The memorial service was confusing; for it contained far more references to her husband than to her.

Frances Hammer died in December 1989. Here she is celebrating an earlier occasion with her husband.

Later at his house, Hammer received guests and I noted that oddly very few spoke to him —preferring to cluster among themselves and thus to avoid the awkwardness of mouthing pleasantries with a man who did not welcome small talk. When I spoke with him, he immediately asked me to do something about The Prince of Wales. "Get him more involved and off that farming kick. Weston and I can't do everything."

Some things had not changed; but as a new year began, it was clear that there would be bitter battles in the court over Frances Hammer's estate, which she left entirely to her niece, Joan Weiss. Weiss in turn sued Hammer for half the value of his estate, reportedly on the grounds that Mrs. Hammer had provided the essential funding that made possible his later fortune. (Books like Epstein's recent exposé of Hammer provide details on this sad denouement.) That case would remain in the hands of lawyers until finally in 1994 it was thrown out.

For us the whole affair was ominous. We had expected some donation from Frances Hammer's estate, and we had not anticipated the series of claims that stockholders and the Weiss family would make that could conceivably entail Hammer's estate for a very long time indeed. The publicity, especially with respect to Hammer's using Oxy money to build the museum to house his art collection (estimated to be worth $300,000,000), was bad indeed and displaced what good he had done. Although we were not worried that the stockholders might succeed in forcing Hammer personally to repay what Occidental had provided the college from its corporate charitable giving, it made any conversation with prospective donors extremely awkward.

One of the issues upon which Hammer had strong opinions was Gourlay's successor in the London office. He felt it should be someone who knew how to run a business. Others wanted a UWC alumnus. Certainly it was unclear what mandate the new person would have to move ahead, especially as grumbling about the increase in contributions asked from the individual colleges had grown much louder. Albert Sloman had established a financial task force to analyze the situation not only in the International Office but also in the individual colleges so as to provide a clear notion of just what our needs were. To some extent it resembled the report Burch Ault and I had prepared five years earlier, but there was a new twist: it was to review the managerial aspects of the movement to see if there were improvements that could be made there that would enhance the financial prospects. Like any such undertaking, necessitating interviews on each campus and the compilation of extensive data, it would require more time than allotted and would not be available in time for the next International Council meeting slated for Duino, Italy, in March of 1990.

Our board had voted in November against increasing our liability from 105 English pounds to 130 pounds per student—a response which caused much consternation in London. It had always troubled us that one-half of the international office's budget depended on the fees asked from each college. Moreover, particularly irritating was the fact that they did not set the figure until after we had set our budget for the coming year. That Venezuela paid nothing initially and Waterford had a scaled-down per head fee only complicated matters. Hence, our board decided to blow the whistle on this process. At that same board meeting, we indicated that there had been 90 inquiries from prospective buyers about the Castle, but no one had bothered to visit. In an attempt to raise substantial new money, Chairman Courtelis had approached the Prince on a fund-raiser for

1990 in the States: he was turned down. On the plus side, a new board member, Jon Huntsman, chairman of the board of the Huntsman Chemical Corporation in Salt Lake City, established a $500,000 scholarship fund. The directors also agreed to authorize $150,000 for new faculty housing.

In the fall we had concluded that we should seek a new dean of studies from outside, to bring new ideas, new procedures, and presumably new perspectives on what we were doing. Neil Hunter had done well, but everyone agreed we might gain much by a new person. Our search was disappointing initially. Good candidates, at least on paper, withdrew for a variety of reasons: local schooling, remoteness, or no job for the spouse. During a winter of sparse snows, we grew increasingly concerned about the caliber of our pool. Late in the season we would select Dr. K. Don Jacobusse, a highly experienced teacher of English and head of an upper school in Santa Monica, California.

This fall had also proved difficult for the local bear population. A poor berry crop in the higher mountains drove them down to the campus for easier pickings. The black bears were sufficiently large to justify a warning about getting too close to them. One even invaded our backyard for apples; others became adept at opening the dumpsters. Then came the bats. The third floor of the administration building was their most recent choice of residence. All staff were trained in the careful removal of these creatures. In the Castle we had begun a systematic sealing off of the entry points so that we could finally clean out the remains from the estimated 2000 bats which had long made the attics their home. We discovered that there are very few "batologists" in the country; ours flew in from Wisconsin to oversee the project.

Since we could not assemble a quorum for a winter board meeting, the executive committee met in Los Angeles in April, 1990. The first action was to change the by-laws to require only two board meetings a year. The main topic of discussion was the future of the Castle. Not having found anyone seriously interested in restoring it for a compatible use, we used the winter to review other options. We evolved a plan whereby we would renovate the south-facing wing and northwest wing to house 98 students and to provide three faculty apartments. We would not attempt to fix up the ballroom area or the upper regions of the southeast wing—merely the minimal stabilization of the trusses. The interiors would require only modest redesign and largely cosmetic work. The largest investment would be in plumbing, electrical, and heating. Code would require a sprinkler system as well. The estimates were encouraging: $2,500,000. If we were able to proceed with this scaled-down version, we would tear down some of the later, architecturally unredeeming, additions made on the north side around the kitchen area.

As this all represented an effort to do some long-range planning with respect to physical facilities, we concluded that we should also present to the directors an outline of the other needs; namely, an indoor recreational center, an infirmary, and further improvements in the residence halls. To lend the exercise some precision, we began to attach figures to the overall capital-improvements program. That was formidable: some four million would be needed to accomplish these projects. As we had very little money to divert to such a program, we realized that we would need to launch a capital campaign to raise the requisite money. After a visit with Chairman Courtelis in Miami, we came up with an alternative way to move ahead, especially with the Castle. If we added 50 fully supported students, we felt we could break even and thus save drawing down on our reserves for scholarship purposes. A strong motivation for this proposal was the thought that we could thus arrest the further deterioration of the Castle. It was also a reluctant concession to those who had repeatedly asked that we find more paying students. Everyone had always agreed that it would be far better if the college were using the historic landmark rather than Marriott.

During this period Louise and Alec Courtelis played a major role, here shown with Armand Hammer at a dinner party.

At the April meeting it was agreed that we should try to raise the four million for improvements to the physical plant; but the executive committee did not think it wise to borrow money in the meanwhile to begin renovations in the Castle. Their reticence was understandable. We concluded that we would put the plan on hold and prepare for a major fund-raising event in Palm Springs, California, in 1991.

Meanwhile one person had come to campus to inspect the Castle carefully. The person claimed to have funds in a Luxembourg foundation. Having once before visited the campus and talked with admissions about enrolling her talented son, she was familiar with our programs and expressed the wish to contribute by renovating the Castle. She stayed at the local hotel, ate her meals on campus, and eventually did her laundry in the dorm. When she gave a reference on her finances that turned out to be a trailer in a park in Denver, we then undertook the delicate maneuver to disengage her from the campus. By this time everyone was either bemused or baffled by her continued presence, in the same outfit, day after day. Producing piles of papers and not inappropriate questions, she still contended that she wanted to undertake the project. Eventually security put her on a bus to Denver. We were learning that the Castle could attract many interesting potential investors but very few qualified buyers.

The mild winter and a shift in the emphasis within our service programs led to a better balance between face-to-face community service and rescue operations. Even campus service, a program we had introduced to require every first-year to do at least one full week of help around the campus in cleaning, washing vehicles, and the like, was working well. Life in the residences was quieter; and with the introduction of aerobics and circuit training as activities, there seemed to be more interest in physical exercise. It had always been an anomaly that institutions so insistent on outdoor service training should be so relaxed about other forms of physical activity.

Two other developments on campus had raised interesting possibilities. First, a conference on the environment had led to the inevitable question: should the United World Colleges take on the environment as a major plank in its programs? At one point the IB had tried to introduce a new curricular option on appropriate technology. It did not catch on. Environmental studies was another option. Given the Prince's interest in the Third World and rural farm management, some felt a new emphasis on environmental issues would be shrewd. That did not catch fire either.

What did appear to offer some practical returns for the colleges was the appointment of former students as instructional interns. We had brought Sandra Thomas ('84) from New Zealand when she finished her history studies there to help handle an overload in that field. She remained to cover for Ivan Mustain when he took a leave to study Korean history. Similarly in biology we had invited another New Zealander, Nina Stupples ('85), to assist. Such individuals could bring fresh hands to the service programs as well. They served as models for students and, as someone ruefully remarked, offset the aging process in the faculty. The plan seemed sufficiently promising that the college expanded its use of former students in various fields over the subsequent years. For once visas were not a problem since it constituted a training program in the eyes of the Immigration Service.

While we were seeking solutions to the Castle, everyone was wondering what solution would be found for the International Office. With Gourlay's departure in March, the question had become very important. But what was most disheartening was the widespread criticism of the London office, much justified and some the product of a distrust that had been allowed to fester. With new colleges proposed in Hong Kong and Norway, with the question of Bulgaria once again before the board, with a working party investigating the possibilities of sites in Nigeria and Ghana for another rural training UWC, there was a clear need for leadership at the center or a substantial reorganization. When no one was nominated prior to the International Council assembling in Italy, the office called in a search firm to help. In this regard the financial task force report could be significant.

The International Council meeting in April at the College of the Adriatic had good attendance. Courtelis concluded that he should attend and visit another UWC to see what others did. He was impressed by the site in Duino, amused at their having problems with a Castle also, and discouraged by the absence of leadership on the International Board. All the heads agreed to spend some time separately together, a pleasant and useful exercise involving as always too much food from both the Italians and Slovenes. Officially the meetings were a success since over 30 national committee chairpersons were present; but it did not lead to any increase in contributions from them or to a reorganization of the office. Again people approached me about being available for the director general's position; again I reminded them that we had critical issues to resolve at the college and, with Hammer's advancing age, I could not leave. That would prove prescient, but it was also easy to say because it had become clear to me and Courtelis that

At a meeting at Duino, Italy, all the UWC heads met, conferred, and then relaxed. Left to right front row: Andrew Stuart (Atlantic) Lu Lockwood, David Sutcliffe (Adriatic), Ted Lockwood with Kathleen Watson in the foreground, Enid Eyeington, Anne Macoun, Elizabeth Sutclifee; standing: Dick Eyeington (Swaziland), Tony Macoun (Canada), Pat Stuart, Luis Marcano (Venezuela) and his wife. Taking the picture was David Watson (Singapore).

many members of the International Board held the heads in low regard and could not envision one of them serving in this capacity—not even David Sutcliffe who obviously knew more about the movement than anyone else. Only years later would they turn to Sutcliffe for help.

Two occasions in Italy were particularly entertaining. In the very formal council chambers in the city of Trieste, the Prince made his customary pitch for the movement to help solve poverty in the Third World by founding more agricultural colleges. I was asked to pose the first question. We both grinned because I could only inquire as to whether solutions did not require the kind of political sophistication which the IB UWCs were best situated to provide. The other encounter with Prince Charles occurred in a crowded reception at the Hotel Europa near the end of the conference. He came up to Lu and me and immediately said: "You do a lot about politics in Montezuma. I just don't understand why they don't talk about political action here in Duino." No doubt an unfair observation, it did cheer us up on a gray afternoon.

Graduation on May 25, 1990, was spectacular. The tent was magnificently decorated as an English garden scene. Nearly 900 people came to lunch. As the Kluge auditorium could not accommodate everyone, television monitors were set up in the lobby. Congressman Vanderjagt from Michigan was the speaker for this occasion. Since he was returning to Canada, Bruce Ives in economics handed the diplomas to Hammer. One

Students surround Hammer at his last commencement, May 1990.

hundred and six students graduated. Representing them was Rachel Ozer from Canada. In his remarks, the last he would deliver at a graduation, Hammer noted: "The most important lesson you have learned, however, is that although you came together from far-flung points on the globe, you soon came to realize that you and your classmates shared common bonds that transcend the boundaries of nationalism, ideology, and creed. You are joined together today more by your hopes and dreams than separated by your differences."

The ceremony turned out to be longer this year since Hammer had brought with him friends from Soka University in Japan. He hoped that we might develop some joint projects and thus garner some new support for the college. The greetings, when combined with translations, took longer than they deserved; but it offered some promise that, alas, did not materialize when Courtelis and Hammer were in Japan a month later. Sometimes, oddly enough, Hammer did not remember that people were out to win his favor by giving as little in return as possible. To everyone at the ceremony Hammer did not seem well; for he had to sit on a cushion and accept assistance in walking to the podium. But his voice was strong and his enthusiasm undiminished.

The year had ended well, and there was some hope that, given a bit more time, we would surmount our traditional problems. Certainly we hoped that as we entered the second decade of our history, we would have conquered our growing pains.

20: THE DEATH OF THE FOUNDER

The summer was a busy one. By 1990 we had learned how to attract good programs, turn a good profit, and win new friends. In particular, our IB workshops were the best in the west and attracted 265 participants. The new dean arrived and he concentrated on becoming familiar with the academic policies and programs. There was an uptick in the community as we looked forward to a new class of students.

The major event of the summer, however, took place in London. The executive committee would interview three candidates for the position as director general. As neither Hammer nor Courtelis could attend, I went to London House. A close vote installed Mr. Bill Bentley, vice-chairman of Royal Shell for European operations, as the new officer. At the same time the report from the financial task force became available. A long and flawed summary probably read by few, the report did identify some changes it felt would improve operations. The executive committee should be enlarged and assume full powers since the International Board was ill-equipped to act and too large to work effectively. In turn that committee accepted the report's recommendation that there be an operations committee consisting of the heads which would meet with the director general twice a year to review operations and to make recommendations to the executive committee. Kingman Brewster's idea, in which I had fully concurred and then argued for, came into being. Its first task would be to suggest the most efficient and cost-effective way in which the central office could operate in serving the colleges as well as the movement as a whole. Finally, it seemed that we might, with the help of a new director general, move ahead constructively on the many issues before the UWCs. As for fund-raising, the issue which had led to the creation of the financial task force, there was a recognition that the first need was for each college to cultivate to the maximum its own constituencies. Beyond that there were merely exhortations to find new monies for the movement. In a sense, the report was reassuring: no UWC was in desperate straits even though both Swaziland and Venezuela were short on funds. The report did not comment on the fact that no college had adequate reserves against unanticipated emergencies. Finally, the report sidestepped the issue of scholarships versus parental contributions.

What would happen next depended largely on how Bentley went about his task. He soon indicated that he would visit each of the UWCs and meet individually with each of us before he prepared any recommendations. It would be February of 1991 before we would confront various options.

Meanwhile, the daily business went forward in Montezuma. Despite Courtelis's and my efforts, the directors did not respond to the capital campaign. Each visit or telephone call had a familiar ending: "I am just not in a position to contribute anything more. You really need to find some new sources." It is true that some had been particularly generous and their response was understandable. Others were tired or had been approached by too many other charities. The conclusion was unavoidable: we would have to postpone the capital campaign. Courtelis and I estimated it would take three to five years to raise this money for improvements to the physical plant— since we had to approach people about scholarship support as well. Hammer turned a deaf ear.

To put these matters in perspective, I had written a long letter to the members of the board. Clearly the program had been a success; the college was highly regarded in academic circles. The co-curricular programs had improved each year; and probably this UWC was more politically active than any other. The faculty had remained strong. Operational routines were well established although they needed codification against a future when not everyone would remember how things had been handled. Surprisingly to many the Montezuma site had served the college well. Las Vegas had proved very hospitable and had been a good location for services. The gaunt structure on the hill was the most obvious disappointment. As I concluded, "Reflection on what has happened since 1981 quite properly brings a warm glow, and we are indeed grateful to our benefactors for our good fortune. But the pioneering days are over and we have reached a plateau . . ."

These matters came before the board on September 12, 1990. By this time we had 33 directors. We reported that we had enrolled a total of 202 students from 70 countries, including our first representative from Czechoslovakia, soon to become the Czech Republic. We had increased tuition to $12,500 as other UWCs made their adjustments and the dollar slid a bit. No one was particularly happy to hear that plans for new colleges in Hong Kong and Norway were moving forward, and especially not that the movement might start another agricultural college in Ghana.

No doubt some of the disenchantment derived from the imbalance we faced in the new budget for the coming year. We had made strong cutbacks, but that did not deflect the argument for more full-paying students. Again Irani emphasized the need for each member to contribute, where possible, $100,000 annually. Approving this in principle, the board then instructed the president to identify which members could afford that levy. There was agreement also to seek new members but no attempt to review other matters at this meeting, particularly the matters which the education committee had considered.

For that committee I had summarized the various goals which the institution had set itself. As a United World College we were not trying to duplicate what the normal educational system provided. We wished to be distinctive. We wanted to be more than an extraordinarily good IB school. The only way the investment others had made could be justified, I argued, was for this small institution to be distinguished in unusual ways. With an exuberance that comes to the typewriter occasionally, the paper set forth a new version of the aims we felt made the college significant:

The constructive use of power
Awareness of the world political situation
The understanding of complexity
The honing of the mind
The maintenance of a truly international perspective
A search to improve the human condition
A rigorous academic program
Freedom of inquiry ["Freedom in the mind can become freedom for the mind"]
Cultural interaction
Personal growth, including the study of values
Respect for the environment and
A commitment to action.

As the committee talked, and subsequently the faculty also, we were trying to identify those aspirations, and attitudes, that could become so pervasive on the campus that we might over time hope to make a constructive contribution to education and society. These could become, in effect, the criteria according to which we measured our various programs. And like so many such statements of goals, there was a summary paragraph that is included here since it became part of a prolonged UWC debate on the aims of the movement:

"In summary, this college strives to address persistently the political issues, the prospects before us in the late 20th century. We hope students sense the complexity of modern civilization and sort out what is manageable from what will take longer to resolve. In addressing the human condition, we seek to lessen the conflict we face in our search for a future secure for all mankind. We want to improve the environment we inhabit. In acting compassionately and sensitively, we hope to sustain the freedom so essential to the growth of the individual and the richness of society."

We felt that these avowedly moral mandates could distinguish our effort from that of other private institutions. We did need to hold high the idealism which had led to the founding of such colleges if we were to maintain our distinctiveness.

Another year, our ninth, had begun on campus. The Kellogg Foundation had provided funding for extending conflict resolution training to the other colleges. With the situation in the Persian Gulf, coffee table discussion and the Friday night world affairs sessions became more popular and heated. Once again, students were prone to criticize the United States. We had always contented that situating a UWC in one of the Superpowers (however limited the meaning of that term) was different from being located in Victoria or Duino. A conference on the relationship between religion and politics focused on Islam, the Irish question, and Latin America. Of course, the unrest in Eastern Europe sparked a lot of conversation as well, and the growing violence and rising poverty in Sub-Saharan Africa was yet another concern on student minds.

On December 10, at around ten in the evening, we received a telephone call that Dr. Hammer had passed away that evening at age 92. He had attended the board meeting in September; we had talked twice on the phone; but for nearly two months no one had heard from him. Not even the staff in Los Angeles were aware of how serious his illness was; and, although Dr. Rosamaria Durazo had become a member of the board and had been serving as Hammer's closest medical adviser, we had known virtually nothing about his deteriorating condition. Everyone had become so accustomed to his involvement with the United World Colleges that, as Prince Charles remarked, "I had somehow grown to believe he was almost indestructible."

Tributes flowed from everywhere. For the moment anyway, his controversial life yielded to the recognition that he had accomplished astonishing things during his many different careers. President George Bush summarized many of those sentiments: "Armand Hammer's memory will long be enshrined in the hearts of his many friends, including world leaders in government and the private sector, and in the institutions to which he gave so much of his time, energy and resources. He will be sorely missed." And as Sir Ian Gourlay was to say at London's Grosvenor Chapel on January 21, 1991: "They say that no one is indispensable. Maybe this is so. But some are irreplaceable, and the Doctor surely stands securely in that category, touching as he did, across the whole span of this century, the lives of countless people from diverse countries, in his oft-expressed desire to leave the world a better place.

"If in life we are in the midst of death, and the events of the [Gulf War] grimly remind us that in peace we are in the midst of war, that peace is a delicate flower requiring constant nurturing, and that we have to be resolute in its protection. Armand Hammer himself . . . sewed deals together across ideological barriers, parleying with heads of states and bringing his compassion to bear at scenes of world disasters like those in Mexico, Armenia, and Chernobyl." Later that view would be severely challenged by authors like Edward Epstein.

The funeral service in Los Angeles was a deliberately small affair at which, indecorously, the speakers from different faiths all claimed his soul. No one knew who would claim his estate: that would come later. On January 4 in Los Angeles in the courtyard of the new museum just completed behind Occidental's headquarters, there was a memorial service. Four of our former students were asked to make remarks: Offi Susser from Israel, Ricardo Zemella of Venezuela, Leroy Lim from Singapore, and Wong Chau Chi from Hong Kong. Again the praises were sung, but by now speculation had begun about his estate; and Courtelis and I used the occasion to meet with his lawyers to discuss what would happen. In a last conversation I had had with Hammer, he had once again assured me that the college would receive one-half of his holdings in Oxy, approximately $15,000,000. Then the lawyers explained that he had elected to separate his estate into two parts. One part was to take care of his outstanding debts, such as an unfinished pledge to the Metropolitan Museum of Art. Once those bequests were executed (but not including any gift to the college), the balance of the estate would go to the Armand Hammer Foundation. What had become clear was that whatever amount remained in his estate after payment of debts would be smaller than the public had assumed.

There were other curious provisions. The college was to receive $100,000 and his papers and memorabilia. This gift was a surprise since a year earlier Hammer had signed a document at a reception in Washington conveying his papers to the Library of Congress. We had no place to house the collection; and, after Lu and I had inspected the four large rooms in which they were stored, we concluded that we would have to add a storeroom on the back of the auditorium to handle the transfer. We did so, but neither the papers nor the money have come to the college. In one sense that was fortunate since it would require a substantial job to sort, index, and then organize the materials so that others could use the collection, which includes old Russian clocks, pieces of jade, innumerable pictures of Hammer in various situations, in addition to his papers. In another sense, it represents yet another promise broken.

What was clear was that the Foundation would handle matters, including a basket full of court challenges. Curiously, after having served for years as the trustees of the Foundation, Morrie Moss and Arthur Groman had been "retired" in September of 1990 and Hammer's grandson, Michael, and his wife, Dru Hammer, became the Trustees who would now review matters. Courtelis, who had played a major role in gaining from President Bush a pardon for Hammer's illegal contributions to candidate Richard Nixon, was shocked by these provisions.

We all knew that an era had come to an end and that we now faced a critical situation at the college, particularly in view of Hammer's having failed to provide any additional funding. It was indeed a tragedy in that what might be a time for genuine outpourings of thanks for a remarkable man became edged with unseemly controversy over

Michael and Dru Hammer, who became executors of the Armand Hammer Foundation in 1990.

his legacy. His art had immediately become the property of Occidental Petroleum to prevent its being seized by anyone else and as compensation for the money the company had advanced to build the museum, some $90,000,000. Mrs. Hammer's niece, Joan Weiss, had sent police to Hammer's home immediately following his death, in the early hours of the morning, to prevent anything being removed; and she shortly thereafter reaffirmed her decision to seek half of the estate and half the value of the art collection. (It was tempting to remark that this could happen only in Los Angeles.) Of immediate concern also was the relationship which the college might or might not enjoy with Occidental Petroleum.

Armand Hammer had made the college possible; and we always knew, while he was still alive, that we could turn to him. He might not concur with what we recommended, but he would not let the institution fail. Now we were missing that assurance. We were entering a transition. There were innumerable questions for which we lacked the answers.

21: THE TRANSITION BEGINS

In January of 1991 the transition to a series of new arrangements began. The first questions revolved around our relations with the Los Angeles office. Did we still need such an office? How many board members from that area would wish to remain involved with the college since so many had joined because of Hammer? How should we best proceed with the Armand Hammer Foundation and with the trust?

Of course, the answers would depend in part on the response of Occidental Petroleum and Michael Hammer, Armand's grandson and now executor for both the Foundation and Hammer's estate. I prepared an analysis for each of the key questions. Perhaps the easiest was the continuation of a separate office in Los Angeles. We had profited from its providing excellent publications at no cost to the Montezuma budget. It had established contacts, especially among Hammer's friends, that we could not duplicate. On the other hand, we confused others, and sometimes ourselves, by having two offices. Running all public relations from Montezuma would reduce the cost substantially, but ironically it would add to the college's budget by some $75,000.

The decision was made in Los Angeles: on February 14th the office closed and all the materials relating to the college were shipped in 273 boxes to New Mexico. We had appreciated the help Carolyn Walker, Florence Ajamian, Shelly Von Berg, Karen Leja and her associates had long provided, but in many ways it made far better sense to bring home as many of the operations as possible at what was obviously an opportune time.

Curiously though, and fortunately, there appeared to be no move by Oxy to disengage itself, but there were many questions concerning future relations that needed clarification. At times we in Montezuma had been exasperated by the financial strings by which we were attached to Los Angeles, but we could not be ungrateful for the support which the corporation and Ray Irani in particular had provided. It had been indispensable; yet, there could be no gainsaying that this connection had hampered some of our fund-raising, puzzled board members, and raised critical questions in our accreditation. In short, it was an important element in any long-range financial planning. Again, in discussions with Irani, Chairman Courtelis and I discovered a genuine commitment to assist what most regarded as Hammer's finest memorial. We arranged for the next meeting of the board to take place in Los Angeles.

That meeting on February 13 handled the necessary routine matters, including a tentative budget for the next year, but was dominated by speculation concerning the future of the college. Fortunately the Lounsbery Foundation had given us a grant to help with seeking new supporters. The board also concluded that we should meet at least once a year at Montezuma and also consider a convenient location like Dallas where people could assemble near the airport. Participation had been a problem and would only grow worse. Therefore, the chairman and I wrote each member to inquire whether he or she would continue to serve and be able to participate in our deliberations. It was a risky move, but essential if we were to know how active a board would remain available to perform the necessary fiduciary responsibilities. Some were willing to remain active; others did not respond; and soon still others indicated that they were resigning. There were no surprises. Courtelis and I talked about rewriting the by-laws and reconstituting the board, but there were enough other concerns to preempt that move for the moment.

Development was another major concern. Hammer had been pivotal in both identifying prospects for us to approach and in finding funds from friends but he had prevented any systematic approach. In fact, he had raised false hopes more times than not by promising us instead the profits from prospective business deals, all of which fell through, such as the Korean truck project, TV coverage of Russian sports, and proceeds from his autobiography. Happily, Courtelis had played an important role in trying to find other constituents and in analyzing out how we could effectively mount a campaign. Our discussions at his home in Miami or at a desk in Los Angeles had a familiar ring. "The Hammer name is no longer an asset," he would observe, "but we are stuck with it. The foundation has its hands full with both major and minor lawsuits aimed at depleting its resources and claiming whatever is left of Hammer's estate. The leeches are already at work. We're stuck with having to work with what we have, minimizing our deficits until we get some new money, and finding some new angels." Courtelis had no illusions despite his optimism about the college. We had begun a review of our experience with foundations and the answer was obvious: very few would provide assistance to an institution which, in their view, Hammer had guaranteed to underwrite. We did not have access to state or federal funding. Burch Ault had rejoined us in a consulting role, thanks to the Lounsbery Foundation once again. We had long felt that we should involve wealthy, prominent New Mexicans in the enterprise, and Ault and I laid out a list of those whom we would approach over the year.

But there were few who could make substantial contributions initially since, as so often happens in asking charitably minded individuals, they would have to discontinue giving to something else. Cultivation required time. We also felt we should identify some key people in Texas and Arizona, if possible, since they might have a stronger tie to the area than those in New York or Los Angeles. In short, all of us concurred: individuals were the key. The question haunting us was whether we would have the time to achieve these goals, given our continuing imbalances and limited reserves. Could we make it through the next two years? Courtelis and I were convinced we could although the evidence to support that hope was skimpy.

There was a curious coincidence at this point. As we debated how we would face an uncertain future, the movement as a whole was beginning to debate how it should position itself at the beginning of a new decade and a new century. It was to be the major topic for a meeting of the heads and the new director general, Bill Bentley, who had arranged for the group to take over a small hotel north of Henley-on-Thames. We had long proposed gathering away from London at a spot that would permit walking but not other appointments. That we had a blizzard during our two-day conference that February reinforced the commitment, soaked the walking shoes, and increased the bar bills. Bentley wanted to know what gripes we had. Our forbearance was remarkable and misleading; for by then the heads felt that we could take over some of the admissions/national committee functions on a regional basis and do a better job at no special cost. Everyone was also uneasy about the cost of the alumni organization (Network) and its progress in compiling information that would not only show how distinguished UWC graduates had become but also how willing and able they would be to support the colleges. We did not spare the director general further cautions about agricultural UWCs. It was useful but inconclusive. Yet, one sensed that Bentley would not let it lie there—just as he would not abide for long our failure to pay the difference between last year's levy on the college and this year's request. It may have been the low point in relations between the center and the colleges — even though we felt encouraged by Bentley.

At Montezuma there was a mood of uncertainty among the faculty and staff. Presidential reassurances about the future were not as persuasive as they would like. It also became increasingly unclear whether the new dean would remain beyond one year. And such proved to be the case. Fortunately we found a very good successor in Barbara Johnson, then running a large school in Cairo, Egypt. The discomfort had been real but short-lived, and I am convinced that the situation would never have seemed so inauspicious had we not been struggling with the bigger question of what would happen to the college now that Hammer was dead.

Of course, the answer was that little had changed. The graduating class was strong and would achieve excellent results. Admissions for the fall of 1991 appeared very strong indeed. Conflict resolution had proved to be popular and effective as a special program.

A mild winter had given some respite to the search and rescue crews.

New Mexico's Governor Bruce King addressed the 1991 graduates in his inimitable style as the 94 students prepared to head on to universities. Of course, some students and faculty who had complained about previous commencements being expensive and meaningless LA "shows" now complained about the scaled-down festivities. Gone was the great spread of white canvas. Gone was the press conference. Gone also was the sumptuous buffet, replaced by what we called our "Tiffany sack lunches." For some reason the baguettes did not have the same appeal as roast beef. To honor his grandfather, Michael Hammer spoke briefly, saying that the college was "one of his greatest achievements and brought him the most joy." In many ways the student speaker, Ian Chisholm from Canada, best summarized what it meant to be at Montezuma: "The UWC pushed us to find our absolute limits; emotionally, physically, socially, academically and in our ideas . . . Today we will walk in different directions, but towards the same place." We also recognized our first official retirement when Nathaniel Mann stepped down from teaching math since 1982.

At a meeting after graduation, it was necessary to reestablish a sense of community among faculty and staff; for the year had taken its toll of good humor and courtesy. There had been too many instances of a lack of professionalism; there were too many chips on too many shoulders. We all sought to redress whatever grievances existed, or were perceived to exist. It had always been one of the strengths of the institution that we could reestablish a sense of community after disappointments. Yet, it was apparent that the passage of time had sapped the spirit of the earlier years among those who had worked so hard for so long. The college was aging; the college was moving in a new direction inevitably; and the spirit of adventure which had marked the eighties was yielding to a reassessment.

That reevaluation of the United World College experience would dominate the international discussions and the next meeting of the board. The summer went by quickly, marked once again by an outstanding and overly subscribed IB workshop in August. One surprise this summer was the amount of rain we received. Not only were the customary barbecues dampened and the trips to the Santa Fe Opera wet, but the Gallinas also rose to spectacular heights and swept away the ford we used to enter the campus.

22: THE TENTH YEAR

The tenth year opened full of enthusiasm. The new dean, Barbara Johnson, welcomed the 104 entering students. This time we had more girls than boys. The only disappointment was the failure of some countries to continue their scholarship support. Despite increasing the comprehensive fee by $1,000 we did not receive more tuition income. A summary of the admissions effort provides some clues as to the source of students and the continuing appeal of the program. We had received over 1,000 requests within the United States for applications but only 150 forms were completed, a surprise until we remembered that once informed, many students discovered that it was not what they had assumed or could effectively pursue. Seventy-five were interviewed; 27 came to Montezuma and eight went to the other UWCs. Twenty-two states in this country were represented, to join the 72 countries. Of the 27 U.S. first years, two were Afro-American, three were Hispanic, one was Vietnamese and one Native American. Six students were full-paying and the rest needed on average 60% scholarship support. The Hugh O'Brien Youth Ambassador program continued to account for a third of the applications, but now alumni and friends were the largest source of inquiries. Obviously numbers did not provide an answer to our success; that lay in the strong reputation we had so quickly built and which would remain critical for the future.

In looking around the campus in the fall, it was gratifying to see how large some of the trees planted ten years earlier had grown, how the new auditorium now blended into the landscape, and how lush the grass had grown. There was an irresistible charm to the location, often captured by our art instructor, Colin Lanham, in his watercolors so gladly received as recognition for long and devoted service when faculty left.

In September the International Office organized another retreat, this time at Jesus College at Oxford University. The heads gathered, argued, and listened to other staff and alumni give their views of what made the UWCs distinguished and different. Bentley was insistent on our identifying just what makes us so great. In addition, what were the important values which we sought to convey? Beyond the obvious excellence of the academic program and the selective, diverse student body, we had some problems identifying what really makes the UWCs different. We talked about cultural sensitivity, the service ethic, the sense of personal responsibility, the cooperative spirit which infused so much that occurs on the campuses. When the conversation veered toward leadership, alumni dissented just as they had in 1985.

But some were willing to consider political sophistication a good goal. Among values, dedication to freedom, justice, and peace had sufficient resonance and enough meaning in practice to be acceptable on the masthead. There was a curious reluctance to sense a moral mandate as central to our mission, for example, a commitment to improving the human condition in whatever ways each might find possible. In keeping with the political correctness of the times, people did not want to sound preachy. In one sense that was understandable since, as many would claim, an "old-boy" network still prevailed among the senior staff within the UWC movement; in another sense it was a disappointment that we could not engender a bit more of the crusading zeal that had launched the movement in the first place.

Perhaps of greater moment were the discussions about organization and practices. Again Bentley challenged standing assumptions. He argued that we needed a corporate image and central direction. We had no sales pitch and very modest public relations. Experts in PR confirmed his contention but could not persuade us we needed a Coca-Cola campaign. They did agree with my contention that we were operating as a loose confederation without a clear sense of direction; hence, it was very difficult to come up with a common approach to PR, fund-raising, or corporate destiny. In trying to agree on that direction, we ended up accepting the notion that we should consider restructuring on lines of a holding company with three major divisions under it: the IB colleges, the agricultural management programs, and the special short programs like that in the Andes or on Malta. We would form something called a United World Trust, and it could invite other similarly-minded operations to join in over time. It was part of a growing sentiment that we needed something more, something new if we were to remain in the forefront of international school programs. Thinking of the plans for the Scandinavian UWC in Norway, we discussed both the Red Cross and Habitat for Humanity as organizations with which we might develop both special projects and a third-year option. Bentley interjected that any program like the UWCs must grow if it is to prosper. We could not agree, however, on how large we wanted to become for the simple reason that we felt there were too many problems in the present operations that needed attention first.

When we turned to finances, Bentley did not conceal his horror at the fragility of the whole program. He challenged the network to get on its own feet and to provide support to the colleges from their graduates. Again a clear mission and a corporate identity would make raising money around the world more effective, he argued. No one disagreed, but no one felt particularly optimistic because the track record was unimpressive. Again it seemed that we would not make much progress as a movement until we had re-established a strong sense of cooperation among all the elements, especially with the central office. As had happened in the past, we spent a few minutes relocating the central office to other parts of the world. Then surfaced the argument on behalf of full scholarship support as a truly distinguishing feature of the UWCs. Singapore dissented immediately; but Bentley had anticipated this argument and on one of his charts bluntly indicated that it was not possible to do without parental contributions and survive. By this time London had developed some ideas for fund-raising: these received polite consideration.

The discussion which might have led to some fundamental revisions tapered off. It had been helpful; it had led to some clarifications on admissions, publicity, and the like; but there was no sense that we were on the move toward a bright new future. The meeting did not provide the new director general with the mandate he had wanted, and it did not take much foresight to anticipate he might resign in due course. And he did primarily because he received no support for his efforts from the International Board and clearly only limited enthusiasm from other constituencies.

I was disappointed because I had hoped we might change the mood toward the International Office, perhaps recapture some enthusiasm from Prince Charles (who was now threatening to resign) and restate our mission in a fashion that would help us in Montezuma get through this period of anxiety quickly and optimistically.

That was not to be the case. Ironically, during a conference on UWC goals this same fall of 1991, our third attempt to use a conference to acquaint new students and faculty with the purposes to which we were committed, we discovered yet again the impatience of younger people with the inability of the movement to coordinate its activities more effectively. Students wanted to do more after they graduated by taking a third year serving elsewhere in the world. One of our own graduates, Francisco "Chico" Ferreira (Brazil 1986), teaching economics at Pearson College, reiterated his conviction that improving the human condition was less daunting and less remote than seeking world peace. He warned against excessive expectations.

In a quite different vein, by this time Alec Courtelis and I had decided against changing the by-laws and creating a new board of trustees. We proposed to concentrate on finding new members to replace the eight directors who had resigned after Hammer's death and to study our finances and fund-raising prospects yet again. At this time we held in cash and securities $22,700,000. We had finished the previous year with slightly less than two million in our reserve fund. The outlook for May 1992 was a further reduction of that reserve by $700,000.

The refrain was familiar: we needed to increase our funds substantially. I had already concluded that I should spend more time meeting with board members to engender greater support, and in locating new prospects. To that end we promoted Barbara Johnson to vice-president for academic affairs so that she could handle more of the daily business while I was away. Business operations under Al Romero were running smoothly, and my own office functioned well in my absences due to Diane Nieto's efforts. We opened an inexpensive office in Santa Fe where I could concentrate on development. We studied all the foundations yet again and began the slow process of trying to engage their interest. We talked with people in Santa Fe and elsewhere to develop a list of possible new members.

When the board assembled at Montezuma on October 18, 1991, ironically half of those attending were members of the U.S. Committee in New York. Relations had improved considerably after Hammer's death. Only Alec Courtelis, Michael and Dru Hammer, and two new members, Neil Chur, head of a Buffalo corporation building and managing nursing homes, and Rosamaria Durazo, Hammer's personal physician during his last years whom he had appointed to the board at the last moment, represented what was left of the original board. I reported about the situation in London and the fact that Prince Charles would soon step down and that we would also soon need a new chairman for the International Board.

Our own situation did not add cheer to the occasion. Even our ability to stay within budget, despite taking over the functions of the Los Angeles office, did not dispel legitimate concerns about the future since in the end we could not avoid unfavorable imbalances. After ten years we were still caught in a fiscal squeeze-play.

We did use the occasion to present a series of proposals for the future. Called "A Program for the Future," it sought to identify the essential elements we needed: a mission, supporters, leadership from the board, and a plan of action. We laid out our needs, largely financial assistance for scholarships and endowment, but also for capital improvements over the balance of the decade. We reviewed the sources of support for this program and again came to individuals as the key. When Hammer had been alive, it had not been possible to take the time for such a discussion. Now it was critical that we lay out the appropriate background and then at the next meeting move to an implementation strategy. The members responded well, and they enjoyed walking around the campus and meeting with the students.

The fall had two national days, European and Asian. There was no sign that either energy or enthusiasm had slackened: these events remained highlights, especially with the stage of the new auditorium available for lavish shows in the evening. Theater had also gained from the move into better quarters. A performance of the Mozart Requiem in collaboration with New Mexico Highlands University was a superb demonstration of what was possible even in a smaller community like Las Vegas. Life had been as busy as ever. Early snows and intemperate weather increased the number of searches during the fall. Thanksgiving seemed but the prelude to Christmas. When the departures occurred in December, we were impressed by the numbers flying back to their homelands. Was it the sign of growing affluence among the students, or merely a reflection of the temporary recession in the United States making cheaper fares available? We were to hear more rhetoric about economic conditions the coming year as the presidential election heated up and the Ross Perot charts puzzled both veterans and newcomers to American politics.

In January we reviewed on campus the situation at the college in preparation for the board meeting at the Dallas airport in February. There was continuing concern not only about finances but also about the wider issues before the movement. We had accepted the new statement of our mission which London had produced:

> "Through international education, shared experience and community service, United World Colleges enable young people to become responsible citizens, politically and environmentally aware, committed to the ideals of peace, justice, understanding, and cooperation, and to the implementation of these ideals through action and personal example."

But we had limited confidence that the new director general, Jeremy Varcoe, a former British foreign service expert, could foster fresh enthusiasm within the movement. He had had extensive diplomatic experience and planned to visit Montezuma along with other campuses to acquaint himself firsthand with what was happening. His visit was reassuring in its compliments but divisive in its insistence that the movement had to expand its agricultural training programs. At our Oxford meeting the previous fall, it was clear that Simon Bolivar still did not fit comfortably into the movement and that Singapore was increasingly critical of getting so little in return for its annual levy. Galen Weston, chairman of the board at Pearson College in Canada, had talked with me about this situation and as a key player on the International Board, he was wondering what to do about the international chairmanship, which he would not accept. We were to return to this issue later in the year.

It was the first time we were to try a board meeting at an airport. Since Occidental had offices in Dallas, it permitted persons like Irani to combine company business with a meeting of the college's directors. We had been fortunate to add James Taylor, another Oxy executive and parent of Karen, an '87 graduate, to the board in anticipation of his pending retirement to live in Santa Fe. Louisa Sarofim from Houston, president of the Brown Foundation, attended the meeting as a new director, along with Jon Huntsman, Jr., ambassador-designate to Singapore. Unhappily Sherry Lansing had just resigned because of the pressure of business at Paramount studios. Everyone understood that we were reaching a critical point in the finances of the college. We had frozen salaries, not that such a move was so unusual at this time in education. Many school systems and universities were cutting back and instituting tough austerity measures. America was not in an ebullient mood.

When we announced that our deficit for the next year would be $683,000 and that we would not have enough reserves to pay off faculty and staff should we need to, Irani took umbrage and declared such a projection unacceptable. It was an encouraging upbraiding because it demonstrated both his personal concern and Occidental's continued presence and possible additional support. Michael Hammer, however, indicated that the Foundation could not help in any substantial fashion because it had to keep all its funds available in the event of adverse rulings in the court cases it still faced. Discussion led to the proposal that we increase our tuition income by taking in 35 U.S. students, with special emphasis on their ability to pay. We had flirted with that idea frequently, but neither the admissions pool nor our experience encouraged us to move that direction. We would try now.

The board agreed that each director should approach three new people who could help the college. (That did not happen except with two directors.) The president would visit with all directors not attending to ascertain their level of interest. In executive session we reviewed the personnel reductions which we planned to make to cut some $150,000 from the 1992-93 budget. I would go on half-pay and less than full-time; Lu would retire from running alumni relations; security would lose one person along with the business office. We would use an intern in the math vacancy. All these moves, hardly desirable, would make a difference but would not solve the deficit. We would have to press for more money from national committees and hope the U.S. Committee could rally enough money to cover those attending other UWCs, a saving of some $200,000.

That did not happen either, but it reminded others of our need. We were asked to mount a more aggressive development campaign. As usual, people did not understand the time it takes to cultivate new sources of support. In one sense the meeting had been worthwhile: the business got done and people became involved. In another sense, it illustrated the weakness of meeting in a place like Dallas: the directors did not see the students and did not have time to get to know one another better—something which could easily offend a newcomer. In short, it lacked the kind of enjoyment that the Montezuma setting could provide.

When I reported these board decisions to the faculty and staff at a dinner in the campus center, there was an understandable gasp. [We had been holding periodic dinners for faculty and staff in the campus center since we had ample funds from the Sasakawa fund for precisely these purposes.] For the most part, they accepted the challenge we had received; some even admitted that they could hardly go anywhere else and have such good support and superior students. Senior faculty like Hannah and Dan Tyson took on the challenge. We had, in effect, made the transition about which we were all so worried.

We had come to grips with those further, stringent measures which we had to take, and the sky had not fallen. We were accepting a certain leanness that was necessary for the future. We all knew what had to be done. There was one disconcerting question: was I going to remain as president or did the move to half-pay and less than full time presage my retirement? Although I had been thinking about leaving, and quite properly so, I did not know how to answer that question other than to say that I would remain until the financial future of the institution had been assured.

Two other steps offered some hope of closing the gap on the roughly $500,000 shortfall we could anticipate each year for at least another few years. Following the board meeting, I had gone to Los Angeles to meet with Ray Irani and Michael Hammer to recommend that we use the foundation and trust to assure that the next two years of imbalances would not become severe drains on our reserves. The Armand Hammer Trust agreed to my request that it advance 100 per cent of its income each year. That would add $200,000 to our income even though in prospect the rate of return would begin to decline as a consequence of the lowering of interest rates generally. At the same meeting Michael Hammer agreed to distribute from the foundation $250,000 for each of the next two years even though certain legal claims outstanding might conceivably intervene, especially if the sale of paintings from the Hammer collection could not be used to offset those claims. Combined with our savings, these moves gave us time while we sought the requisite new donors.

We had also concluded that it was mandatory to commit more money and effort to that development campaign. As someone who had always been troubled by the rate of return from development offices (knowing that some organizations spent fifty cents on expenses for every dollar raised), I was not anxious to move in that direction; but we had little choice. But what was more vexing was a sense that, no matter what resolutions we took at a meeting, we did not have a board sufficiently committed to the institution—"in love with the place"—that we could mount an effective campaign to erase worries about the future.

From the beginning the board had responded as a group accustomed to acquiescing in corporate plans without ever grasping what a vast difference there is in serving on a non-profit board with ultimate fiduciary as well as legal responsibility. We were now forced to ask people to become active without their having had the necessary training. In numbers the board had shrunk to 21, of whom at least seven were inactive. John Kluge had resigned; Arthur and Miriam Groman could no longer participate despite their genuine interest, and even Seamus Malin felt it impossible to continue.

As we looked for assistance in fund-raising, Neil Chur recommended we recruit Russell Gossage from Trinity University in San Antonio, Texas, where he had been a successful vice-president in college relations. He and a Santa Fean, Seymour Gormley, joined the office, now relocated to a somewhat larger, even less expensive, and considerably colder suite in Santa Fe's Cordova Road area. We began to codify all the information we had on foundations and narrow down the list to those most likely. Even then we had little luck in eliciting support, but we could at least reassure everyone that we had done the requisite background analysis and initial approach.

We studied corporations and sought help from the directors on seeking donations. It did not lead anywhere, most likely because companies were aware of our ties to Occidental Petroleum; or, as was so often the case, unwilling to believe that Hammer had left us in the lurch. Once again we were back to individuals. And in this respect we were disappointed in the assistance our new consultants offered. I continued to work primarily off the list which Ault and I had compiled months earlier. We visited people; we elicited some interest and many wishes for good fortune; but we did not succeed in capturing any big prizes. Nor had contributions from the board increased. We were merely in a holding pattern.

23: PASSING ON THE BATON

That pattern did not change during the spring of 1992. But it was a time when we would see the departure of two who had served most diligently since July of 1982: Al Romero as Business Manager and Diane Nieto as assistant to the president. Our staff celebrations at the end of the year included an increasing number of certificates to those who had completed ten years of service. The college was building a history of dedicated service.

Yet, when we held our graduation in May, 1992, students responded with the same degree of exuberance; the guests were full of both gratitude and warmth; and the cheers went up as the graduates filed across the platform. Dr. Wendy Lee Gramm from the Commerce Department in Washington was the speaker. A native of Hawaii, she spoke eloquently about the hard work which had brought her family from the sugar fields to executive positions from which they would seek to preserve their heritage and give something back to their community. As student speaker, Orit Gidali from Israel emphasized how much all of them had changed in two years. It was nice to note that the crowds who came for what had always been a colorful ceremony unlike any other in New Mexico had not substantially diminished since the Hammer years. It was still an important landmark.

We reached another landmark when we celebrated our tenth anniversary in November of 1992.

Everyone wanted to do something to mark the anniversary. We decided to begin with a banquet at the Quail Run Resort in Santa Fe on November 14. Twenty-eight students greeted the 130 guests whom the college had invited, both to tell them the UWC story and to entertain them after the dinner. It was a successful evening, and even those who had attended many celebratory affairs in Santa Fe were moved when the students marched in with their countries's flags. And, happy to add, the dinner did lead to some contributions and two new, important members of the board, Bill and Nancy Anixter, living in Albuquerque after retiring from business in Chicago. They had established a scholarship earlier and now would become even more vigorous supporters of the college. The other events planned for the tenth year included a special dinner for the students on campus, a charity run on behalf of Somalia (a way to raise the community's awareness of such tragedies) and a summer reunion for graduates. We were also learning another lesson: the terrible problems confronting students from the former Yugoslav republic. With two students from Serbia and two from Montenegro, we reviewed yet again what the world can do when confronted with such crises. Over the ten years we had known other such incidents, but none as sad as that of the Bosnian situation.

In November of 1992, the movement also celebrated the opening of the Li Po Chun United World College in Hong Kong. Lu and I represented the United States and Montezuma at the dedication on the entirely new campus, just a few miles from the Chinese border. Beautifully situated on a bay in the New Territories near Shatin, the college had constructed a strikingly modern set of buildings. Prince Charles reflected on the opening of Atlantic College thirty years earlier and then speculated about the importance of this UWC in the heart of the most densely populated part of the world. It was to be his last official act at a college. In chatting with His Royal Highness, we were surprised by his concern about what Hammer had failed to do for Montezuma. Most enjoyable was seeing some former students like Fiona Siu Wing-Sum ('86) from Hong Kong and Charlotte Brenner ('85) from Germany.

With others we discussed what we could do about a replacement for Prince Charles and the appointment of a new board chairman. At the International Board's business session, it was agreed that a small committee should immediately tackle these issues; and that committee (Galen Weston, Lady Jane Prior from the Atlantic College Board, and myself) concurred that we should find an International Board Chairman first. That we would accomplish by early in 1993 when Mark Hoffman, an American financier living in London, accepted the position. Because we individually would be talking with possible candidates, I tried to find out the exact status of Prince Charles, when he was actually stepping down, etc.. The London office was opaque and never officially notified anyone until well after the event. As it happened, I found out directly in a response to a letter I had written the Prince informing him of my plans.

As was now customary, the heads talked among themselves about all the usual misgivings and hopes. Then we enjoyed the hospitality provided by David Wilkinson, founding principal at Li Po Chun and his wife, Veronica, on a boat cruising Hong Kong's many harbors. With new heads coming on board, it was clear that the movement needed some further effort at bringing greater cohesion, a task left to the coming spring when we would gather again at Atlantic College under Jeremy Varcoe's direction.

That meeting was marked by some bitter discussions over who could raise money where on behalf of which constituency within the movement. It had always been a question, especially for the United States, but one which had been muted simply because so few efforts had been mounted to find new funds. For example, Swaziland had always let us know when they were approaching people in the States for support: it was seldom an issue since the individuals were not likely donors to Montezuma. Similarly, Atlantic College had always been cooperative in allowing the U.S. to have its galas in England. Of course, since the donors were primarily American and Canadian, there was no competition; but there could have been some resentment, particularly when AC was asked to provide entertainment.

Sensitive to that possibility, Hammer had given some modest contributions to Atlantic in 1989. What was much more difficult to define was any approach from the central office to prospects in countries where UWCs were located. It was reminiscent of the debate Kingman Brewster had held about fund-raising turf; and it was regrettable that it had not been solved then. For the issue was further complicated by the thought that each college might approach special ethnic groups on each other's terrain. Despite a commendable attempt by London to do some fund-raising from the center, it just did not go far and later would recede. Yet, despite the experience, the board would continue to admonish the central office and itself of the importance of finding funds but never look to its own membership. Only Hammer, Weston, and Sir Q.W. Lee, chairman of Li Po Chun UWC, ever stepped up to the problem. Once again, there was no resolution by the international corporation of how to delineate between the efforts of the individual colleges, so clearly responsible for their own financial welfare and for supporting the central office, and the call for funds from the movement as a whole.

During the fall also our own board had reached some important decisions. It met at a hotel near the Dallas airport. Since Alec Courtelis could not make the meeting, he and I met in Chicago just prior to the board's assembling in Dallas. He was tired; I was concerned whether the board would do anything; and we both knew that we had to reach an agreement on my retirement. By this time, I felt that before the close of 1992 I could put the financing needed in place, and both Lu and I were wearing down. We needed to organize for a search.

All of this was not pleasant to discuss. Nor were the results of the development campaign encouraging. We were both edgy; we had become victims of the long struggle to bring financial stability to the institution; and we felt, no doubt, that Hammer had unfairly left us with an immense problem and no resources. We knew that we had probably chosen the wrong consultants to achieve our fund-raising goals. In short, we were frustrated. In one of those cramped cubicles at O'Hare Airport we reached an agreement which I would carry to the board.

At the Dallas meeting Irani sat in the chair and sufficient numbers came that we could execute our business. Directors were pleased to hear that tuition income had exceeded our estimate by $40,000. Our new budget reflected the reductions we had set in motion in the spring. We would remain under four million in expenditures and would still have over a million in reserves in June of 1993. Sometimes a director would ruefully observe that I had mastered the technique of scaring everyone with projections and then lowering their blood pressure when the reports came in at the next meeting.

That was not true, but at least it was better than showing even gloomier prospects. What was more important was that the Brown Foundation had agreed to a three-year challenge grant: they would give $200,000 once we raised at least $300,000 in each calendar year. That grant assured the future, thanks to Mrs. Sarofim. Among others the Anixters had also pledged substantial scholarship money annually. Applications for admission had risen significantly. It all sounded promising to the board. Even a proposal to shorten the name of the college received bemused consideration but no action. Then we went into executive session.

I announced my intention to retire during the summer of 1993. Some were surprised; some were concerned; and some agreed to help with the search although Courtelis would quite properly make the final determination. Gossage and Gromley made their report on development efforts thus far. Even though their observations about the need for more help from the Board were appropriate, they fell on deaf ears. Consultants seldom stir people to action. Burch Ault had been helpful, especially in identifying new supporters, but the president alone would carry the burden until a new constituency was in place. The executive session closed quietly and people went their respective ways.

When we returned to Montezuma and again met with faculty and staff over an excellent dinner, sparked with some good wine, people were surprised and then full of questions about how we would proceed, how we would organize the search, and what kind of person we would consider for the position. These were good questions for which the board had not provided much guidance. In general, we knew that the next president should be a younger person with sufficient international experience to understand some of the challenges of working with the movement as well as foreign students. As the faculty discussed the qualifications with me, we concluded that it would help if the person had some residential preparatory school experience, was married, and quite obviously was willing and able to raise money. There was considerable sentiment for having the new person be able to concentrate on learning about the college before spending chunks of time away on fund-raising. There would need to be some reorganization since alumni affairs, public relations, and development were all being covered by *ad hoc* arrangements—deliberately designed not to commit the new person to any built-in pattern or persons. Fortunately the new president would have an experienced person as deputy head.

What became apparent very quickly was that the directors were not in a position to take any part in finding suitable candidates, much as they did wish to screen the candidates at the appropriate time. Therefore, we set up the basic mechanics for the search at

Montezuma; and I went through the customary sources for likely people. There was some awkwardness in the process since I was working out of Santa Fe primarily. Somehow we managed to organize the requisite materials for the more interesting candidates and do the "reading" of the portfolios with very few snags. The pool was slow emerging despite the wide net we cast during the fall.

We had an unanticipated opportunity to visit with a possible candidate in December in Houston, just prior to a trip to South Korea where we were hoping to set up a national committee. Louisa Sarofim had a reception for a representative from World Learning, Inc., formerly the Experiment in International Living, in Brattleboro, Vermont. Philip Geier and I had a chance to chat; then it was on to Korea where we were able to bring that country into those sponsoring UWC students.

While we were reviewing presidential credentials, we had to prepare materials for a meeting of the board on January 25, 1993. The main issue would be the progress we were making on finding a new president; but there were other issues, including the inevitable financial review. By then we were making some progress on finding the matching grant of $300,000. We were able to report, surprisingly, that for the first time we had achieved 75 countries being represented at the College—no doubt the most diverse of all the United World Colleges. It hardly seemed possible that 203 young people from so many different backgrounds could be living in this pocket of New Mexico.

A practice we had introduced at board meetings was to have Barbara Johnson present a report on the college as seen from her office. There was no question that over the years our record-keeping, registration, and grade reporting had improved greatly. By this time many universities like Harvard, Vanderbilt, Chicago, and New York had welcomed early decision candidates. What was troublesome now was the decline in foreign scholarship assistance at even the most eminent colleges. For students from Africa in particular this trend was a severe disappointment.

The college was employing more former students as interim instructors, especially to cover for faculty who had earned a sabbatical. They were popular with the students; they brought fresh energy to activities; and generally they were well overworked. After having secured a firm place for conflict resolution in the overall program of the UWCs, we now wanted to encourage the introduction of a course to supplement Theory of Knowledge.

At the suggestion of Colin Jenkins, head of Atlantic College, we were working on a course which would have segments prepared by faculty at the different colleges, all aimed at improving our understanding of the current global situation. World affairs had long been an optional Friday night feature, but time had limited its contribution. Everyone agreed that we now needed a component, hopefully part of the IB curriculum, dedicated to global issues. Johnson also summarized for the board the artist-in-residence program we had long run in cooperation with the State of New Mexico, which covered half the cost. We had introduced a community service leadership training program alongside an environmental awareness project. Each year we had an Armand Hammer Day during which students could spend the entire day with their community service assignment in Las Vegas. With obvious pride, Johnson summarized the accomplishments of the students: winner of the National Peace Essay, first in the state's 1993 science board contest, first in the science Olympiad, first and second places in the State's math contest—all marks of the institution's continuing academic excellence.

In the narrative we have chosen to emphasize here these achievements are easily forgotten; but the core program had proved extraordinarily invigorating for everyone. The level of conversation was astonishing, in the classroom, the dining hall, and the dorms. So long as we could insulate to some degree the people in Montezuma from the strains that had always existed and, in truth, provided a fascinating challenge for the chief executive, then the mission would be successful.

As if the schedule were not full enough, in 1992 we had had to prepare for another site visit from the North Central Association of Schools and Colleges. With help from our biologist, Margaret Summerfield, we assembled in two impressively thick volumes the information required of an institution. Then came the visit in November, a quiet confirmation by the visiting team of the accuracy of what we claimed we were doing. The team was astonished — and then worried. They had no question about continuing our accreditation; they had nothing but admiration for the students and faculty; and they included many very pleasant compliments in their report. "This is a very fine school, with far more to commend than to recommend." But, as is always the case in such studies, the recommendations were more indicative than the overall endorsement. The physical plant was satisfactory, but the college needed indoor recreation facilities and a new infirmary. No surprise there. The committee raised questions about the appropriateness of trying to find more full-paying U.S. students in view of the institution's mission. They also felt that student residential life would prosper if the dorms were less crowded. Throughout the college they felt that there were not enough computers for a modern-day operation. The library could use more staff. Needless to say, much of the team's concern centered on the finances of the institution. They noted that the college "finds itself spending all of its surplus, eroding its endowment, and, in effect, mortgaging the future of the college for the sake of the present." Finally, there was genuine concern that the search for a new president would deflect the board from its continuing need to plan for the future.

To the board this report was an irritant, preferably to be dismissed since we had unanimously gained reaccreditation, than to be read carefully. To those most familiar with the history, it was familiar litany, but it was yet another indication of the need to recruit new directors who would have a better understanding of this kind of pre-university school. We had often talked over dinners about the possibility of disengaging from the United World College movement, but even those most anxious to solve our finances through becoming a tuition-supported private academy had to recognize that, without the international student body and the distinctive programs we offered, we would be in an unfavorable competitive position with respect to long-established and heavily endowed private schools like Exeter and Andover. In fact, the challenge was to review what we were doing, some of which had been eagerly emulated on other campuses, and find new ways to promote international learning.

The board meeting ended with the hope that a new president could be selected by April and report by fall. The board selection committee had indicated that it would assemble in Chicago once we had narrowed down the list and interviewed the leading candidates on campus. As vice-president Barbara Johnson was one of the candidates, we strove to limit consideration to a "final four." Winnowing down the list from the one hundred applicants, most of whom had reasonable qualifications, was a strenuous exercise, even with the help of the faculty committee. The guest room was a busy place. We tried to have each person spend two days with us at the college. If necessary, I would also discuss the job at great length separately. Most candidates were sufficiently struck by the mission that they were prepared to accept the opportunity if the job were offered. This was a change from the deanship which, for outsiders, had had less appeal. From all the deliberations and meetings, we concluded that four should meet with the committee in Chicago. There was a discernible difference between those leading candidates and the next four or five possibilities.

The committee met at the City Club in Chicago, a location which made it easier for everyone to be present on neutral ground near a hub airport without hearing the jets overhead. As the first and only occasion on which the directors would meet these persons, it was critical that there be sufficient time both to talk with the candidates and then to talk among ourselves. I had tried to schedule everything sensibly. Barbara Johnson was the first to be interviewed, a kindness on her part and an excellent initial experience for the committee since they knew her and could evolve a style of interview that would be more relaxing and, hopefully, more informative than one with a stranger might have provided. It was an exhausting exercise those two days. As so often happens, the committee had comparatively little difficulty, in the end, in selecting their recommendation for confirmation by the entire board, which would meet within two weeks. What was less comfortable was the task left to the president to notify the unsuccessful candidates, at least one of whom had to be keep on board until acceptable terms had been worked out with the new person.

Philip O. Geier, vice-president for external affairs of World Learning, Inc., in Brattleboro, Vermont, was selected. He was appropriately young, 44, and had a strong academic background. A graduate of Williams College, he held a master of arts in history from the Maxwell School of Public Affairs at Syracuse University, where he also earned his Ph.D. in American studies. Twice recipient of Fulbright awards, he had the kind of international experience everyone hoped we would find in a new president. When the news reached campus, no one was surprised by the choice even though there were some who might have wished one of the other candidates had been successful. To the faculty parents on campus, the fact that Amy and Phil had three children of school age was a great boon.

In effect, the selection of a new president marked the end of the transition. After Hammer had died in December of 1990, we had gone through two and a half years with minimum damage, as it were, and in many ways much progress. The new president would have the opportunity to review where we were and then to make constructive changes. The mood was welcoming. I remarked at the time:

> "It is the kind of occasion that prompts some reflections on institutions and on this one in particular. Many have observed that the history of colleges in this country reflects changes in society and the fortunes of other institutions. For example, before the Civil War there were many denominational colleges that could not survive our massive internal upheaval. The arrival of a publicly supported system of higher education shifted the emphasis of many universities. Most recently economic factors have determined that some smaller institutions either consolidate or disburse their assets. Institutions have astonishing resilience against social changes, but as often as not, their fate depends on the foresight of faculties and administrations—and their governing boards.
>
> "This college, placed so uniquely within the structure of American education, and dedicated so securely to international cooperation, needs now to reconsider its role and to determine what modifications time and conditions suggest are appropriate. It does not have the leisure to sit back. Not only are there major issues in the world that could critically affect the United World Colleges, such as political disarray in many areas and economic disjunction, but also there are curricular questions within the International Baccalaureate that need resolution.
>
> "There is no denying also that the financial premises upon which, *de facto,* the movement has been operating face revision if we are to continue to blend successfully the idealism of philanthropic support with governmental backing in some instances and parental contributions in others. Pragmatism has played a more prominent role in our success than we wish to admit—a most common ingredient in the most eminent institutions."

To these general observations one could easily add the list of particular challenges at Montezuma. Certainly to the board, the election of a new president was a welcome departure from normal business, and the April 5th meeting in Dallas went smoothly with a goodly number of directors present. There were a few dissents from the proposed salary and benefits for the new president, the perennial risk for a board which had not given much thought to these matters before. In this regard the board followed UWC tradition: when long-serving members retired, even when Prince Charles stepped down, there was never any mention of their contribution.

This year, as graduation approached, Lu and I had very strongly mixed reactions: we were finishing a project, fascinating and worthwhile; we were officially retiring; and we were moving to a new home in Santa Fe. We had to sort through everything, ready the desk for a new person, and decide what to do with the materials that twelve years had seen mount from the basement to the top floor.

Geier and I arranged another airport meeting in Chicago so that we could spend a weekend, undistracted, and review confidentially all the matters which might be of greatest moment to a new president. We did not cover everything; but it was a worthwhile way to decide how best to proceed. One touchy matter was the announcement of the chairman that I would remain as president of the board of directors. Geier and I concluded that it would be far preferable to have me available as a quiet consultant. Then he could establish his own style with the board. We also planned that, although he officially was to take office on July 1, 1993, we would remain to handle the business of the college

Over the yeaers graduates of the college assembled for reunions. Here students join Hammer, the Lockwoods and Carolyn Walker at a Los Angeles meeting.

through mid-August. We would be at the reunion of the classes of 1984 and 1985; we would confirm all the admissions commitments for the fall; in short, we would try to put in place all the pieces needed to open another year. We even planned to visit the Geiers in Vermont. (Of course, there were some who could never understand why the first two presidents had to come from that little green mountain state in New England.)

Graduation was the usual festive affair. During the awarding of degrees our collie, Farah, who had somehow gotten out of the house and was sitting with Lu in the front row, concluded that it would be her last chance to receive a degree. Accordingly she beckoned to my voice and joined the students going up the steps to the podium. She received strong applause. John Lombardi, president of the University of Florida, was the guest speaker. And Courtelis gave both Lu and me kind words for our effort. Farewell parties are always difficult, and this year's was no exception. Then we packed and moved with our three animals to the heights north of the city of Santa Fe.

EPILOGUE

It had been 15 years since the decision to open a United World College in the United States. This account provides a brief glimpse into what happened to make The Armand Hammer United World College of the American West possible. It is neither exhaustive nor objective, but it does seek to provide some clues as to why things happened as they did, both at home and abroad. Clearly there is another story about the students and people who worked with them over the years, that collection of portraits which could form an impressionist rendering of "life at Montezuma."

Institutions tend to measure their success by what their alumni accomplish in later life. Harvard and Yale and Berkeley and MIT point with pride to their illustrious graduates. There is little doubt that ours will distinguish themselves in different arenas around the world. But those recognizable achievements may be less important than what each student carried away from the two years at the college. We often editorialize about the attitude of people, especially in a time when there is great unease in the world, on the assumption that if they felt differently, if they spoke more understandingly, and showed greater compassion, somehow the world would be a better place. Even if we grant just partial validity to such an assumption, then what happens to young people during the years when education may have its greatest impact becomes as important as anything we can possibly teach. The success of this college will depend on what those students think and do differently in the years ahead.

It would be unbecoming to ask whether, in light of the unfilled promises and the anguish of constant uncertainty, the enterprise was worth the effort. Obviously it was, but it could have gone farther had Hammer done what he had said he would. We lived with an irony: we were indeed fortunate to be in northern New Mexico where we could formulate our own programs without continuous intervention from the founder and his staff, but we never gained full control over the instruments so essential to that task.

This narrative has its repetitive moments since the college's financial insecurity was so often the topic of conversation. We never feared that the college would not prevail, but it was never certain in what style. Admittedly, few non-profit enterprises prosper without a struggle over funding, but in this instance it was an unnecesarry irritant. We should have achieved a better balance between dreams and delivery.

Of course, it is not uncommon for a benefactor to spend much time and money in the initial phases of a project and then to turn his attention to other matters. He had numerous other projects demanding his attention in his last years, and his interest trailed off once he was convinced that this memorial was in place and operating fairly well. Once he had made sure that his name would be attached permanently to the college, he was reluctant to put more money into the enterprise except in that curious instance when unexpected profits from the Hammer Galleries left him with a $500,000 tax embarrassment which he avoided by conveying that bonus to the college.

In this regard Lu and I remember two curious conversations. The first took place soon after the college opened. Hammer remarked: "Ted, I'll never let you down." Then in September of 1990, he asked: "Ted, you won't let me down, will you? Make sure the college continues."

Hammer never approached a project in a fashion that was not alloyed with a personal motive that detracted from essentially generous and at times brilliant moves. Nor did he forsake using money to influence the outcome in his various undertakings. In this case, he was misled by some who had vastly underestimated what it would cost to establish and then to maintain a United World College in keeping with the international guidelines. Perhaps he felt that we could either change those in due course or ignore them. London's inability to decide whether to level with the man about their misgivings no doubt fueled Hammer's decision to try to shape the movement to his liking, something which in the end he could not achieve. The very indecision that characterized so many UWC operations was a safeguard against any takeover.

Much more difficult to conclude is how many missed opportunities there were. No doubt we could have done things differently. We lived within the constraints of the International Baccalaureate which, despite its immense strengths that were so significant in our obtaining wide acceptance academically, did not encourage faculty to propose changes. Or we lacked the ingenuity to work around those limitations. We aimed high, and that did require the level of financial support that Hammer had promised but could not fully deliver. Once those expectations were established, then it became increasingly difficult to suffer the periodic setbacks that we received in our planning. In effect, we could not plan with much hope that we would reach our goals.

We made mistakes, but by and large we (by which I mean all the faculty and staff) accomplished an incredible amount over the years in establishing what is undoubtedly one of the best such international institutions for young people in the world. In that context complaints may appear petty, but disappointments are always a part of the story—and at least a few of ours were unnecessary—just as descriptions of our overall success cannot be excluded.

The board of directors, whose meetings so often appear in this narrative, was hamstrung for the first eight years. It lacked a mandate so long as the Honorary Chairman could so readily alter its agenda, prevent any thoughtful discussion, and move to go to lunch so peremptorily. But around the edges the necessary business got done and on occasion there were significant debates about such matters as admissions, three-year programs, and financial solutions.

Yet, it was difficult to gain closure; too often things were left to being worked out by the chairman and the president. The directors themselves were prominent people whose willingness to take on this assignment was always surprising; and for their contributions one has to be grateful since clearly they could have used the time and effort in other causes. They were sincere in their admiration for the program; they were kind and supportive; and for all their attentions we are most grateful. What we could not achieve until the last two years was a real engagement of the board with the future of the college. No doubt in this regard our location militated against their appreciation of the undertaking.

It is not possible to compare the founding of this institution with any other and then draw any legitimate conclusions. It was, and remains, one of a kind. And, once again, Hammer made sure it would always be so since in the document setting up the trust, he gave its governors the power to revoke their support should there be another United World College in the United States.

As we have never listed the countries from which our students came, and still come, they appear in this epilogue: Argentina, Australia, Austria, Bahamas, Barbados, Belgium, Bermuda, Bhutan, Bolivia, Botswana, Brazil, Bulgaria, Canada, Cayman Islands, Chile, China, Colombia, Costa Rica, Cyprus;, Czechoslovakia, Denmark, Ecuador, Egypt, Ethiopia, Finland, France, Germany, Ghana, Greece, Guatemala, Hong Kong, Hungary, India, Indonesia, Ireland, Israel, Italy, Jamaica, Japan, Jordan, Kenya, Lesotho, Malaysia, Mexico, Montenegro, Morocco, Nepal, Netherlands, New Zealand, Nicaragua, Nigeria, Norway, Pakistan, Panama, Paraguay, Peru, Philippines, Poland, Portugal, Russia, Senegal, Serbia, Sierra Leone, Singapore, Spain, Suriname, Swaziland, Sweden, Thailand, Turkey, Turks and Caicos, Uganda, United Kingdom, Uruguay, United States, Uzbekistan, Vanuatu, Venezuela, Zimbabwe.

To all those who have worked with us on this project, to all the graduates who spent time at Montezuma, we extend both our thanks and our best wishes.

SOURCES

This history relies primarily on materials in the archives at the United World College; for example, board minutes, letters, and documents in the administrative files. In addition, I maintained a dictated history of important events, conversations, and trips to various meetings. Of course, memory of both the critical and the amusing episodes plays a major role in reconstructing the story.

There are a number of written materials about Armand Hammer. None of them devote much space to the United World College or even to events like the Palm Beach gala in 1985. For instance, the autobiography which Hammer commissioned with Neil Lyndon refers to the college very seldom, on pages 511 through 514 mainly. But it is interesting to read this book: *Hammer*, G. P. Putnam's Sons, New York 1987. Lyndon has now concluded that Hammer was quite a different person from the one portrayed in this account. Steve Weinberg, *Armand Hammer: The Untold Story,* Little, Brown, New York, 1989 devotes a few pages to a description of the collaboration with Prince Charles. Carl Blumay with Henry Edwards, *The Dark Side of Power: The Real Armand Hammer,* Simon & Schuster, New York 1992 took a far less charitable view of Hammer's venture in New Mexico, claiming that Hammer considered it a "rathole" for his money. Most recently Edward Jay Epstein has provided an equally critical view in *Dossier: The Secret History of Armand Hammer*, Random House, New York, 1996. He devotes only two pages to the college even though many not friends of Hammer would agree that founding this institution was probably the finest charitable effort the man undertook.

For the best account of the IB and international schools, one can read A.D.C. Peterson, *Schools Across Frontiers: The story of the International Baccalaureate and the United World Colleges,* Open Court, Lasalle (Illinois), 1987.

There are innumerable books on Prince Charles, most of which do not mention the college and make only passing reference to Hammer. However, there are some interesting accounts in Jonathan Dimbleby, *The Prince of Wales: A Biography*, William Morrow, New York, 1994, that suggest the Palace had a different view of the Prince's involvement with Hammer than others have asserted.

The articles which others wrote about the college repeat for the most part what is in this history. In fact, there is distressingly little literature about the United World Colleges, individually or collectively, one further reason for publishing this account.

INDEX